India-Brazil-South Africa Dialogue Forum (IBSA)

T0271828

The establishment of the IBSA as one of the principal platforms of South-South cooperation is one of the most notable developments in international politics during the first decade of the twenty-first century. While the concept is now frequently referred to in discussions about the global South, there has not yet been a comprehensive and scholarly analysis of the history of the IBSA grouping and its impact on global order.

This book:

- Offers a definitive reference history of the IBSA grouping (India, Brazil and South Africa)—a comprehensive, fact-focused narrative and analytical account from its inception as an ad hoc meeting in 2003 to the political grouping it is today;
- Situates the IBSA grouping in the wider context of South-South cooperation and the global shift of power away from the United States and Europe towards powers such as Brazil, India, and South Africa.
- Provides an outlook and critically assesses what the IBSA grouping means for global order in the twenty-first century.

Offering the first full-length and detailed treatment of the IBSA, this work will be of great interest to students and scholars of international organizations, international relations, and the global South.

Oliver Stuenkel is an Assistant Professor of International Relations at the Getulio Vargas Foundation (FGV) in São Paulo, where he coordinates the São Paulo branch of the School of History and Social Science (CPDOC) and the executive program in International Relations. He is also a non-resident Fellow at the Global Public Policy Institute (GPPi) in Berlin. His research focuses on rising powers—specifically on Brazil's, India's, and China's foreign policy and on their impact on global governance.

In 2012 he was part of the Brazilian delegation at the track II meetings in New Delhi and Chongqing in preparation for the fourth and fifth BRICS Summits.

Routledge Global Institutions Series

Edited by Thomas G. Weiss
The CUNY Graduate Center, New York, USA
and Rorden Wilkinson
University of Sussex, UK

About the series

The Global Institutions Series provides cutting-edge books about many aspects of what we know as "global governance." It emerges from our shared frustrations with the state of available knowledge—electronic and print-wise, for research and teaching—in the area. The series is designed as a resource for those interested in exploring issues of international organization and global governance. Since the first volumes appeared in 2005, we have taken significant strides toward filling conceptual gaps.

The series consists of three related "streams" distinguished by their blue, red, and green covers. The blue volumes, comprising the majority of the books in the series, provide user-friendly and short (usually no more than 50,000 words) but authoritative guides to major global and regional organizations, as well as key issues in the global governance of security, the environment, human rights, poverty, and humanitarian action among others. The books with red covers are designed to present original research and serve as extended and more specialized treatments of issues pertinent for advancing understanding about global governance. The volumes with green covers—the most recent departure in the series—are comprehensive and accessible accounts of the major theoretical approaches to global governance and international organization.

The books in each of the streams are written by experts in the field, ranging from the most senior and respected authors to first-rate scholars at the beginning of their careers. In combination, the three components of the series—blue, red, and green—serve as key resources for faculty, students, and practitioners alike. The works in the blue and green streams have value as core and complementary readings in courses on, among other things, international organization, global governance, international law, international relations, and international political economy; the red volumes allow further reflection and investigation in these and related areas.

The books in the series also provide a segue to the foundation volume that offers the most comprehensive textbook treatment available dealing with all the major issues, approaches, institutions, and actors in contemporary global governance—our edited work *International Organization and Global Governance* (2014)—a volume to which many of the authors in the series have contributed essays.

Understanding global governance—past, present, and future—is far from a finished journey. The books in this series nonetheless represent significant steps toward a better way of conceiving contemporary problems and issues as well as, hopefully, doing something to improve world order. We value the feedback from our readers and their role in helping shape the ongoing development of the series.

A complete list of titles appears at the end of this book. The most recent titles in the series are:

Making Global Institutions Work (2014)
Edited by Kate Brennan

Post-2015 UN Development (2014)
Edited by Stephen Browne and Thomas G. Weiss

Who Participates in Global Governance? (2014)
Molly A. Ruhlman

The Security Council as Global Legislator (2014)
Edited by Vesselin Popovski and Trudy Fraser

UNICEF (2014)
Richard Jolly

The Society for Worldwide Interbank Financial Telecommunication (SWIFT) (2014)
Susan V. Scott and Markos Zachariadis

The International Politics of Human Rights (2014)
Edited by Monica Serrano and Thomas G. Weiss

India-Brazil-South Africa Dialogue Forum (IBSA)

The rise of the global South?

Oliver Stuenkel

Routledge
Taylor & Francis Group

LONDON AND NEW YORK

First published 2015
by Routledge
2 Park Square, Milton Park, Abingdon, Oxfordshire OX14 4RN

and by Routledge
711 Third Avenue, New York, NY 10017

First issued in paperback 2016

Routledge is an imprint of the Taylor and Francis Group, an informa business

British Library Cataloguing in Publication Data
A catalogue record for this book is available from the British
Library

Library of Congress Cataloging in Publication Data
Stuenkel, Oliver.
   India-Brazil-South Africa dialogue forum (IBSA) : the rise of the
global south / Oliver Stuenkel.
   pages cm. – (Global institutions ; 89)
Includes bibliographical references and index.
1. Brazil–Foreign relations–India. 2. Brazil–Foreign relations–South
Africa. 3. India–Foreign relations–Brazil. 4. India–Foreign
relations–South Africa. 5. South Africa–Foreign relations–Brazil. 6.
South Africa–Foreign relations–India. 7. India-Brazil-South Africa
Dialogue Forum. I. Title.
   F2523.5.I4S78 2014
   327.81054–dc23
               2014008862

ISBN 13: 978-1-138-28803-4 (pbk)
ISBN 13: 978-1-138-78908-1 (hbk)

Typeset in Times New Roman
by Taylor & Francis Books

Contents

List of illustrations		viii
Acknowledgments		x
List of abbreviations		xi
	Introduction	1
1	The history of IBSA: first steps	11
2	Towards institutionalization	37
3	IBSA's institutional structure	66
4	Does IBSA matter?	93
5	The politics of South-South cooperation: towards a new paradigm?	117
6	IBSA: rising democracy promoters?	129
7	Conclusion	154
	Appendix: timeline of events	158
	Select bibliography	168
	Index	170
	Routledge Global Institutions Series	175

List of illustrations

Figures

1.1 Brazilian exports to India and South Africa as a share of total Brazilian exports 12
1.2 Indian exports to Brazil and South Africa as a share of total Indian exports 13
1.3 South African exports to Brazil and India as a share of total South African exports 13
1.4 Brazilian imports from India and South Africa as a share of total Brazilian imports 14
1.5 Indian imports from Brazil and South Africa as a share of total Indian imports 14
1.6 South African imports from Brazil and India as a share of total South African imports 15
1.7 Trade between India and South Africa in US$ million 15
1.8 Trade between Brazil and South Africa in US$ million 16
1.9 Trade between Brazil and India in US$ million 16
3.1 IBSA's institutional structure 68
4.1 Intra-IBSA trade flow (1995–2012) 95
4.2 India's trade diversification (2003–12) 98
4.3 Brazil's trade diversification (2003–12) 98
4.4 South Africa's trade diversification (2003–12) 98

Tables

3.1 Number of meetings of the IBSA working groups (since 2003) 68
3.2 Number of meetings of nongovernmental forums (since 2003) 81
4.1 Intra-IBSA trade flow (1995–2012) 96

4.2   Democracy and institutional agreement   111
A.1   IBSA timeline   158

Boxes

1.1   From Third World to global South   21
1.2   The first meeting of IBSA foreign ministers   25
1.3   Meeting of IBSA foreign ministers on the sidelines of the
      58th UN General Assembly   27
2.1   First meeting of the Trilateral Commission   40
2.2   Meeting of IBSA foreign ministers on the sidelines of the
      59th UN General Assembly   40
2.3   Second meeting of the Trilateral Commission/Third
      meeting of IBSA Focal Points   41
2.4   Third meeting of the Trilateral Commission   42
2.5   First IBSA Summit   43
2.6   Fourth meeting of the Trilateral Commission/Ninth
      meeting of IBSA Focal Points   45
2.7   Meeting of IBSA foreign ministers on the sidelines of the
      62nd UN General Assembly   46
2.8   Second IBSA Summit   46
2.9   Fifth meeting of the Trilateral Commission   48
2.10 Third IBSA Summit   48
2.11 Sixth meeting of the Trilateral Commission   50
2.12 Meeting of IBSA foreign ministers on the sidelines of the
      64th UN General Assembly   50
2.13 Fourth IBSA Summit   52
2.14 Meeting of IBSA foreign ministers on the sidelines of the
      65th UN General Assembly   52
2.15 The IBSA satellite program   53
2.16 Foreign ministers meeting   54
2.17 Seventh meeting of the Trilateral Commission   55
2.18 Foreign ministers meeting at the 66th UN
      General Assembly   55
2.19 Fifth IBSA Summit   56
2.20 Meeting of IBSA foreign ministers on the sidelines of the
      68th UN General Assembly   60
6.1   South Africa and the Mugabe regime   141

Acknowledgments

The students in my undergraduate, graduate, and executive classes at Fundação Getulio Vargas in São Paulo and Rio de Janeiro greatly contributed to this volume through their participation during our discussions. My colleagues Matias Spektor, Elena Lazarou, Alexandre Moreli and Marcos Tourinho at the Center of International Relations have provided useful guidance and support throughout the writing process. I would also like to thank the countless academics, journalists, and policy makers who agreed to be interviewed for this book—in São Paulo, Rio de Janeiro, Brasília, New York, Pretoria and New Delhi. Due to frequent travel and a considerable teaching load in recent years, I could not have written this book without the outstanding research assistance of Bruno de Marco Lopes, Camila do Amaral, Suellen Aguiar, Thiago Kunis, Victoria Pisini and Mariela Won. In addition, Salomão Cunha Lima and Ana Patricia Silva have been essential in providing a first-class working environment at FGV's School of Social Sciences (CPDOC) in São Paulo.

Abbreviations

AIDS	acquired immunodeficiency syndrome
ANC	African National Congress
BRIC	Brazil, Russia, India and China grouping
BRICS	BRIC grouping after inviting South Africa in December 2010
CPLP	Community of Portuguese Language Countries
DRC	Democratic Republic of the Congo
DTI	South Africa Department of Trade and Industry
EU	European Union
FDI	foreign direct investment
FTA	free trade agreement
G3	Alternative name for IBSA (India, Brazil and South Africa)
G7	Group of 7
G8	Group of 8
G20	Group of 20
G77	Group of 77
GCIS	Government Communication and Information Services
GDP	gross domestic product
GNP	gross national product
HIV	human immunodeficiency virus
IBSA	India-Brazil-South Africa Dialogue Forum
IBSAMAR	India-Brazil-South Africa maritime cooperation
IMF	International Monetary Fund
IPS	Inter Press Service
ITAC	South Africa International Trade Administration Commission
LDCs	least developed countries
MDGs	Millennium Development Goals

MERCOSUR Southern Common Market (Brazil, Argentina, Uruguay and Paraguay)
MINUSTAH United Nations Stabilization Mission in Haiti
NAM Non-Aligned Movement
NAMA Non-Agricultural Market Access
NED National Endowment for Democracy
NEPAD New Partnership for Africa's Development
NGO nongovernmental organization
NIEO New International Economic Order
NPT Non-Proliferation Treaty
OAS Organization of American States
OECD Organisation for Economic Co-operation and Development
PPP purchasing power parity
PT Brazilian Workers' Party
PTA preferential trade agreement
R2P Responsibility to Protect
SACU Southern African Customs Union
SADC Southern African Development Community
SANEF South African National Editors' Forum
SAPA South African Poultry Association
SSC South-South cooperation
TFTA trilateral free trade agreement
TRIPS Trade Related Aspects of Intellectual Property Rights
UN United Nations
UNASUL South American Community of Nations
UNCTAD United Nations Conference on Trade and Development
UNDP United Nations Development Programme
UNGA United Nations General Assembly
UNSC United Nations Security Council
US United States
USAID United States Agency for International Development
WG Working Group
WGHS Working Group on Human Settlements
WHO World Health Organization
WTO World Trade Organization
ZANU-PF Zimbabwe African National Union–Patriotic Front

Introduction

This is a group to spread goodwill and the message of peace—we are not against anyone.

(Celso Amorim[1])

We are overcoming historical, geographic, cultural and mental barriers that have always made us look to the North rather than the South.

(Luiz Inácio Lula da Silva[2])

In 2003, three emerging powers created the "India-Brazil-South Africa (IBSA) Dialogue Forum." It was established following negotiations among India (Prime Minister Atal Bihari Vajpayee), Brazil (President Luiz Inácio Lula da Silva), and South Africa (President Thabo Mbeki) during the 2003 Group of Eight (G8) summit in Evian, France. The three had been invited to the summit as observers, yet they felt that the invitation had been merely symbolic. "What is the use of being invited for dessert at the banquet of the powerful?" Lula later said. "We do not want to participate only to eat the dessert; we want to eat the main course, dessert and then coffee."[3]

Only three days later, India's Minister of External Affairs Yashwant Sinha, Brazil's Foreign Minister Celso Amorim and South Africa's Minister of International Relations and Cooperation Nkosazana Dlamini-Zuma met in Brasília, in what they called a "pioneer meeting," and formalized the IBSA Dialogue Forum through the adoption of the "Brasília Declaration."[4] As Celso Amorim argued several years later, when IBSA had institutionalized the grouping, it was "time to start reorganizing the world in the direction that the overwhelming majority of mankind expects and needs."[5]

A commitment was made to place the IBSA process within the ministerial bureaucracies of each participating country and to select sectors in which they would actively seek to develop cohesive policies.

As a result, IBSA established 16 trilateral working groups in areas such as agriculture, the environment, defense and energy. Ministerial-level gatherings were held in New Delhi in 2004, 2007, 2008 and 2011; Cape Town in 2005; Rio de Janeiro in 2006; in Somerset West (South Africa) in 2011; and Brasília in 2009. The meetings, bolstered by five presidential summits held in Brasília in 2006 and 2010, Tshwane/Pretoria in 2007, and New Delhi in 2008 and 2011, seemed to strengthen the three countries' commitment to this process while attempts to develop joint positions in other multilateral forums underlined the growing influence that IBSA had obtained in global politics. The IBSA Forum thus emerged in a context of the rise of emerging powers and international institutions' apparent difficulty in reflecting a shift of power away from Europe and the United States to rising states such as Brazil, India and South Africa.

Yet why exactly did India, Brazil and South Africa create the grouping and what has it achieved in its 11-year history? Has it helped emerging powers align their positions and increase their negotiation power in international forums? Most importantly, has it promoted stronger ties between rising democracies in the global South?

The dominant position established powers have traditionally held in global affairs is slowly eroding.[6] For better or worse, the group of those countries with the power to make a difference internationally is changing. As new powers rise to the fore, the world's decision-making elite will most likely become less Western, with fewer common interests and more ideologically diverse.[7]

While some are skeptical about whether a shift of power is indeed taking place, it seems difficult to contest that the increased prominence of global challenges such as climate change, failed states, poverty and mass atrocities has contributed to a growing consensus that emerging countries such as Brazil, India and China are indispensable in the effort to develop meaningful solutions.[8] Global summits can no longer claim legitimacy and inclusiveness without inviting countries like Brazil and India. While the US National Intelligence Council's 2005 *Global Trends* report still predicted that the United States would remain the "single most powerful actor economically, technologically and militarily,"[9] the 2009 issue predicted "a world in which the US plays a prominent role in global events, but … as one among many global actors."[10] The 2013 report was even more emphatic, arguing:

> The world of 2030 will be radically transformed from our world today. By 2030, no country—whether the US, China, or any other large country—will be a hegemonic power. The empowerment of

individuals and diffusion of power among states and from states to informal networks will have a dramatic impact, largely reversing the historic rise of the West since 1750, restoring Asia's weight in the global economy, and ushering in a new era of "democratization" at the international and domestic level.[11]

The value of exports from developing countries to other developing countries (South-South trade) now exceeds exports from poor countries to rich ones (South-North trade).[12] By comparison, in 1985, South-South trade only accounted for 7 percent of overall trade.[13] India's Tata Group and Reliance, Brazil's Petrobras, Vale and Embraer, and South Africa's De Beers are just a few examples of emerging economy multinationals striding onto the global stage. The transition from the G8 to the Group of 20 (G20) in 2008 was one of the most powerful symbols of this shift towards a more multipolar order.

Even though growth rates in several large countries in the global South slowed markedly after 2011, the overall trend of multi-polarization—the emergence of many centers of power, as compared to the bipolarity of the Cold War—creates a necessity to understand emerging powers' views. Yet uncertainty remains on many important questions of international affairs, regarding the ideas and perspectives that inform emerging powers as they seek greater visibility and the capacity to influence the global agenda.[14]

How do rising powers like Brazil, India and South Africa—located on the periphery of both international institutions and the global distribution of power, countries that seek to change their position in the present context of the internationalization of authority—behave, react and construct a discourse?[15] In principle, the three countries in question are in agreement with the broad precepts of international order, and the system-wide benefits it produces for them are far too copious to bring about any profound changes. In addition, US hegemonic power fails to pose an existential threat to them.[16]

In this context, it is important to note that there is no consensus on what constitutes an emerging power or a rising power. While China, for example, is at times called a rising power,[17] others argue that it is well established within today's institutions such as the United Nations (UN) Security Council.[18] Brazil and India are at times called middle powers,[19] rising powers[20] or emerging powers,[21] the latter two terms being used interchangeably here, as is common.[22] Both rising power and emerging power imply that a state accumulates power (primarily economic power but possibly also political and military power) at a higher rate than others, which may lead it to seek to alter the global order in its favor.

Liberal institutionalist theorists assume that the rising powers' domestic political system matters. They predict that democracies are more likely to engage in international institutions than non-democratic regimes.[23] They expect democratically organized emerging powers to become "responsible stakeholders,"[24] adapt to the existing norms and align with the status quo, the Western-dominated system of liberal internationalism. Specifically, liberals argue that establishing trust between liberal democracies is easier, and that they tend to seek international collaboration to create a more transparent, predictable and stable system, thus maximizing the gains of international collaboration.[25]

In addition, there is a systemic liberal institutionalist argument about why rising powers—even non-democratic ones—are likely to integrate: they face a Western-centered system that is, as Ikenberry stresses, "open ... and rule-based, with wide and deep political foundations,[26] a force that will enmesh and entrap even the most powerful."[27] The Western order, which Roosevelt had conceived to "ensure the end of beginning of wars,"[28] is "hard to overturn and easy to join."[29] Emerging actors encounter an environment in which they will be able to rise. Finally, due to unprecedented economic interdependence through trade, investment and commercial flows with others, non-established rising powers will seek to strengthen global governance to maintain economic stability.[30]

Those in the realist camp, on the other hand, understand the system according to the distribution of power[31] and predict that the rising powers will not "play by the West's rules."[32] They generally expect emerging powers to use their "newfound status to pursue alternative visions of world order"[33] and challenge the status quo, for example by joining hands with other rising powers and mounting a counter-hegemonic coalition.[34] Rising powers could create a parallel system with, as Weber puts it, "its own distinctive set of rules, institutions, and currencies of power, rejecting key tenets of liberal internationalism and particularly any notion of global civil society justifying political or military intervention."[35] In the same way, Krasner expects that once the balance of power moves against the West, emerging powers will create different principles,[36] for example by introducing countervailing power against the US-led Bretton Woods institutions.

Indeed, all three IBSA members have questioned the foundations that underlie the global order, expressing differences of opinion on the scope of cooperation, the location of rules and the allocation of authority. In so doing, the IBSA countries have posited fundamental disagreements over substantive policies of the postwar liberal consensus. At the extreme, liberal internationalism has been interpreted by

Brazilians, Indians and South Africans as a form of liberal imperialism, and the power of the hegemon at the center of the liberal order has been portrayed by them as a menace at least as threatening as anarchy in the international system. The result has been a critical challenge to the liberal internationalist project in several areas.

Partly as a consequence, several Western observers believe the "rise of the rest" will have negative consequences. They believe that countries such as Brazil, India and South Africa are "irresponsible stakeholders,"[37] that emerging powers' aid policies would make the world more "corrupt, chaotic, and authoritarian" and that they were "rising spoilers."[38]

In the aftermath of the terrorist attacks of 11 September 2001, the reappearance of the South-North divide as a defining axis of the international system is of great significance. In this context the emergence of a group of Southern countries actively challenging the position and assumptions of the leading states of the North is an especially important phenomenon.[39] Rising powers' decision to institutionalize their cooperation—for example in the form of the BRICs/BRICS (Brazil, Russia, India, China, and later South Africa) or IBSA are often seen as attempts to create anti-hegemonic blocs keen on undermining global order. In this context, the establishment of the IBSA grouping as one of the principal platforms of South-South cooperation[40] is one of the most curious developments in international politics during the first decade of the twenty-first century. While the concept is now frequently referred to in discussions about the global South,[41] there has not yet been a comprehensive and scholarly analysis of the history of the IBSA grouping, which should precede any debate about its impact on the global order. This lack of analysis is surprising because the IBSA countries' decision to organize regular summits can be seen, along with the creation of the G20 and the BRICs grouping, as the most significant innovation in global governance of the global South in recent years.

This book thus has two main goals. First, it seeks to offer a definitive history of the IBSA grouping—a comprehensive, fact-focused narrative and analytical account from its inception as an ad hoc meeting in 2003 to the political grouping it is today (Chapters 1–3). This includes a detailed description of its institutional structure. Second, it seeks to provide a critical analysis of South-South cooperation and assesses how far cooperation between the three IBSA members has any meaningful implications for the future of the global order (Chapters 4–6). Where can India, Brazil and South Africa cooperate, and has the grouping increased their capacity to speak with one voice? Answering these questions first is indispensable in order to discuss meaningfully the broader questions about emerging powers and the future of the global order.

To provide insight into the three IBSA countries' motivations, the book relies on interviews with more than 100 government officials, diplomats, policy analysts and academics from the IBSA countries, which I have been able to conduct over the past three years. I have benefited from exceptional access to key policy makers, partly in the context of my participation in the BRICS track II summits in Brasília (Brazil), New Delhi (India) and Chongqing (China) between 2010 and 2012 as part of Brazil's academic delegation.

For example, a conversation with Brazil's Foreign Minister Celso Amorim about IBSA's origins reveals Brazil's strong preference to work with democracies over deepening engagement with the BRICS grouping, which includes Russia and China. In a similar way, Indian foreign policy makers pointed out during the conversations that a platform of rising democracies that did not include China would make it possible to discuss common challenges such as human rights and inequality more openly. Yet how far is this pro-democracy rhetoric reflected in actual policy? Are ties between India, Brazil and South Africa really stronger than their respective ties to China? Interestingly enough, interviews with business representatives in the IBSA countries reveal a profound skepticism regarding the importance of the other members, compared to more important economies in their neighborhood. The majority of private sector leaders interviewed had never heard of the IBSA grouping.[42]

The results of the interviews will be contextualized by the relevant economic and political data of each period. This will make it the first full-length and detailed treatment of the IBSA grouping's history and analysis of its impact. The book thus seeks to provide a thorough analysis of intra-IBSA cooperation—telling the story from the group's origins until the potentially identity-shaping political grouping it was at its height in 2010, when it served as an important platform for frequent policy meetings and engagement on business, cultural and academic levels, to its possible decline and the debates about whether or not to merge it with the BRICS grouping. In short, the book provides a critical "historical biography" of the IBSA concept and a political contextualization.

The book also aims to serve as a basis for others to conduct theoretical research and explain how to understand the creation of the IBSA grouping—for example, why did the three countries in question decide to create their own club, rather than inviting other emerging democracies such as Turkey, Mexico and Indonesia? What is the importance of these so-called "informals" for international relations theory? Beyond the official objectives of promoting South-South cooperation mentioned in the different summit declarations, what are the underlying strategic aims for cooperating? After more than one decade, to what extent has IBSA delivered on these stated objectives?

This study is thus designed as a primary reference of the history of IBSA for both specialists and the general reader. It evaluates the IBSA Summits which, having started in 2003, serve as the pillars in the history of institutionalization. The analysis moves into several areas of cooperation, ranging from education, research and health care to agriculture, and assesses what lies behind the rhetoric of cooperation. This will help answer questions such as whether the IBSA platform has the potential to turn into an anti-hegemonic bloc, which are generally answered without any serious understanding of what intra-IBSA cooperation actually entails.

The reader learns about a considerable degree of multi-level cooperation between governments in the context of the IBSA grouping. In 2011, negotiators from IBSA countries traveled to Damascus, Syria, in an attempt to initiate a dialogue with the Bashar al-Assad regime about a possible ceasefire. Understanding the IBSA grouping, in short, is an important element when discussing today's ever more multipolar world.[43]

Notes

1 In Darlene Miller, "South Africa and the IBSA Initiative: Constraints and Challenges," *Africa Insight* 35, no. 1 (2005): 52–57.
2 In Felipe Seligman, "Brazil, India and South Africa Optimistic about Future Ties," *IPS News*, 13 September 2006, www.ipsnews.net/2006/09/trade-brazil-india-and-south-africa-optimistic-about-future-ties/.
3 In Daniel Kurtz, "Guest Post: Defending the IBSA Model," *Financial Times*, 29 April 2013, blogs.ft.com/beyond-brics/2013/04/29/guest-post-defending-the-ibsa-model/?Authorised=true#axzz2hho4pJ6d. Also: Daniel Kurtz-Phelan, "What is IBSA Anyway?" *Americas Quarterly*, Spring 2013, www.americasquarterly.org/content/what-ibsa-anyway.
4 India-Brazil-South Africa Dialogue Forum (IBSA), "Brasília Declaration," 6 June 2003, www.ibsa-trilateral.org/index.php?option=com_content&task=view&id=48&Itemid=27.
5 Celso Amorim, "Os Brics e a Reorganização do Mundo," *Folha de S. Paulo*, 8 June 2008, www1.folha.uol.com.br/fsp/opiniao/fz0806200807.htm.
6 Randall Schweller, "Emerging Powers in an Age of Disorder," *Global Governance* 17, no. 3 (2011): 285–97.
7 See, for example: Parag Khanna, *The Second World: How Emerging Powers are Redefining Global Competition in the Twenty-first Century*

(New York: Random House, 2009); Fareed Zakaria, *The Post-American World* (New York: Norton, 2009); and Dilip Haro, *After Empire: The Birth of a Multi-Polar World* (New York: Nation Books, 2010). For the most important example of the contrary view, see Stephen G. Brooks and William C. Wohlforth, *World Out of Balance: International Relations and the Challenge of American Primacy* (Princeton, N.J.: Princeton University Press, 2008); and Simon Serfaty, "Moving into a Post-Western World," *The Washington Quarterly* 34, no. 2 (2011): 7–23.

8 Andrew Hurrell, "Hegemony, Liberalism and Global Order: What Space for Would-be Powers?" *International Affairs* 82, no. 1 (2006): 1–19, 3.

9 National Intelligence Council, "Mapping the Global Future—Report of the National Intelligence Council's 2020 Project," 2004, 8.

10 National Intelligence Council, "Global Trends 2025: A Transformed World," November 2008, 2. A similar argument is found in: Gideon Rachman, "Is America's New Declinism for Real?" *Financial Times*, 24 November 2008, www.ft.com/cms/s/0/ddbc80d0-ba43-11dd-92c9-0000779fd18c.html.

11 National Intelligence Council, "Global Trends 2030: Alternative Worlds," December 2012.

12 "O for a Beaker Full of the Warm South," *The Economist*, 19 January 2013, www.economist.com/news/finance-and-economics/21569747-poor-co untries-other-poor-countries-matter-more-rich-ones-o-beaker.

13 UNCTAD, *Handbook of Statistics 2009* (Geneva: United Nations, 2009), unctad.org/en/pages/PublicationArchive.aspx?publicationid=2381.

14 Randall Schweller and Xiaoyu Pu, "After Unipolarity: China's Visions of International Order in an Era of U.S. Decline," *International Security* 36, no. 1 (2011): 41–72.

15 Mônica Herz, "New Directions in Brazilian Foreign Relations," Woodrow Wilson International Center for Scholars, 28 September 2007.

16 Layne points out that the United States does not threaten emerging powers' sovereignty and calls it a "liberal hegemon." Christopher Layne, "The Unipolar Illusion Revisited," *International Security* 31, no. 2 (2006): 7–41, 16–17.

17 See, for example, G. John Ikenberry, "The Future of the Liberal World Order," *Foreign Affairs* 90, no. 3 (2011): 56–68; and Ann Florini, "Rising Asian Powers and Changing Global Governance," *International Studies Review* 13, no. 1 (2011): 24–33.

18 Alastair Iain Johnston, "Is China a Status Quo Power?" *International Security* 27, no. 4 (2003): 5–56.

19 Chris Alden and Marco Antonio Vieira, "The New Diplomacy of the South: South Africa, Brazil, India and Trilateralism," *Third World Quarterly* 26, no. 7 (2005): 1077–95.

20 See, for example, Andrew Hurrell, "Lula's Brazil: a Rising Power, but Going Where?" *Current History* 107 (2008): 51–57.

21 Stephen Philip Cohen, *India: Emerging Power* (Washington, DC: Brookings Institution Press, 2002).

22 See, for example, Schweller, "Emerging Powers in an Age of Disorder."

23 Michael Doyle, *Ways of War and Peace. Realism, Liberalism and Socialism* (New York: W.W. Norton and Company, 1997).

24 Philip Stephens, "Rising Powers do not Want to Play by the West's Rules," *Financial Times*, 20 May 2010, www.ft.com/intl/cms/s/0/f9f1a54e-6458-11d f-8cba-00144feab49a.html.

25 G. John Ikenberry, "The Rise of China and the Future of the West," *Foreign Affairs* 87, no. 1 (2008): 23–37.
26 Ibid.
27 Hurrell, "Hegemony, Liberalism and Global Order," 19.
28 Jed Rubenfeld, "The Two World Orders," *The Wilson Quarterly* 27, no. 4 (2003): 22–36.
29 Ikenberry, "The Rise of China and the Future of the West."
30 Thomas L. Friedman, *The Lexus and the Olive Tree: Understanding Globalization* (New York: Farrar, Straus and Giroux, 2000).
31 Many scholars measure "critical mass" (population and territory), economic capability (GNP), and military capability as objective determinants of power, to which they sometimes add force postures, "strategic purpose," and "national will," which are less objective. Doyle, *Ways of War and Peace.*
32 Stephens, "Rising Powers do not Want to Play by the West's Rules."
33 Amrita Narlikar, "Bargaining for a Raise," *Internationale Politik*, 2006, ip-journal.dgap.org/en/ip-journal/topics/bargaining-raise.
34 Guimarães distinguishes between "normal" and "confrontational" states, categorizing Brazil as one of the latter. Samuel Pinheiro Guimarães, *Quinhentos Anos de Periferia* (Porto Alegre, Brazil: Contraponto, 1999).
35 From Steven Weber and Bruce W. Jentleson, *The End of Arrogance* (Cambridge, Mass.: Harvard University Press, 2011), 11. Nazneen Barma, Ely Ratner and Steve Weber, "A World Without the West," *National Interest* (July–August 2007). The authors identify a "third way" between alignment and confrontation, yet their scenario contains many elements of confrontation, as it is hardly possible simply to "ignore" the Western-dominated system without causing considerable friction.
36 Stephen D. Krasner, *Structural Conflict: The Third World Against Global Liberalism* (Berkeley, Calif.: University of California Press, 1985).
37 Jorge G. Castañeda, "Not Ready for Prime Time," *Foreign Affairs*, September/October 2010, www.foreignaffairs.com/articles/66577/jorge-g-castaneda/not-ready-for-prime-time; and Stewart Patrick, "Irresponsible Stakeholders?" *Foreign Affairs*, November/December 2010, www.foreignaffairs.com/articles/66793/stewart-patrick/irresponsible-stakeholders.
38 Moises Naím, "Rogue Aid," *Foreign Policy*, 1 March 2007, www.foreignpolicy.com/articles/2007/02/14/rogue_aid; Schweller. "Emerging Powers in an Age of Disorder," 285–97; and Matias Spektor, "A Place at the Top of the Tree," *Financial Times*, 22 February 2013, www.ft.com/intl/cms/s/2/9c7b7a22-27bb9-11e2-95b9-00144feabdc0.html.
39 Alden and Vieira, "The New Diplomacy of the South," 1077.
40 South-South cooperation describes the exchange of resources, technology, and knowledge between developing countries, including trade, investment, development assistance and other financial flows. South-South cooperation was grown considerably over the past decade. For example, Brazil's trade with Africa increased between 2000 and 2012 from US$4 billion to $28 billion. Partly as a consequence, Brazil has now 37 embassies on the African continent, more than the United Kingdom, and China is Africa's most important trading partner. China has also become Brazil's, South Africa's and India's most important trading partner over the past years, growing at higher rates than North-South trade. Trade between Africa and the BRICS

has grown so fast that it now even exceeds intra-BRICS trade. China, India and Brazil are also increasingly active as so-called "emerging donors," both in Africa and in their respective neighborhoods.

41 The term "global South" refers to developing nations in Africa, Central and Latin America, and most of Asia. It therefore includes countries that are not in the Southern hemisphere, such as India and China.

42 For more information, see: Oliver Stuenkel, "Can the BRICS Co-operate in the G-20? A View from Brazil," *SAIIA*, 3 December 2012, www.saiia. org.za/occasional-papers/can-the-brics-co-operate-in-the-g-20-a-view-from-brazil.

43 I present some related arguments in previously published articles in *Third World Quarterly* and a policy paper written for the UN High Level Panel on post-2015 development challenges.

1 The history of IBSA

First steps

- **A disconnected South**
- **Why IBSA? Three motivations**
- **IBSA's origins**
- **Joint action: IBSA and the patent case**
- **IBSA at the WTO: uniting the South**
- **Conclusion**

After providing a brief overview of relations between India, Brazil and South Africa after the end of the Cold War, this chapter recounts the intellectual origins of IBSA, the motivations that led the three countries to create the grouping, and two instances of successful cooperation—one immediately before and one after IBSA's birth in June 2003.

> IBSA is a unique model of transnational cooperation based on a common political identity. Our three countries come from three different continents but share similar worldviews and aspirations.
>
> (Manmohan Singh[1])

> What unites these nations from different continents are "big political ideas," which are best summarized in the premise of South-South solidarity.
>
> (Suzanne Graham[2])

> International politics, as are all forms of politics, is not only about who gets what, but also, and perhaps more fundamentally, about how people are treated.
>
> (Philip Nel[3])

A disconnected South

Both economic and political ties between India, Brazil and South Africa historically have been relatively insignificant.[4] There are some exceptions. For example, India was the first country in the world to isolate the apartheid regime in South Africa in 1946 and raise the issue at the UN, aside from recognizing the African National Congress (ANC) and allowing them to build a mission in New Delhi.[5] Yet overall, interaction during most of the Cold War was sporadic and of little long-term consequence.[6] Largely due to their limited participation in the global economy and the geographic distance between the three countries, India, Brazil and South Africa knew little about each other until the early 1990s. Trade between the three, as Figures 1.1–1.6 show, grew during the 1990s, but remained very low as a percentage of the three countries' overall trade.

It was only in 1994 that India reestablished political and economic ties with post-apartheid South Africa by setting up a joint India-South Africa ministerial commission. Despite such efforts, however, South Africa only represented 1 percent of India's total exports during the period 1995–2002 (see Figure 1.2).[7] This was largely due to trade barriers and the lack of transport and communication infrastructure between the two countries.

Brazil and South Africa, for their part, had closer ties than India and South Africa during the apartheid period, yet they were only minor trading partners. Brazilian governments initially kept bilateral relations with the apartheid regime despite international

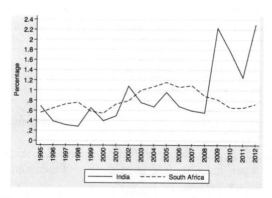

Figure 1.1 Brazilian exports to India and South Africa as a share of total Brazilian exports
(UNCTAD statistical database (UNCTAD STAT), unctad.org/en/pages/Statistics.aspx)

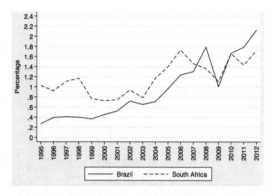

Figure 1.2 Indian exports to Brazil and South Africa as a share of total Indian exports
(UNCTAD statistical database (UNCTAD STAT), unctad.org/en/pages/Statistics.aspx)

condemnation, and in the 1960s, Brazil was the most important Latin American exporter to South Africa.[8] In 1974, Brazil's President Ernesto Geisel decided to end bilateral relations with South Africa and openly condemned the apartheid regime.[9] In the early 1990s, economic and political relations were once again established and President Fernando Henrique Cardoso became the first Brazilian president to make an official visit to South Africa in 1996. Yet similar to India-South Africa relations, trade ties between Brazil and South Africa remained insignificant throughout the 1990s (see Figure 1.8).

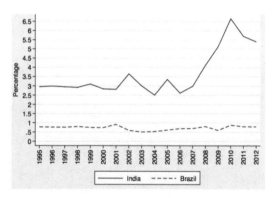

Figure 1.3 South African exports to Brazil and India as a share of total South African exports
(UNCTAD statistical database (UNCTAD STAT), unctad.org/en/pages/Statistics.aspx)

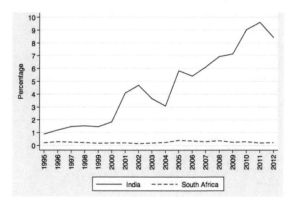

Figure 1.4 Brazilian imports from India and South Africa as a share of total Brazilian imports
(UNCTAD statistical database (UNCTAD STAT), unctad.org/en/pages/Statistics. aspx)

Ties between Brazil and India remained least significant of all—largely due to the great geographic distance that separates the two. Until well into the 1960s, there was not a single trade agreement between them, and no more than 20 Indian visas were issued for Brazilians annually, most of them for diplomats.[10] As Brazil's former Foreign Minister Lampreia points out, alignment was often spontaneous and coincidental, rather than planned.[11] While Brazil was geopolitically tied to the United States, India turned out to be much more aligned with the

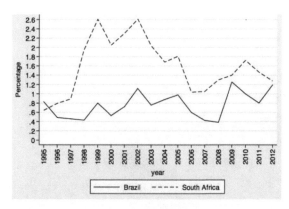

Figure 1.5 Indian imports from Brazil and South Africa as a share of total Indian imports
(UNCTAD statistical database (UNCTAD STAT), unctad.org/en/pages/Statistics. aspx)

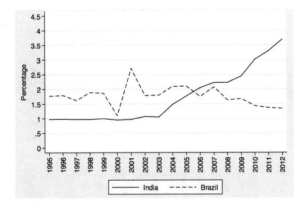

Figure 1.6 South African imports from Brazil and India as a share of total
South African imports
(UNCTAD statistical database (UNCTAD STAT), unctad.org/en/pages/Statistics.
aspx)

Soviet Union.[12] In 1976, at a time when the communist party was still
prohibited during the military dictatorship in Brazil,[13] a constitutional
amendment was passed to make India a socialist republic.[14] Ten years
later, India unofficially invited Brazil to turn into a full member of the
Non-Aligned Movement (NAM) to balance leftist radical countries,
but Brazil declined and preferred to remain an observer.[15] Throughout
the decades bilateral ties remained minimal, and in 1990, fewer than
100 Brazilians lived in India (see Figure 1.9).[16]

Yet after the end of the Cold War, Brazil and India began to liber-
alize their economies and pragmatically decided to diversify their

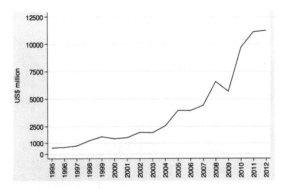

Figure 1.7 Trade between India and South Africa in US$ million
(UNCTAD statistical database (UNCTAD STAT), unctad.org/en/pages/Statistics.
aspx)

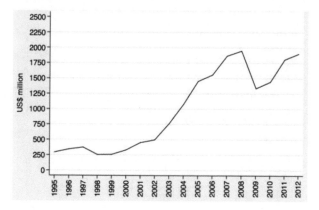

Figure 1.8 Trade between Brazil and South Africa in US$ million
(UNCTAD statistical database (UNCTAD STAT), unctad.org/en/pages/Statistics.
aspx)

partnerships. While not abandoning traditional allies in Europe and
North America, Cardoso carefully articulated and implemented Brazil's new global strategy, which involved stronger ties with other developing countries such as India. Cardoso visited India in 1996; President
Narayanan paid a return visit in 1998. Yet despite this political
approximation, trade ties remained extremely weak. Trade with India
represented less than 2 percent of Brazil's overall economic exchanges
between 1990 and 2000.[17]

Things changed when Brazil's President Lula da Silva took office.
Early on, he envisioned stronger ties with India. Critics pointed out

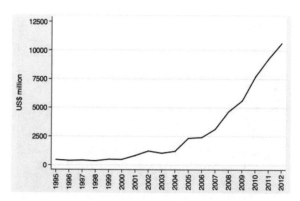

Figure 1.9 Trade between Brazil and India in US$ million
(UNCTAD statistical database (UNCTAD STAT), unctad.org/en/pages/Statistics.
aspx)

that the weak commercial links between the two did not justify a political alliance, reflecting that Brazilian foreign policy has traditionally been dictated by trade links. Lula, on the other hand, envisioned a political alliance as a starting point, from which trade links would be systematically fostered.[18] The creation of IBSA and a stronger emphasis on South-South ties is generally seen as a key element of President Lula and his Foreign Minister Amorim's foreign policy strategy between 2003 and 2010.[19] This move proved highly innovative. As Faria, Nogueira and Lopes point out, "irrespective of Brazil's insertion in any specific moment in history (equidistant, pragmatic, autonomous ... , responsible, assertive, etc.), the focus regarding national development was always tied to the relationship with the North—the motor of the global economy."[20]

The institutionalization of the trilateral IBSA grouping, then, symbolized, more than anything, a genuine effort to revise this tradition of mostly focusing on the world's established powers. No longer did Lula seek to design South-South ties complementary to relations with the North; from now on, they would be built in their own right.[21]

Why IBSA? Three motivations

As this brief historical overview shows, economic ties between IBSA countries were weak at the beginning of the twenty-first century, despite a low-level rapprochement during the 1990s. Why, then, did the three countries decide to create the IBSA Forum? What led these governments to devote efforts and resources to increase relations with faraway partners? What are the incentives for cooperation between India, Brazil and South Africa in the different working groups and nongovernmental forums?

We can point to three broad motivations that led decision makers in the three countries to initiate discussions about the creation of a platform. The first is to obtain greater independence and autonomy from established actors, i.e. the Group of 7 (G7), by diversifying partnerships. The concept of autonomy can be described as the capacity of a state to implement decisions based on its declared objectives, without interference by other actors or events beyond its borders. Autonomy requires the mobilization of power resources in the periphery: regional alliances against the center, integration (political and economic), and the improvement of negotiation techniques constitute the strategies to achieve this goal.[22] The IBSA Forum can thus be understood as an attempt to gain autonomy and greater independence from the economic core by diversifying partnership and strengthening economic and political ties to non-traditional members outside of their region. Senona writes that the goal of IBSA must be "political and economic cooperation aimed at unshackling and empowering these emerging, but still developing countries towards a path of sustained economic growth and development as well as catapult them to political iconism in a world of hegemonic North."[23] The concept of autonomy can be traced back to the "autonomous school" of Helio Jaguaribe in Brazil and Juan Carlos Puig in Argentina, who, influenced by Raul Prebisch, focused on reducing dependence on the United States in order to promote economic development in the global periphery or the so-called "Third World."[24]

In this aspect, the India-Brazil-South Africa Forum can be seen as an heir to attempts to establish international institutions in the global South during the Cold War. Writing about the creation of the NAM in 1955, Jacqueline Anne Braveboy-Wagner argues:

> one of the major aims of the global south nations has been to challenge the perceived inequality of the international status quo, achieve visibility for their concerns, and reduce their economic and political dependence on the north. To attain these ends, they have had to establish channels for the promotion of alternative norms and strategies.[25]

In a similar vein, Doyaili, Freytag and Draper write that one of IBSA's main "underlying value[s] is one of equity in international relations, an ethic that has long animated various South-South processes from at least the time of the Bandung forum in 1956."[26]

According to Nel, the goal of redistribution is premised on a more fundamental unfinished struggle of developing countries. This is the struggle for recognition of developing countries as full and equal partners in the society of states, but also as states with specific development needs that are too often ignored in the "spurious universality promoted by the developed North." The struggle for recognition focuses on inclusive multilateralism and "non-indifference" towards the development needs of the global South.[27] One of IBSA's concerns, in short, may be to change the way in which developing countries are treated in the society of states.

At the same time, the identification of IBSA with an ideological notion of the South must be assessed with caution. After all, emerging economies such as IBSA operate in a very different context, and have different needs, from many other poor developed countries. The usual North-South divide that existed in the 1970s has evolved into a new and far more complex international hierarchy with the IBSA countries, forming a sort of "intermediate level." As Vieira and Alden argue, their "interests, influence, and bargaining capabilities are closer to those of the advanced industrial world than to the development needs of the 'old South'."[29] The creation of IBSA may be partly motivated by a need for greater autonomy, but this cannot be understood as a simple continuation of the traditional economic and political demands of post-colonial states. This tension that exists between IBSA's "developing country rhetoric" and its divergent interests from smaller and poorer countries (and hence the growing difficulty to represent them) is a defining element when discussing IBSA's role in the global order. Given their stake in the system (and the benefits it provides), IBSA declarations suggest that South-South cooperation is not meant to eliminate and replace already existing North-South cooperation[29]—even though leaders' rhetoric may at times suggest otherwise.[30]

The second goal of institutionalizing South-South cooperation in the form of the IBSA Forum was to enhance the socialization process between emerging powers—for example, by exchanging best practices and identifying new areas of economic and political cooperation with formerly little-known actors. IBSA represents a necessary platform for galvanizing South-South cooperation and promoting greater understanding between three important parts of the developing world.[31] This goal can also explain the creation of working groups, which will be described in more detail in Chapter 3.

In light of how little IBSA countries know about each other, policy makers frequently argue that India, Brazil and South Africa face many similar internal challenges—ranging from socioeconomic inequality and low levels of public education to rapid urbanization—and that exchanging views and experiences could be a productive exercise for policy makers. Socialization is a key dimension of South-South cooperation (SSC) as it implies that "the three countries share similar social challenges and could learn more from each other's social policies and programs to address these challenges. Socialization then happens through knowledge sharing for capacity building through the different working groups."[32]

Finally, the third goal was to increase political leverage in international negotiations by working together with other countries in the global South, and to combine forces to pursue a specific reformist agenda in global politics. IBSA serves as a forum in which the three can discuss their own agenda and collectively present their positions on different global governance issues. This does not only concern working on specific issues within international institutions, but also reforming these institutions themselves to gain greater space. As Flemes argues, "from IBSA's perspective, the current international economic and financial architecture has not served the interests of the poor in developing countries."[32] Raja Mohan writes that IBSA "is about middle powers aspiring for a larger role by working with each other,"[34] and Fabricius points out that the key goal for IBSA members was to "increase the clout of the developing world."[35]

Looking back to the first decade of the new century, Matias Spektor writes that "the US went to war in the Middle East, Europe faltered, Asia rose, and the institutions that governed the world were evidently no longer up to the task. Unsettling as they were, these transformations opened up a new world of opportunities."[36]

Mzukisi Qobo alludes to a similar fact by writing that the world's established powers "were not only experiencing economic decline, but also waning intellectual and moral authority."[37] Kornegay sees the creation of IBSA as part of a larger process of turning global order into a multipolar, post-Western world moving toward the democratization of global governance in a "culturally diverse world."[38] Finally, Monica Hirst writes that "the IBSA coalition has built on niche diplomacy to deal with pressing realities in the developing world in defense of a non-westernized approach."[39]

The IBSA countries thus felt there was a common denominator in their desire to reform global institutions, and believed that by strengthening ties they could enhance their capacity to achieve their goals. From the very beginning, UN Security Council reform was therefore one of the central themes of the IBSA meetings. Qobo argues that IBSA's goal was to "establish a powerful counter-force to the dominant pole represented by the G8."[40] IBSA thus seems to have been a natural evolution for three countries that have, since the end of the Cold War, acquired a "prominent place in the bigger picture of International Relations, whether for their increasing regional importance or for their political activism in the multilateral environment."[41] Brazilian diplomats have summarized these goals by arguing that IBSA's objective was to "reshape the forces of globalization to make them more amenable to emerging powers' desires, interests and needs."[42] In a sense, the creation of IBSA was also the result of frustration that emerging powers' rise had not resulted in the reform of global governance for which they had hoped.[43]

At the same time, some have argued that IBSA is not an obvious successor of older forms of South-South solidarity based on multilateralism, but a vehicle for the development and increased projection of power in international affairs of its three members. This would imply, as mentioned above, that there is some tension between individual advancement superseding South-South solidarity.[44]

Indeed, the creation of IBSA and the group's members' growing global ambitions inevitably leads to questions about their regional role. India, Brazil and South Africa are often seen as "pivotal states"[45] that have a growing influence on international affairs. Yet at the same time, they also face limitations—being characterized as mere "regional powers" and "middle powers," the latter of which has been subject of ample debate.[46] Given their contested leadership position in their respective regions, their legitimacy to represent other countries in their vicinity is limited. Critics thus point out that IBSA's discursive strategy that focuses on its representative capacity is a mere fig leaf for a hard-nosed and self-interested attempt to turn into permanent members of the great power club. This dilemma is a key characteristic of the IBSA grouping, and possibly explains why cooperation with other regional powers is seen as a necessary element of each member's strategy to articulate a more global strategy. Geldenhuys argues that "a regional power could use the region as a springboard for a global role."[47] Some observers and IBSA policy makers privately respond that a restrained discourse will simply not be enough, and that "speaking in the name of the South" carries more weight.[48]

Box 1.1 From Third World to global South

The concept of the global South has become popular among analysts and policy makers over the past decades, replacing the term "Third World"—which referred to Africa, Asia and Latin America, that is, the countries located roughly in three Southern continents which share a history of underdevelopment and colonialism—and were often members of the NAM and the Group of 77 (G77). "Global South," by contrast, seems to be more neutral and less tied to the region's troubled past—and thus more apt for articulating a new narrative that no longer implies weakness, but which may also be tied to positive aspects such as high growth and the capacity to influence the global agenda.

In the 1960s and 1970s, the new developing nations were economically weak, strongly dependent on trade and investment links with the North and resentful about the legacy of colonialism. Arguing that there was strength in numbers, they gathered in a vast array of entities, led by the NAM, G77 at the UN, and the UN Conference on Trade and Development (UNCTAD). Speaking from weakness, they developed proposals like that of the New International Economic Order (NIEO), demanding large-scale transfers of resources from North to South. Though some Northern leaders listened to them (such as the drafters of documents like the Brandt Report), the South had little with which to back up their demands beyond their undeniable voting power in the UN General Assembly. As a consequence, they frequently ended up empty handed.[1]

The leaders of the global South no longer ask for aid, as Third World movements had done, but for a place at the table of the powerful. As large developing countries rise to the fore, they are able to speak from strength, not from weakness. Demands include a greater voice in the International Monetary Fund (IMF), the World Bank, and UN Security Council (UNSC) reform. China's role as the largest holder of US debt in the world is yet another sign of a new power dynamic between the North and the South, which was nonexistent during the twentieth century.

The creation of IBSA, in a sense, is thus a powerful symbol of this change.

Note

[1] Jorge Heine, "From Third World to New South," *The Hindu*, 27 April 2010, www.thehindu.com/opinion/lead/from-third-world-to-new-south/article412600.ece.

At the same time, IBSA countries' limited global reach also presented opportunities. Strengthening ties also seemed like a risk-free undertaking at the time, precisely because intra-IBSA ties were so low and because IBSA members' sphere of influence was previously limited. As Samuel Pinheiro Guimarães, a Brazilian diplomat and influential thinker during the Lula administration, points out in *Five Hundred Years on the Periphery*, "despite the differences between Brazil and other large peripheral states, inasmuch as they share common characteristics and interests and are far away from one another, they do not have direct competitive interests and are therefore able to construct common political projects."[49]

According to Zélia Roelofse-Campbell, "the main objective of IBSA is to speak with one voice at multilateral organisations. In a world of asymmetric economic power relations, developing countries had often felt marginalized … "[50] In response to this situation, as early as 2001, two years prior to the creation of IBSA, South Africa's President Thabo Mbeki argued:

In relation to possible future rounds of the WTO [World Trade Organization], our policy will be to seek to bring developing countries around a common agenda the so-called G-South. It is evident that only a co-ordinated response from the South will be able to secure sufficient concessions from the powerful industrialized countries.[52]

In a sense, goals described here do not differ much from what the developing countries have always sought to obtain. Like their predecessors who opposed neocolonialism and promoted an NIEO, India, Brazil and South Africa continue to be concerned about the unequal distributional outcomes of the global political economy. As their predecessors did, they also seek to influence the processes of a number of global regimes in order to secure better results for them and for their allies among the non-aligned countries of the world. This shows that the IBSA states are as committed to obtaining a redistribution of power, wealth and privilege in the global economy as was the first generation of post-colonial leaders.[52] Following earlier leaders, they prefer negotiation and dialogue with the North as the means to achieve such redistribution, rather than overthrowing the system. Similar to their predecessors, they see South-South solidarity and cooperation as a means to strengthen their position in the North-South dialogue.

What makes IBSA different from previous generations, however, is that they include a novel element in their overall argument—namely, that emerging powers are successful and that the rise of the global South is set to change fundamentally the distribution of power in global affairs. IBSA's *raison d'être* is profoundly influenced by this narrative. Emerging powers are far more influential than ever before, and they have the ambition to shape the global debate. Second, given the benefits they enjoy and which have contributed to their rise, they have a stake in today's structures, and are less willing to destabilize the status quo. As a consequence, they seek to balance a relatively status quo-oriented economic agenda that does not question the liberal elements of today's political economy with a more change-oriented foreign policy that seeks to rebalance and reform structures of global governance.

Considering these three motivations, IBSA can thus be characterized as both a strategic alliance for the pursuit of common interests in international institutions also as a platform for trilateral South-South cooperation.[53]

IBSA's origins

Although India, Brazil and South Africa had been invited to join the G8 (through the creation of the so-called Outreach 5 during the G8 meetings) the three felt that they were not being truly included in one of the world's most exclusive clubs.[54] It was time to create a "G8 of the Global South"[55]—an idea that had first surfaced among ANC members in the early 1990s, before the party took power in South Africa.[56]

South Africa's President Mbeki first articulated and promoted the idea of a trilateral platform in January 2003.[57] Chris Landsberg affirms that "IBSA is widely recognized, even by India and Brazil, as the brainchild and strategic idea of South Africa."[58] He further explains that:

> A strong boost was given to the eventual idea when foreign policy activist, Deputy President Thabo Mbeki started to openly punt the idea of the need for a "G8 of the South" or "G-South," as a potential counterweight to the powerful and dominant G8; as a powerful South bloc to engage the G8. The aim: extract commitments from the industrialised North on issues of trade, debt eradication, global social policy, aid, and global power relations. The idea of a G-South was key in the eventual establishment of IBSA.[59]

By then, Thabo Mbeki had already approached Brazil, China, Egypt, India, Mexico, Nigeria, and Saudi Arabia to join South Africa in forming the "G8 of the South," but eventually only Brazil and India showed serious interest in the offer.[60]

When, already President, Mbeki came to Brazil in January 2003 to attend the inauguration of President Luiz Inácio Lula da Silva, they discussed ways to strengthen ties. Later in 2003, a number of meetings between foreign ministers led to the idea of establishing a regular forum. The presence of the heads of state of India, Brazil and South Africa at the G8 summit in Evian, France, in 2003 offered the opportunity for the first high-level meeting where the common policy agenda of IBSA was presented to the wealthiest nations in the North. This led to the formalization of the partnership with the Brasília Declaration of June 2003.[61]

While South Africa's president may have had the initial idea, Celso Amorim, Brazil's foreign minister at the time, who enjoyed ample support from his president, soon turned into the key person to bring the grouping to life.[62] Amorim also affirmed that while South Africa's foreign minister suggested a larger grouping in early 2003 (including countries such as Saudi Arabia), he convinced Zuma that the grouping should be limited to three countries.[63]

Box 1.2 The first meeting of IBSA foreign ministers

Place: Brasília, Brazil
Date: 6 June 2003
Participants: Brazil's Minister of Foreign Relations Celso Amorim, Minister of External Affairs of India Pranab Mukherjee, and South Africa's Foreign Minister Nkosazana Dlamini-Zuma
Significance: Creation of the IBSA grouping
Results: IBSA was formalized and launched through the adoption of the Brasília Declaration, specifying cooperation in IBSA on three fronts: first, as a forum for consultation and coordination on global and regional political issues, such as the reform of the global institutions of political and economic governance, WTO/Doha Development Agenda, climate change, terrorism etc.; second, trilateral collaboration on concrete areas/projects, through working groups and people-to-people forums, for the common benefit of the three countries; and third, assisting other developing countries by taking up projects through the IBSA Fund, which would be established earlier.

When the three foreign ministers met in Brasília in June to discuss the details of the grouping, they particularly emphasized their belief that articulating their strategic visions in a united manner could increase their leverage. In the Brasília Declaration,[64] countries "agreed on the need to reform the United Nations, in particular the Security Council. In this regard, they stressed the necessity of expanding the Security Council in both permanent and non-permanent member categories, with the participation of developing countries in both categories."[65]

The need to reform the UNSC would become a principal *leitmotif* of all subsequent IBSA summits. In addition, they "identified the trilateral cooperation among themselves as an important tool for achieving the promotion of social and economic development and they emphasized their intention to give greater impetus to cooperation among their countries."[66]

Perhaps most importantly, the declaration, while welcoming the expansion of economic growth and the accompanying rise in the standard of living in several developing countries in recent years,

underlined their concern "that large parts of the world have not benefited from globalization."[67] At the same time, the IBSA grouping
clearly did not proclaim the desire to create an alternative global order
that provides greater rights to the developing world—the word
"reform" only appears once in the document. Rather, the initiative is
firmly placed within the framework of the existing international order
and the rules that undergird it, as the Brasília Declaration makes clear:
"Respecting the rule of international law, strengthening the United
Nations and the Security Council and prioritizing the exercise of
diplomacy as means to maintain international peace and security."[68]

In addition, IBSA's democratic character and potential commitment
to defending human rights immediately became part of IBSA's overall
rhetoric—an issue that will be analyzed in detail in Chapter 6. In
Brasília, leaders promised to coordinate their behavior in the UN
Human Rights Council and reaffirmed their commitment to the universality of human rights.[69] Both the decision not to include China and
the prominence of democracy in the declaration gave the IBSA
grouping a normative gloss: the Declaration reads that "this was a
pioneer meeting of … three countries with vibrant democracies … "[70]

Prime Minister Singh stressed that IBSA's normative approach
reflected a common identity of its member states and thus a key element of the grouping's overall purpose. In his closing remarks, he said:
"IBSA is a unique model of transnational cooperation based on
common political identity. Our three countries come from three different continents but share similar world views and aspirations." In sum,
IBSA's main objectives, according to its early pronouncements, were to
promote:

- South-South dialogue, cooperation and common positions on issues
  of inter-national importance;
- trade and investment opportunities between the three regions;
- poverty alleviation and social development internationally;
- turn collective strengths into "complementary synergies"; and
- cooperation in a broad range of areas, namely agriculture, climate
  change, culture, defense, education, energy, health, information
  society, science and technology, social development, trade and
  investment, tourism and transport.[71]

An additional meeting among the countries' foreign ministers took
place in September at the margins of the 58th UN General Assembly
(UNGA) in New York, during which they reiterated their willingness

to strengthen the "G-3," an alternative name for the IBSA grouping which has since fallen in disuse.[72]

Box 1.3 Meeting of IBSA foreign ministers on the sidelines of the 58th UN General Assembly

Place: New York, United States
Date: 24 September 2003
Participants: Brazil's Minister of Foreign Relations Celso Amorim, Minister of External Affairs of India Pranab Mukherjee, and South Africa's Foreign Minister Nkosazana Dlamini-Zuma
Results: The three countries agreed to cooperate on international forums and multilateral discussions, seeking to fight poverty and hunger, improve education, health and sanitation, and further UN reform. In addition, they agreed to move ahead in setting up the IBSA Fund with the aim of combating poverty and hunger.[1]

Note

[1] India-Brazil-South Africa Dialogue Forum (IBSA), "Press Release on the Occasion of the 59th Session of the United Nations General Assembly," 23 September 2004, www.ibsa-trilateral.org/images/stories/documents/foreign_ministers/IBSA_MIN_PRESS_UNGA59.pdf.

However, even after the meeting in September, few analysts believed the outfit had much potential.[73] The first IBSA Summit was received by the international media with neglect and skepticism.[74] Indeed, from the very beginning, many observers pointed out that despite the acronym's attractiveness and its capacity to offer an easy account of a new distribution of global power, the category was inadequate for a more rigorous analysis given that the differences between the IBSA countries far outweighed their commonalities. During the first years after its creation, few academics wrote about the grouping.[75] This can partly be explained by the low connectivity between the three countries: in 2003, total trade among IBSA countries stood at less than US$4 billion, and political ties were still incipient.[76] In addition, several observers saw it as a mere re-edition of Third Worldism of the 1970s.[77] Yet it is also important to recognize that the creation of IBSA was visionary, given that, at the time, the question of emerging powers was not as widespread as it would be five years later during the financial crisis that led to the institutionalization of the BRICS grouping.[78]

Policy makers decided to establish intra-IBSA cooperation on three levels. First, leaders of government would meet during the IBSA summits. Second, the so-called Trilateral Commissions would organize cooperation between the ministries and coordinate meetings between the ministers. Finally, collaboration would take place through the so-called Focal Points, which would be responsible for the activities of the Working Groups, whose tasks include, among others, the IBSA Fund. The Focal Points meet regularly, managing the overall activities of the IBSA Forum.

Yet it must also be asked why these particular countries decided to join forces. What do they have in common? There are several reasons to consider these three states as regional powers with relatively similar characteristics and ambitions. Aside from their important regional role, they have articulated some global ambitions.[79] Brazil has a continental scale and regional preponderance, both economically and militarily. It has about half of South America's population, territory, and gross domestic product (GDP). South Africa is a mid-sized, regionally important state, having only 6 percent of the population of sub-Saharan Africa, but a third of its GDP.[80] India is an emerging global power, with one sixth of the world's population and an increasingly important economy with a global reach. They share the ambition to shape the agendas and outcomes of their regional settings, with mixed success. All three rely on a preponderance of material and ideational resources and institutional capacities to project and defend their interests and values beyond their immediate borders and create, to differing degrees, cohesion in their respective regions by providing one or more public goods on which this cohesion depends.

Joint action: IBSA and the patent case

The creation of IBSA in June 2003 was by no means an untested experiment. An example of India, Brazil and South Africa cooperating successfully took place prior to the formation of the grouping. By that time, the three countries were actively involved in lobbying for an agreement to address the negative effects of the WTO Agreement on Trade Related Aspects of Intellectual Property Rights (TRIPS), thus representing a major concern in the developing world, as it limited their access to cheap medicines. The campaign led to the 2003 WTO General Council Decision (the "TRIPS Waiver"), which allowed developing countries to export locally produced generic drugs to countries facing public health crises, thus ensuring poor countries' access to cheaper versions of on-patent pharmaceuticals.[81]

In this context, IBSA member countries led the G21 lobby that succeeded in reducing the negative effects of TRIPS on patents that enforce high costs of HIV/AIDS drugs in developing countries, especially in Africa. An interpretative statement of the 2001 Doha Declaration made clear that TRIPS should not prevent states from fighting public health crises. Since then, the TRIPS agreement has provided for "compulsory licensing," allowing governments to issue licenses for drug production for the domestic market without the consent of the patent owner (usually located in the United States or Europe).[82]

IBSA at the WTO: uniting the South

A few months after the grouping's genesis the three countries acted together in the most impressive manner. In September 2003, at the WTO Ministerial Conference in Cancún, IBSA generated considerable political momentum in the multilateral arena. After developed countries prepared a joint text on agricultural trade, which would have perpetuated their right to subsidize their domestic agricultural sectors, developing countries responded by submitting an alternative. This marked the beginning of the G20+ coalition in the Doha Round agriculture negotiations. In the process, Brazil's foreign minister wrote later, IBSA helped create a developing world bloc within the WTO which played a decisive role in changing the negotiating model of the organization.[83] According to him, IBSA succeeded in convincing a group of 21 developing countries to block the final agreement. The G20 also rejected the so-called Singapore issues, which include trade facilitation, transparency in government procurement, competition policy and investment.

Indeed, even diplomats from European countries affirmed that the IBSA grouping was instrumental in bringing the Doha Round of negotiations to a halt by insisting on discussing the gradual liberalization of agricultural subsidies in the developed world.[84] Brazil and India jointly prepared the first draft of the G20+ response text and then collaborated with the other countries—including South Africa—that became members of the developing country bloc.[85] The IBSA countries "had a powerful moral voice in that they were major democracies in the developing world and had a clear normative proposition about the reform of global governance institutions."[86] It was in Mexico that a kind of Third World solidarity that had not defined

North-South relations since the 1970s briefly resurfaced as developing countries collectively resisted the industrialized world.

More important than having altered the global trade agenda and forcing industrialized countries to reassess their policies, however, several policy makers from the global South pointed out that 2003 marked a fundamental change in the overall dynamics of multilateralism.[87] Vieira and Alden even affirm that "the unified stance of resistance shown in Cancun by major players in the developing world marked the beginning of a new era in the international relations of the third world."[88]

This has led commentators to describe IBSA as the "central axis of the South" and the "hard core" of the G20 developing nations in the WTO. For White, IBSA "has played a pivotal role in shaping the global trade agenda over the past three years."[89] This was largely due to the developing world's previous incapacity to find a common denominator and maintain intra-group discipline.[90] Without Brazil's and India's leadership, several participants in the negotiation commented, the G20 would not have been able to adopt the common negotiating position necessary to reject the proposal made by the developed world.[91] At the same time, however, it is difficult to prove how far the creation of IBSA had anything to do with this process, or whether Brazil and India would have assumed a leadership role even without the creation of the platform. What one can say for sure is that the creation of the IBSA grouping in 2003 powerfully symbolized the beginning of a more assertive stance by developing countries in multilateral forums, and a willingness to increase South-South cooperation in specific instances such as agricultural negotiations at the WTO.

There were also critical voices. Flemes, for example, argued that:

> the G-3 has not always spoken on behalf of the global South. It is true that the WTO negotiations have failed because the industrialized countries have not been willing to reduce their agricultural subsidies to a sufficient extent, but the G-3 has not been representing the net food importers, most of whom are the least developed countries (LDCs), which are not interested in the reduction of the agricultural subsidies in Europe and the United States that keep prices low. The majority of the LDCs are Sub-Saharan African, South Asian and Latin American countries, which have not felt represented by their "regional leaders."[92]

Since Cancún, the G20+ has turned into a key actor in the Doha Round agriculture negotiations, allowing developing countries to act as agenda setters, a role traditionally played by the European Union (EU) and the United States in multilateral negotiations. Looking back, the IBSA grouping's capacity to cooperate was perhaps most surprising because Brazil's and India's key priorities differed substantially. While India's main aim was to protect its extremely large and unproductive number of farmers, Brazil is the most productive agricultural power in the world and it sought to obtain greater market access for its exports. In the area of financial services, retail trade and construction, the interests of South African companies supported a policy of closing the doors to foreign participation. In the industrial goods segment, India did not show willingness to make concessions and reduce the high tariffs practiced in specific sectors.

Yet thanks to continuous cooperation, Brazil and India have been able to continue their cooperation in the area, even representing the G20+ on other occasions, such as the G5 or "Five Interested Parties," which played a key role during agricultural negotiations in Geneva in 2004 and in Hong Kong in 2005.[93] The three members of IBSA also coordinated their actions in Hong Kong during the "Non-Agricultural Market Access-11" (NAMA-11), which played a role in the Doha Round's non-agricultural market access negotiations.

Conclusion

As this chapter shows, 2003 marked the first high point of South-South cooperation after historically insignificant ties up to the 1990s. The IBSA grouping can be seen as an attempt by three emerging countries to reduce their economic dependence on the industrialized world, reduce mutual ignorance about each other, and increase their leverage to reform international institutions. Successful cooperation immediately after the grouping's creation in the realm of trade policy was seen as evidence that if they found a common denominator, emerging powers could obtain much greater international influence than previously thought.

Notes

1 *Closing Remarks by Prime Minister Manmohan Singh at the 2nd IBSA Summit*, 17 October 2007.
2 Suzanne Graham, "South Africa's UN General Assembly Voting Record from 2003 to 2008: Comparing India, Brazil and South Africa," *Politikon: South African Journal of Political Studies* 38, no. 3 (2011): 416.
3 Philip Nel, "Redistribution and Recognition: What Emerging Regional Powers Want," *Review of International Studies* 36, no. 4 (2010): 963.

4 Antônio Carlos Lessa, "Brazil's Strategic Partnerships: An Assessment of the Lula Era (2003–10)," *Revista Brasileira de Política Internacional* 53 (2010): 115–31, 123.
5 Research and Information System for the Non-aligned and Other Developing Countries, ed., *Trinity of the South: Potential of India-Brazil-South Africa (IBSA) Partnership* (New Delhi, India: Academic Foundation, 2008), 23.
6 For a description of the history of Brazil-India relations, see: Oliver Stuenkel, "Seeing India Through Brazilian Eyes," *Seminar* 630 (2012): 2–5.
7 Folashadé Soule-Kohndou, "The India-Brazil-South Africa Forum a Decade on: Mismatched Partners or the Rise of the South?" *Global Economic Governance Programme Working Paper* 2013/88, University of Oxford, November 2013.
8 Wayne Selcher, *Brazil in the International System* (Boulder, Colo.: Westview Press, 1981).
9 UNCTAD, *Handbook of Statistics 2009*.
10 Stuenkel, "Seeing India Through Brazilian Eyes," 2–5.
11 Luiz Felipe Lampréia, "Liderança em Desenvolvimento," *Estado de São Paulo*, 3 May 1998.
12 Stephen P. Cohen, "India Rising," *The Wilson Quarterly* 24, no. 3 (2000): 32–53.
13 Edson Telles and Vladimir Safatle, *O que Resta da Ditadura: A Exceção Brasileira* (São Paulo: Boitempo Editorial, 2010), 259.
14 C. Raja Mohan, *Crossing the Rubicon: The Shaping of India's New Foreign Policy* (New York: Palgrave Macmillan, 2004).
15 Maíra Baé Baladão Vieira, "Relações Brasil-Índia (1991–2006)," Master's dissertation, *Universidade Federal do Rio Grande do Sul*, 2007.
16 Ibid.
17 UNCTAD, *Handbook of Statistics 2009*.
18 Amâncio Jorge Nunes Oliveira, Janina Onuki and Emmanuel de Oliveira, "Coalizões Sul-Sul e Multilateralismo: Países Intermediários e o Caso IBAS," in *Brasil, Índia, e África do Sul. Desafios e Oportunidades Para Novas Parcerias*, eds Mônica Hirst and Maria Regina Soares de Lima (São Paulo, Brazil: Paz e Terra, 2009).
19 Amado Luiz Cervo, "Brazil's Rise on the International Scene: Brazil and the World," *Revista Brasileira de Política Internacional* 53 (2010): 7–32; Carlos Aurélio Pimenta de Faria, Joana Laura Marinho Nogueira and Dawisson Belém Lopes, "Coordenação Intragovernamental para a Implementação da Política Externa Brasileira: O Caso do Fórum IBAS," *DADOS— Revista de Ciências Sociais, Rio de Janeiro* 55, no. 1 (2012): 173–220, 174.
20 Ibid., 179.
21 Amado Luiz Cervo and Clodoaldo Bueno, *História da Política Exterior do Brasil* (São Paulo, Brazil: Editora Ática, 1992).
22 Juan Carlos Puig, *Doctrinas internacionales y Autonomía Latinoamericana* (Caracas, Venezuela: Ación Bicentenario de Simón Bolívar, 1980); in Soule-Kohndou, "The India-Brazil-South Africa Forum a Decade on," 9.
23 Joseph Senona, "The IBSA Summit and the Political Economy of the Global South," *South Bulletin: Reflections and Foresights* 25 (2008): 8–10.
24 The main autonomous initiatives take place during the governments of Perón, Frondizi, Cámpora and Alfonsín (in Argentina), and Vargas, Kubitschek, Quadros and Goulart (in Brazil).

25 Jacqueline Anne Braveboy-Wagner, *Institutions of the Global South* (London: Routledge, 2008): 13.
26 Sarah al-Doyaili, Andreas Freytag and Peter Draper, "IBSA: Fading out or Forging a Common Vision?" *South African Journal of International Affairs* 20, no. 2 (2013): 297–310, 300.
27 Nel, "Redistribution and Recognition," 966.
28 Marco Antonio Vieira and Chris Alden, "India, Brazil, and South Africa (IBSA): South-South Cooperation and the Paradox of Regional Leadership," *Global Governance* 17, no. 4 (2011): 507–28, 512.
29 See paragraphs 11–13 of: India-Brazil-South Africa Dialogue Forum (IBSA), "2008 New Delhi IBSA Summit Declaration," 15 October 2008, www.itamaraty.gov.br/temas-mais-informacoes/temas-mais-informacoes/sa iba-mais-ibas/documentos-emitidos-pelos-chefes-de-estado-e-de/3rd-ibsa-su mmit-declaration/view.
30 Cervo and Bueno, *História da Política Exterior do Brasil.*
31 Graham, "South Africa's UN General Assembly Voting Record from 2003 to 2008," 413.
32 Soule-Kohndou, "The India-Brazil-South Africa Forum a Decade on," 14.
33 Daniel Flemes, "Emerging Middle Powers' Soft Balancing Strategy: State and Perspectives of the IBSA Dialogue Forum," *GIGA Working Papers* 57 (2007): 17.
34 C. Raja Mohan, "IBSA Forum, BRIC, Non-Aligned Movement, BRIC," *Indian Express*, 16 April 2010, www.indianexpress.com/news/ibsa-to-bricsa-china-churns-the-new-alphabet-soup/607112/.
35 Peter Fabricius, "IBSA is All Talk and, So Far, No Sign of Action," *The Star*, 27 July 2007, 20.
36 Matias Spektor, "A Place at the Top of the Tree," *Financial Times*, 22 February 2013, www.ft.com/intl/cms/s/2/9c7b7a22-27bb9-11e2-95b9-00144 feabdc0.html.
37 Mzukisi Qobo, "The Role of IBSA in Global Development: 10 Year Review," *DIRCO IBSA Review after 10 Years*, 29–30 April 2013, 3.
38 F. Kornegay, "Democracy, Cultural Diversity and the Question of Hegemony: The South African Dimension within the Context of IBSA," Paper presented at the First Academic Seminar of the India-Brazil-South Africa Dialogue Forum (IBSA), Brasília, 13 September 2006.
39 Monica Hirst, "Emerging Powers and Global Governance," Universidad de San Andrés, 2011, 2, www.udesa.edu.ar/files/UAHUMANIDADES/EVENTOS/PAPERHIRST11112.PDF.
40 Qobo, "The Role of IBSA in Global Development," 1.
41 T. Campos and L. Las Casas, "Similar Roles, Different Strategies: Brazil, India and South Africa Trade Policies," paper presented at the ISA's 50th Annual Convention, "Exploring the Past, Anticipating the Future," New York City, USA, 15 February 2009; in Graham, "South Africa's UN General Assembly Voting Record from 2003 to 2008," 411.
42 Interviews with Brazilian diplomats in Rio de Janeiro, June 2012.
43 Daniel Kurtz-Phelan, "What is IBSA Anyway?" *Americas Quarterly*, Spring 2013, www.americasquarterly.org/content/what-ibsa-anyway; in Sean Woolfrey, "The IBSA Dialogue Forum Ten Years On: Examining IBSA Cooperation on Trade," *Tralac Trade Brief* No. S13TB05/2013, August 2013, 3. See also: S. Cornelissen, "Awkward Embraces: Emerging

and Established Powers and the Shifting Features of Africa's International Relations in the Twenty-first Century," *Politikon* 436, no. 1 (2009): 5–26.

44 C. Moore, "Multilateralism and Trilateralism in the IBSA Partnership: Tensions and Congruities," Conference Papers—International Studies Association, 2008 Annual Meeting, citation.allacademic.com/meta/p_mla_apa_research_citation/2/5/1/8/2/p251820_index.html; in Graham, "South Africa's UN General Assembly Voting Record from 2003 to 2008," 411. However, this notion has been challenged by Alden and Vieira, who see no contradiction between IBSA and South-South solidarity. Chris Alden and Marco Antonio Vieira, "The New Diplomacy of the South: South Africa, Brazil, India and Trilateralism," *Third World Quarterly* 26, no. 7 (2005): 1077–95, 1077.

45 Jeffrey E. Garten, *The Big Ten: The Big Emerging Markets and How they Will Change Our Lives* (New York: Basic Books, 1997), XXV.

46 See, for example: S. Schirm, "Emerging Power Leadership in Global Governance: Assessing the Leader—Follower Nexus for Brazil and Germany," paper prepared for the ECPR Joint Session Workshop on the Rise of (New) Regional Powers in Global and Regional Politics, European Consortium for Political Research, Helsinki, 7–12 May 2007. See also: Andrew Hurrell, "Some Reflections on the Role of Intermediate Powers in International Institutions," Working Paper 244, Latin American Program—Woodrow Wilson International Centre for Scholars (2000), 1–12.

47 D. Geldenhuys, "The Idea-Driven Foreign Policy of a Regional Power: The Case of South Africa," paper prepared for the first Regional Powers Network (RPN) conference at the GIGA German Institute of Global and Area Studies in Hamburg, Germany, 15–16 September 2008.

48 Interviews with South African and Indian policy makers, academics, diplomats and former diplomats, 2012 and 2013, Pretoria and New Delhi.

49 Samuel Pinheiro Guimarães, *Quinhentos Anos de Periferia* (Porto Alegre, Brazil: Contraponto, 1999).

50 Zélia Roelofse-Campbell, "Some Insights into the IBSA Dialogue Forum," in Synopsis, *Policy Studies Bulletin of CPS* 8, no. 2 (2006): 15–17.

51 Department of Trade and Industry, "Industrial Strategy for the Republic of South Africa," www.polity.org.za/html/govdocs/discuss/industrat2/pdf, 15.

52 Nel, "Redistribution and Recognition," 953.

53 Flemes, "Emerging Middle Powers' Soft Balancing Strategy," 6.

54 Soule-Kohndou, "The India-Brazil-South Africa Forum a Decade on"

55 Center for Policy Studies (CPS), "India-Brazil-South Africa in a Multipolar World Synopsis," *Policy Studies Bulletin of CPS* 8, no. 2 (2006): 1.

56 João Genésio de Almeida Filho, "O Fórum de Diálogo Índia, Brasil e África do Sul (IBAS): análise e perspectivas," thesis presented at XLIX Course of High Level Studies in Rio-Branco Institute; in Gilberto F.G. de Moura, "O Diálogo Índia, Brasil, África do Sul—IBAS: Balanço e Perspectivas," in *III Conferência Nacional de Política Externa e Política Internacional "O Brasil no mundo que vem aí"—III CNPEPI—Seminário IBAS*, ed. Fundação Alexandre de Gusmão (FUNAG) (Brasília, Brazil: FUNAG, 2008), 157–31, 9.

57 Some observers argue that while 2003 can be associated most directly with IBSA's creation, the idea of a powerful alliance of the global South evolved thanks to the initiative for a larger and more decisive role for "emerging

powers" in the global financial architecture since the meeting of the "Willard Group" of 22 states in 1998, the creation of the G20 of finance ministers in 1999 under the tutelage of the IMF, and the initiative taken by Japan at the 2000 G8 meeting in Japan to invite President Olusegun Obasanjo of the Federal Republic of Nigeria, President Thabo Mbeki of the Republic of South Africa, President Abdelaziz Bouteflica of the Democratic People's Republic of Algeria, and Prime Minister Chuan Leekpai of the Kingdom of Thailand for consultations with the G8. Since then, most G8 summits have invited additional guests, in an indirect admission that the G8 alone could no longer claim sole authority to solve the world's most pressing problems.

58 Chris Landsberg, "IBSA's Political Origins, Significance and Challenges," *Policy Studies Bulletin of CPS* 8, no. 2 (2006): 4–7.

59 Ibid, 5.

60 Peter Fabricius, "IBSA Defends its Apparent Exclusivity," *The Star (Johannesburg)*, 19 October 2007; in Nel, "Redistribution and Recognition," 961.

61 Vieira and Alden, "India, Brazil, and South Africa (IBSA)," 509.

62 Interviews with Brazilian, South African and Indian policy makers, June 2012.

63 Celso Amorim, *Breves Narrativas Diplomáticas* (São Paulo, Brazil: Benvirá, 2013). Amorim also affirms that he had toyed with the idea of a G3 of Brazil, India and South Africa in early 1994, during his first stint as foreign minister.

64 IBSA, "Brasília Declaration."

65 Ibid., para. 4.

66 Ibid., para. 9.

67 John Cherian, "An Emerging Alliance," *Frontline* 21, no. 5 (2004), www.frontline.in/static/html/fl2105/stories/20040312000306100.htm.

68 Daniel Flemes, "India-Brazil-South Africa (IBSA) in the New Global Order: Interests, Strategies and Values of the Emerging Coalition," *International Studies* 46, no. 4 (2009): 401–21, 402.

69 IBSA, "Brasília Declaration."

70 IBSA, "Brasília Declaration"; Priya Chacko, "IBSA in the Foreign Policy of a Rising India," in *Contemporary India and South Africa: Legacies, Identities, Dilemmas*, ed. Sujata Patel and Tina Uys (New Delhi, India: Routledge, 2012).

71 India-Brazil-South Africa Dialogue Forum (IBSA), *About Us*, ibsa.nic.in/about_us.html.

72 Celso Amorim writes that until mid-2004, policy makers at times referred to the grouping as the G3, as they still considered the possibility of expanding the grouping (see: Amorim, *Breves Narrativas Diplomáticas*).

73 Soule-Kohndou, "The India-Brazil-South Africa Forum a Decade on," 1.

74 Greg Mills, "South Africa: Talk Shop with Offer of Exotic Travel," *All Africa*, 28 March 2006, allafrica.com/stories/200603280330.html. See also: Moura, "O Diálogo Índia, Brasil, África do Sul—IBAS," 10.

75 The first academic article about the grouping was published in 2005 (Alden and Vieira, "The New Diplomacy of the South").

76 Kurtz-Phelan, "What is IBSA Anyway?"

77 Ibid.

78 Ibid.

79 Nel, "Redistribution and Recognition," 957.

80 Gwynne Dyer, "South Africa at 20 is No Post-Apartheid Success Story," *The Salt Lake Tribune*, 15 February 2010, archive.sltrib.com/printfriendly.php?id=7859524&itype=storyID.
81 Flemes, "Emerging Middle Powers' Soft Balancing Strategy."
82 Flemes, "India-Brazil-South Africa (IBSA) in the New Global Order," 411.
83 Amorim, *Breves Narrativas Diplomáticas.*
84 Phone interviews with German and French diplomats, April 2012.
85 Amrita Narlikar and Diana Tussie, "The G20 at the Cancun Ministerial: Developing Countries and their Evolving Coalitions in the WTO," *The World Economy* 27, no. 7 (2004): 947–66, 952.
86 Qobo, "The Role of IBSA in Global Development," 2.
87 Interview with Celso Amorim, April 2013, Rio de Janeiro; and phone interview with Indian diplomat, October 2011.
88 Vieira and Alden, "India, Brazil, and South Africa (IBSA)," 510.
89 Lyal White, "IBSA: A State of the Art," in *South African Yearbook of International Affairs 2003/4* (Johannesburg: South African Institute of International Affairs, 2004), 11.
90 Alden and Vieira, "The New Diplomacy of the South," 1087.
91 Phone interviews with German and French diplomats, April 2012.
92 Flemes, "India-Brazil-South Africa (IBSA) in the New Global Order," 411.
93 Braz Baracuhy, "Rising Powers, Reforming Challenges: Negotiating Agriculture in the WTO Doha Round from a Brazilian Perspective," Working Paper no. 1, Centre for Rising Powers, 2011, 8.

2   Towards institutionalization

- **2004–06: laying the foundations**
- **2007–11: a time of action**
- **2012–14: slowing the pace**
- **Conclusion**

This chapter chronicles the process of institutionalization of the IBSA grouping from its first year of existence until today. The analysis shows that after leaders established the institutional structure of the grouping during the first years, IBSA enjoyed high-level political support and temporarily featured among the three countries' most important foreign policy initiatives. President Lula, in particular, symbolized his country's focus on strengthening South-South ties in general and South-South trade in particular. His successor, however, has given much less attention to the grouping, which led to a crisis in 2013 and a debate about whether IBSA should continue to exist as an independent outfit or whether it should merge with the BRICS grouping.

2004–06: laying the foundations

> The more we speak together the more impact we will have on world affairs.

> (Celso Amorim[1])

> … beyond these regular meetings, the IBSA leaders have failed to translate their statements into real action.

> (R. Beri[2])

On 25 January 2004, Brazil's President Lula met India's Prime Minister Atal Bihari Vajpayee in New Delhi and was the chief guest at

India's Republic Day parade. The visit to India, Lula's 20th foreign trip since assuming the presidency a year earlier, powerfully symbolized his wish to strengthen relations between two of the world's biggest democracies among developing nations. Lula took with him 100 businessmen and -women from 78 different companies in an effort to expand bilateral trade, as well as the Southern Common Market's (MERCOSUR) Eduardo Duhalde, Paraguay's foreign minister, Brazilian ministers and the governors of the Brazilian states of Paraná and Mato Grosso.

The Indian media was full of praise for Lula's seemingly natural appreciation of India's global role, and his talk of a "new trade geography" in the world. Indian policy makers frequently marveled at the Brazilian president's informal and friendly demeanor during the visit. "It seemed as if he had been to India many times before," one said.[3]

In what was seen as a crucial step at the time, India signed a preferential trade agreement (PTA) with MERCOSUR. Lula described the accord as the first step towards future free trade and as the inauguration of a "new era in South-South cooperation." At the same time, he was eager to point out that his strategy to foster South-South ties should not be seen as directed against the West. As he told Brazilian journalists in Rashtrapati Bhavan, the official home of the President of India, immediately after his arrival in New Delhi: "Emerging nations cannot sit and wait for beneficial concessions from the richer nations. Accords such as these should not substitute international relations with developed countries, but complement them."[4]

At the same time, the institutional form of the IBSA grouping also began to take shape. While the first stand-alone IBSA summit between state leaders would not take place until 2006, IBSA's foreign ministers had agreed to come together once a year on the margins of the UN General Assembly in September.

One hierarchical level below the foreign ministers, so-called Focal Points were created, which were crucial in connecting the leaders' political vision with the actual cooperation on the ground. In Brazil, the IBSA Focal Point is the Political Subsecretary for Africa, Asia, Oceania and the Middle East. This post was occupied by Roberto Jaguaribe (2007–10), Maria Edileuza Fontenele Reis (2010–14), and since early 2014 José Graça Lima. In South Africa, the responsible diplomat is Vice-Director General for Asia and the Middle East Jerry Matjila (since 2011). In India, the Focal Point is the so-called Secretary West, a position held by Nalin Surie (2006–09), Vivek Katju (2009–13) and Shri Dinkar Khullar (since 2013).

The Focal Points, who can be considered the key actors in the IBSA Forum, gather once per semester and have met 22 times since the grouping's inception.[5]

Below the Focal Points are the national coordinators. In Brazil's case, this is the Director of the Department of Regional Mechanisms of Itamaraty. In South Africa, it is the Director of the Department for Economic Affairs and Regional Organs. In India, it is the Secretary for Multilateral Economic Relations. The national coordinators are responsible for the coordination of the working groups.

In the Brazilian case, institutionalization at Itamaraty (the Ministry of Foreign Affairs) began in 2004 with the designation of one diplomat as responsible for coordinating IBSA-related activities both domestically and internationally. As administrative demands rose, a proper division was created for IBSA (called "DIBSA") in 2008, which was in turn renamed "Division for the IBSA Forum and the BRICS grouping" in 2010, even though it remained relatively small, with only three designated diplomats, having suffered a staff reduction in 2011—a potential sign that IBSA was no longer a priority for Lula's successor, Dilma Rousseff.

At the Foreign Ministries in Pretoria and New Delhi, similar arrangements were made to institutionalize the grouping around 2004. The decision to embed the IBSA structure in each member's Foreign Ministry was of great importance: had it remained attached to the heads of state, it could have been too closely associated to a particular leader, and a successor could have been tempted not to continue the initiative. This was particularly important as a new government took over in India in 2004, and India's new Prime Minister Manmohan Singh promptly voiced his intention to continue India's commitment to the IBSA grouping.[6]

The first meeting of the Trilateral Commission took place on 4 and 5 March 2004 in New Delhi. On this occasion, the foreign ministers discussed the progress achieved up to this point in the trilateral partnership. They also spoke about issues related to multilateralism and the proposed reforms of the UN, peace and security, terrorism, globalization, and sustainable and social development. The first communiqué issued by the three foreign ministers declared that the IBSA grouping would help "advance human development by promoting potential synergies among the members."[7]

The question of economic South-South cooperation dominated the discussion. Ministers committed themselves to increasing intra-BRICS trade flows to US\$10 billion within three years.[8] In order to achieve this goal, they promised to strengthen business linkages through PTAs and assess additional ways to foster intra-IBSA trade.

Box 2.1 First meeting of the Trilateral Commission

Place: New Delhi, India

Date: 4–5 March 2004

Participants: Brazil's Minister of Foreign Relations Celso Amorim, Minister of External Affairs of India Yashwant Sinha, and South Africa's Foreign Minister Nkosazana Dlamini-Zuma

Results: The countries made the commitment to increase South-South cooperation, reform the UN Security Council and ensure sustainable development alongside the well-being of people to underpin international peace and stability. The "Delhi Plan of Action" identified ambitious programs for strengthening trade, security cooperation, including joint peacekeeping, training and military exchange, cooperation in the area of combating narcotics trafficking and in the arms industry. It was agreed to collaborate in the area of education with special emphasis on quality and gender equality.

(From India-Brazil-South Africa Dialogue Forum (IBSA), "Joint Working Group (JWG) on Education—Introduction," ibsa.nic.in/intro_education. htm)

Foreign ministers yet again convened in September 2004 at the margins of the 59th UN General Assembly.

Box 2.2 Meeting of IBSA foreign ministers on the sidelines of the 59th UN General Assembly

Place: New York, United States

Date: 23 September 2004

Participants: Brazil's Minister of Foreign Relations Celso Amorim, Minister of External Affairs of India Pranab Mukherjee, and South Africa's Foreign Minister Nkosazana Dlamini-Zuma

Significance: The foreign ministers agreed to have closer political consultations amongst themselves and that the permanent representatives in New York would have regular meetings in this regard. Finally, referring to the recently launched IBSA Fund, they announced the launching of the first project to be financed by the fund, in support of agriculture and livestock development in Guinea-Bissau.

(From India-Brazil-South Africa Dialogue Forum (IBSA), "Press Release on the Occasion of the 59th Session of the United Nations General Assembly")

Finally, during the second meeting of IBSA Focal Points held in New Delhi on 29 and 30 November 2004, it was recommended that during the ministerial meeting on education, each IBSA country should offer to organize one roundtable conference each in the three areas of coop-eration, namely, open and distance education, higher and professional education and universal mass education.[9]

Looking back, the year 2004 was thus marked by an unprecedented degree of diplomatic interaction between Brazil, India and South Africa. Foreign ministers met three times during the year alone, underlining the mutual commitment to strengthen ties. While it is hard to pinpoint such unusual activities to one single factor, it seems that President Lula's foreign policy activism and eagerness to strengthen ties with other emerging powers strongly contributed to the IBSA grouping's initial importance. In addition, South Africa's President Thabo Mbeki, while not as much as Lula, had a strong personal interest in foreign policy and traveled frequently—which was often criticized at home.[10]

The second meeting of the Trilateral Commission, held on 10 and 11 March 2005, issued the Cape Town Ministerial Communiqué.[11] Here the ministers proposed a series of joint initiatives to be undertaken. They expressed their commitment to work with the UN towards the conclusion of the Millennium Review Summit in September 2005.

Box 2.3 Second meeting of the Trilateral Commission/ Third meeting of IBSA Focal Points

Place: Cape Town, South Africa
Date: 10–11 March 2005
Participants: Minister of Foreign Affairs of South Africa Nkosazana Dlamini-Zuma, Minister of External Affairs of India Natwar Singh, and Foreign Minister of Brazil Celso Amorim
Results: Cape Town Ministerial Communiqué and the establishment of the IBSA Business Forum.

Notably, the Cape Town Communiqué included one of the most explicit calls for UN Security Council reform. In paragraph 12 of the document:

> The ministers expressed the view that the composition of the UN Security Council no longer represented present-day realities. Bear-ing in mind that decisions of the Council should serve the interests

of the broader United Nations Membership, they highlighted the need for the urgent reform of the Council that would include its expansion in both categories of membership, permanent and non-permanent, in order to render it more democratic, legitimate and representative. Towards this end, developing countries from Asia, Africa and Latin America would need to be included as permanent members on the Security Council.[12]

Brazil's foreign minister repeated this argument during the opening speech at the 60th General Assembly in September, saying that " ... no Security Council reform will be meaningful should it not contemplate the expansion of permanent and non-permanent seats, with developing countries from Africa, Latin America and Asia in both categories. We cannot accept the perpetuation of imbalances that run contrary to the very spirit of multilateralism."[13]

UN Security Council reform stood at the center of international debates when the G4 (Germany, Japan, Brazil and India) circulated a draft resolution on reform to the General Assembly's 191 members in the hope of attracting the necessary two-thirds support.[14] Yet in the end, the proposal failed to be put to vote, since the United States, Russia and China would not endorse the plan and African nations did not support the compromise that would leave new permanent members without veto power. Yet supporters of reform had come closer to their aim than never before, and the episode strengthened the notion among policy makers in Brasília, Pretoria and New Delhi that working together could bring tangible gains.[15] At the same time, it clearly showed that all three IBSA members' claims to regional leadership were highly contested. Rather than giving support, IBSA's neighboring countries had been the most vocal critics of the reform proposal.

Further meetings occurred between the Focal Points in Rio de Janeiro in 2005 and in Vereeniging (South Africa) in late November, during which the creation of additional IBSA working groups was discussed.

Box 2.4 Third meeting of the Trilateral Commission

Place: Rio de Janeiro, Brazil
Date: 28–30 March 2006
Participants: India's Minister for External Affairs Anand Sharma, Brazil's Minister of Foreign Relations Celso Amorim, and South Africa's Minister of Foreign Affairs Nkosazana Dlamini-Zuma
Results: Rio de Janeiro Ministerial Communiqué

The foreign ministers' meeting in Rio de Janeiro saw a further expansion of IBSA-related activities.[16] They agreed to institutionalize the UN-managed IBSA Fund, discussed additional IBSA working groups, and referred to the creation of an IBSA Business Forum to enhance economic ties between member countries. The document described in great detail the obstacles to stronger trade and how government sought to overcome them. Notably, ministers also announced the first stand-alone presidential IBSA summit in Brazil later that year.

Box 2.5 First IBSA Summit

Place: Brasília, Brazil
Date: 13 September 2006
Participants: Prime Minister of India Manmohan Singh, President of Brazil Luiz Inácio Lula da Silva, and President of South Africa Thabo Mbeki
Results: First IBSA Summit Joint Declaration

After several ministerial meetings, President Lula da Silva, President Mbeki and Prime Minister Manmohan Singh held the First IBSA Summit in Brasília in September 2006. This meeting, first suggested by the Brazilian government, can be seen as a high point of IBSA cooperation and a sign of the countries' continued commitment to enhancing ties. While the crisis of 2008 (which would temporarily reduce the West's capacity to influence global affairs) was still several years away, the summit was marked by optimism and a growing assertiveness among emerging powers.[17] At the summit, leaders predicted the coming of "a fair and equitable global order."[18] The steps taken in the meeting, according to Brazilian President Lula da Silva, were fundamental in "overcoming historical, geographic, cultural and mental barriers that have always made us look to the North rather than the South."[19] Quite notably, Manmohan Singh was the first Indian prime minister in 38 years to travel to Brazil, showing how limited bilateral ties had been during previous decades.

Aside from the symbolic rhetoric, the summit largely focused on agreements aimed at stimulating trade between and economic growth in the three countries. President Mbeki expressed his hope that IBSA would soon form a free trade agreement between the three countries:

> Beyond the bilateral agreements, we are exploring the prospect of a Trilateral Free Trade Agreement (TFTA). Such an outcome

would be without precedent in the global trading system ... This agreement should be capable of delivering on the developmental challenges we face, challenges of unemployment, poverty and underdevelopment. The agreements we model should provide leadership and creative economic impetus to the global system of trade, which delivers little to the many and too much to the few.[20]

After a meeting between the countries' representatives, they also agreed to establish an "IBSA Revenue Administration Working Group" to discuss these issues further.[21]

Parallel to the summit, an academic seminar took place in Brasília which brought together researchers to discuss issues of common interest, and to establish ties between universities of the three countries.

In addition to strengthening the academic dialogue, participants and organizers at times mention that the documents produced for and during this encounter should benefit policy makers. Jerônimo Moscardo, president of the Alexandre Gusmão Foundation at the time, argues that "the seminar served as ammunition for the summit of heads of state and government." Yet it remains highly doubtful that the outcome document of the academic seminars has any influence, let alone comes to the attention of diplomats involved in the process.

The three governments also coordinated their standpoints and voting behavior in the NAM conference in Havana (which would take place immediately after the IBSA summit) and the 61st UN General Assembly session, where South Africa was elected a non-permanent member of the UN Security Council (2007–08) for the first time.

Despite the flurry of diplomatic activities and high-level meetings, the general public remained deeply skeptical of the usefulness or significance of the IBSA grouping. In the Western media, the summits were barely commented on. Several years after the creation of the grouping, the number of academics writing about it remained extremely small. Even sympathetic reporting by Indian journalists sounded quite defensive: "Who says summitry of the IBSA kind is a waste of time?" T.K. Arun of India's *Economic Times* asked after the presidential summit in September after citing a long list of potential benefits of the grouping.[22]

While the summits continued to focus on the expansion of trade ties, which indeed grew considerably (albeit from a very low base), policy makers tried hard to identify additional areas of cooperation. Establishing working groups (which will be described in detail below) for many different areas was seen as the best way to establish stronger ties in different areas, such as agriculture, education, health and defense.

2007–11: a time of action

> IBSA is a strong moral force in today's unsettled world.
>
> (Manmohan Singh[23])

In June 2007, three years after his first visit to India, President Lula returned to Delhi promising to "transform" his country's political and economic relations with India through a series of bilateral initiatives and increased cooperation in international affairs.[24] Together with India's Prime Minister Manmohan Singh, he announced the India-Brazil CEO Forum, co-chaired by Ratan Tata and Jose Sergio Gabrielli, then president of Brazil's state oil firm Petrobras. "We are working to transform the strategic partnership (with India) ... it has grown a lot, from 2000 to 2005, exports to India increased by 422 percent and imports from India increased by 343 percent," the president said.[25] Indeed, the two-way trade between India and Brazil had registered a strong increase from $488 million in 2000 to $2.4 billion in 2006, and in Delhi both governments set a bilateral trade target of $10 billion by 2010.[26] Yet at the time, the PTA still had to be ratified by the legislatures of Brazil and Argentina.

A month later, on 16 July 2003, the Fourth Meeting of the Trilateral Commission began in New Delhi. Yet again, the idea of one economic space between MERCOSUR, the Southern African Customs Union (SACU) and India dominated the debate. In an interview with *The Hindu*, an Indian newspaper supportive of the idea of stronger South-South cooperation at the time, Brazilian Foreign Minister Celso Amorim said the emergence of such a large economic space would place India, Brazil and South Africa in a better position to face the North "in a creative, competitive way." At the same time, he acknowledged that the three countries had only so far "scratched the surface" in terms of mutual cooperation, blaming "closed bureaucratic and entrepreneurial practices" for the slow pace, especially when it came to the formation of joint ventures.[27]

Box 2.6 Fourth meeting of the Trilateral Commission/ninth meeting of IBSA Focal Points

Place: New Delhi, India
Date: 16–17 July 2007
Participants: India's Minister of External Affairs Pranab Mukherjee, Brazil's Minister of Foreign Relations Celso Amorim, and South Africa's Minister of Foreign Affairs Nkosazana Dlamini-Zuma
Results: New Delhi Ministerial Communiqué

Foreign ministers yet again gathered in New York at the margins of the 62nd UN General Assembly, during which they mostly discussed trade issues and the development projects supported by the IBSA Fund.

Box 2.7 Meeting of IBSA foreign ministers on the sidelines of the 62nd UN General Assembly

Place: New York, United States

Date: 26 September 2007

Participants: Brazil's Minister of Foreign Affairs Celso Amorim, India's Minister of External Affairs Pranab Mukherjee, and South Africa's Minister of International Relations and Cooperation Nkosazana Dlamini-Zuma

Significance: The foreign ministers mentioned the launch of further projects financed by the IBSA Fund, as well as commenting on the activities by the growing number of IBSA working groups. On trade issues, the ministers welcomed the upcoming meeting in October 2007 of the group responsible for considering the modalities for the envisaged TFTA among MERCOSUR, SACU and India, reflecting certain optimism at the time that a trade agreement could be reached.

On 17 October 2007, the Second IBSA Summit was held in Pretoria, South Africa. Manmohan Singh yet again urged businesses to take the lead in strengthening South-South cooperation: "We have set ourselves a modest target of $15 billion by 2010 for trade among our three countries. My suggestion to our business leaders would be to aim to achieve this by 2009 and then go on to double that by 2012. Business must be pro-active."[28]

Box 2.8 Second IBSA Summit

Place: Pretoria, South Africa

Date: 17 October 2007

Participants: India's Prime Minister Manmohan Singh, Brazil's President Luiz Inácio Lula da Silva, South Africa's President Thabo Mbeki

Results: Tshwane Declaration, Signing of a Tax and Customs Cooperation Agreement, multiple Memoranda of Understanding regarding cooperation on culture, wind power, social themes, health, medicine, public administration and governance.

How can it be explained that IBSA presidents decided to hold yet another summit merely a year after the first encounter in Brasília? Why were they so concerned about increasing trade between each other?

Intra-BRICS activism at the time must be understood in the context of a growing notion that multilateral trade talks were not advancing, largely because rich countries had established a powerful and solid coalition. It was precisely because of this united position of industrialized countries that IBSA leaders were so keen on finding a joint position.[29]

At the same time, the early years of the IBSA grouping was made possible by leaders from Brazil, India and South Africa who all considered foreign policy to be a key element of their overall project. Prior to the summit in Pretoria, for example, both Lula and Singh had visited several African countries.[30] Conscious of this rare coincidence, advisors who participated in these encounters were concerned about institutionalizing the grouping as quickly as possible so that ties would not be undone by future leaders less interested in the IBSA grouping.[31]

Shortly after the Second IBSA Summit of presidents, Roberto Mangabeira Unger, Brazil's Minister for Long-Term Strategic Planning, argued that it was IBSA's goal to "develop a shared geopolitical vision." Countries "had a shared stake in a world that is safe for a plurality of power and vision. Such a world can't be a world that is organized either around duopoly of power of the US and China or a state of latent belligerence between the US and China. Our basic stake is to make the world situation more complicated and richer in sources of thought, of capability, of power."[32]

He further argued that IBSA's significance for the future depended on:

> whether we can transform it into an instrument for the shared development of a model of social inclusive growth and of geopolitical vision that serves the goal of a plurality of power in the world ... Each has to acquire a force in association with the other. Diplomacy is never enough without ideas. We should resist the temptation to retreat, as professional diplomats sometimes do, to a world of power politics bereft of ideological proposals. In a world of democracy, the politics of power and ideas are inseparable. There is a vital burning question ... What will we do to rescue the majority imprisoned in the disorganized economy? The future of our countries and IBSA will turn on the answer we give to this question.[33]

Even though not expressed explicitly, Mangabeira Unger's ideas were undergirded by the assumption that South-South cooperation is the key to a more equal, less exploitative and mutually beneficial kind of inter-national system. This claim will be analyzed in more detail in Chapter 5.

Box 2.9 Fifth meeting of the Trilateral Commission

Place: Somerset West, South Africa
Date: 11 May 2008
Participants: Minister of External Affairs of India Pranab Mukherjee, Minister of Foreign Relations of Brazil Celso Amorim, and Minister of Foreign Affairs of South Africa Nkosazana Dlamini-Zuma
Results: Fifth Ministerial IBSA Communiqué

The fifth meeting of the Trilateral Commission, attended by the IBSA foreign ministers, yet again promised to expand cooperation. Notably, the participating ministers mentioned the first IBSA Joint Naval Exercises which were taking place in South Africa's territorial waters during the time of the fifth IBSA ministerial meeting.

In addition to IBSA, Brazil and India began to engage in the BRIC grouping in 2008. In May 2008, only five days after the IBSA meeting in South Africa, the BRICs foreign ministers held their first stand-alone meeting in Yekaterinburg, after which they issued the first joint BRICs communiqué—a move which, according to Brazil's Foreign Minister Celso Amorim, "said more about multipolarity than words could ever do."[34]

Box 2.10 Third IBSA Summit

Place: New Delhi, India
Date: 15 October 2008
Participants: Brazil's President Luis Inácio Lula da Silva, India's Prime Minister Manmohan Singh, and South Africa's President Kgalema Motlanthe
Results: Third IBSA Summit Declaration

In 2008, President Lula visited India for the third time since taking office, underlining his conviction that Brazil-India ties needed to be strengthened. By 2006, Brazil and India referred to each other as "strategic partners," a move that received considerable attention in India's foreign policy community.[35]

At the Third IBSA Summit, the leaders spoke about ways of better involving civil society in the intra-IBSA activities and argued that the participation of academia, business leaders, editors and women's groups in their respective forums was a crucial step to increase citizens' participation. During the summit, an IBSA Cultural Festival and the first Food Festival took place in New Delhi, coordinated by the IBSA Working Group on Culture. Indeed, in the year 2008 alone, a total of 21 official international meetings had taken place in the context of IBSA (most of them working groups)—an unprecedented number which brought together many government and civil society representatives on different levels. "IBSA has an important role to play internationally. We are meeting against the backdrop of the international financial crisis," Prime Minister Singh said while opening the Third IBSA Summit. "Our voice on how to manage this crisis in a way that does not jeopardize our development priorities needs to be heard in international councils."[36]

The leaders' final declaration included yet another explicit reference to the creation of a free trade agreement:

> With reference to paragraph 8 of the Somerset West Ministerial Communiqué, South Africa, 11 May 2008, the leaders reaffirmed the importance of granting support to the goal of the envisaged MERCOSUR-SACU-India Trilateral Trade Arrangement (TTA) at the highest political level. In this regard, they welcomed the proposal of a MERCOSUR-SACU-India trilateral ministerial meeting in order to promote high-level discussions on the topic.[37]

Yet several policy makers privately admitted that internal constraints and political costs leaders faced were probably too high to achieve a trade agreement.[38] It remains somewhat surprising, then, that leaders kept insisting on including their hope for the conclusion of a trade agreement into every single declaration. In the eyes of Indian and Brazilian businessmen interviewed, this reduced the credibility of the grouping, since the declarations did not reflect how difficult and unlikely it would be to reduce trade obstacles between the three economies in a meaningful way. Several businessmen interviewed argued that the declarations "raised false hopes."[39]

While the IBSA Summit Declaration of 2008 had announced that the fourth summit would take place in Brazil in October 2009, scheduling issues led to its postponement to 2010. After consecutive meetings in 2006, 2007 and 2008, this would be the first year without a presidents' IBSA summit.

The creation of a new grouping may have influenced that decision. On 16 June 2009, Russia hosted the first BRIC Leaders' Summit, which was attended by Brazil's President Lula, Russia's President Dimitry Medvedev, India's Prime Minister Singh and China's President Hu Jintao, in Yekaterinburg. Host Dmitry Medvedev hailed the Urals city of Yekaterinburg as "the epicenter of world politics." The need for major developing world nations to meet in new formats was "obvious," he said.[40] Only a day earlier, Russia had hosted, in the same city, the ninth Summit of the Shanghai Cooperation Organization (SCO), with many observer countries, including a brief visit by Mahmoud Ahmadinejad, who had just been declared the winner of a controversial presidential election in Iran.

The financial crisis at the heart of the global economic core was widely thought to have profound consequences for all countries that participated in the international market. Yet, as *The Economist* wrote at the time, the largest emerging markets were "recovering fast and starting to think the recession may mark another milestone in a worldwide shift of economic power away from the West."[41]

Box 2.11 Sixth meeting of the Trilateral Commission

Place: Brasília, Brazil
Date: 31 August–1 September 2009
Participants: Brazil's Minister of Foreign Affairs Celso Amorim, India's Minister of External Affairs S.M. Krishna, and South Africa's Minister of International Relations and Cooperation Maite Nkoana-Mashabane
Results: Sixth IBSA Trilateral Ministerial Commission Meeting Communiqué

Box 2.12 Meeting of IBSA foreign ministers on the sidelines of the 64th UN General Assembly

Place: New York, United States
Date: 21 September 2009
Participants: Brazil's Minister of Foreign Affairs Celso Amorim, India's Minister of External Affairs S.M. Krishna, and South Africa's Minister of International Relations and Cooperation Maite Nkoana-Mashabane

Yet despite the rise of the BRIC grouping—which due to Russia's and China's membership generated a far stronger reaction in the global media than the IBSA grouping, IBSA-related events continued to take place. While the BRIC grouping dominated the headlines, policy makers in Brazil and India felt that due to IBSA's more sophisticated institutional structure, it could have a more lasting impact on global affairs.[42] During the sixth meeting of the Trilateral Commission, as a consequence, foreign ministers stressed in the communiqué that intra-IBSA cooperation was not confined to governments but also included business communities, civil society, and other people-to-people contacts.[43]

At the meeting, the ministers also hailed the entry into force of the PTA between MERCOSUR and India, as well as the conclusion of the PTA between MERCOSUR and SACU. Still, due to the small number of products included, the business communities of the countries involved did not consider the deal to be consequential.[44]

Returning to the theme of what Brazil's President Lula had once termed "a different kind of globalization," the communiqué pointed out that the ministers:

> Acknowledge the need to ensure that trade agreements and free trade agreements between countries of the South and North provide the necessary "policy space," allowing individual developing countries to construct their own development paths. Also acknowledge the need to forge coherent multilateral policy making and establish mutually supportive systems for governing international trade, monetary and financial relations. Whilst rules are important, existing multilateral governance structures should be reformed to promote development and ensure equity. Development lies at the heart of the future prosperity and stability of the world economy, and, indeed, to the future of globalisation.[45]

In response, Gilley argued that IBSA is "an alliance that seeks to use democratic ideals to effectively reshape the U.N. and other international institutions to serve poor countries better. In a strange way, IBSA is a community of democracies from hell—a group of countries with impeccable democratic credentials who are using that common identity to challenge rather than advance US interests."[46]

The Fourth IBSA Summit took place immediately after the Second BRIC Summit—a decision that, despite India's interest in keeping the two separate—could largely be explained by scheduling difficulties.[47] The two groupings were originally meant to meet over two days, but with China's President Hu Jintao cutting short his visit because of an earthquake in

Qinghai, the India-Brazil-South Africa forum and the Brazil, Russia, India, China group both met within hours of each other on 15 April.[48]

The international media paid very little attention to the IBSA meeting and more to the BRIC Summit, which saw the Russian, Indian and Chinese heads of state in Latin America simultaneously for the first time.[49]

On the occasion of the Fourth IBSA Summit in Brasília in 2010,[50] there were also meetings of the IBSA academic forum, the IBSA parliamentary forum, the IBSA women's forum, and the IBSA editors' forum, pointing to a strong proliferation of activities in the IBSA context.[51] In addition, the 15th IBSA Focal Point encounter was organized, as well as gatherings among IBSA small business CEOs. Also, there was a round table on local governance as well as an exhibit on the IBSA Fund.[52]

Box 2.13 Fourth IBSA Summit

Place: Brasília, Brazil
Date: 15 April 2010
Participants: Brazil's President Luis Inácio Lula da Silva, India's Prime Minister Manmohan Singh, and South Africa's President Jacob Zuma
Results: Fourth IBSA Summit Declaration

For the first time, the IBSA Forum also held a ministerial-level meeting with the foreign minister of Palestine, Riad al-Malki. The IBSA countries had recently started jointly funding sports facilities for the Palestinians in Ramallah. India was represented by Commerce and Industry Minister Anand Sharma. The ministers expressed strong disappointment over the continued construction of settlements by Israel in the Occupied Territories and committed IBSA to support "proactively" the formation of a viable Palestinian state.[53]

Box 2.14 Meeting of IBSA foreign ministers on the sidelines of the 65th UN General Assembly

Place: New York, United States
Date: 25 September 2010
Participants: Minister of External Affairs of the Republic of India S.M. Krishna, Minister of Foreign Relations of Brazil Ambassador Celso Amorim, and Minister of International Relations and Cooperation of South Africa Maite Nkoana-Mashabane

Results: Ministerial Meeting at the margin of the 65th UNGA
Communiqué

In the declaration, the foreign ministers made reference to a meeting
hosted by Indonesia on the sidelines of the General Debate of the 65th
Session of the UN General Assembly, on the situation in Palestine in
which Brazil, India and South Africa participated, as a concrete example
of developing countries meeting to discuss ways of assisting the country. In
a similar vein, the ministers also noted the "historic occasion" in 2011 in
which all three IBSA countries would serve on the UN Security Council.
In the declaration, they stressed the "importance for IBSA to work together on the Security Council with the aim of making the Council more
responsive and transparent in the execution of its mandate."[54]

Box 2.15 The IBSA satellite program

The creation of the IBSA satellite program was announced at
the conclusion of the Fourth IBSA Summit in Brasília in April
2010. Lula da Silva remarked that the satellite would "benefit
the IBSA countries and other friendly countries, providing more
effect in matters of agriculture, transport and telecommunications.
It is a project symbolic of the new stage in our partnership."[1]

The IBSA satellite was supposed to be used for studying climate to help the agriculture sector in the three countries. "Space
weather influences earth weather as well as affecting satellites,"
a South African expert explained.[2] The space weather satellite
would especially study space weather over the South Atlantic.
Rather than buying a satellite from the industrialized world,
IBSA leaders had agreed that IBSA satellites would be smaller
and cheaper, and so more affordable.[3] Singh commented that
strengthening cooperation in science and technology, energy
and ocean research were "the hallmark of the forum."[4] South
Africa's President Zuma, for his part, argued that the satellite
offered "an opportunity to expand our cooperation into
advanced technology, increasing our collective scientific and
engineering capacity. We see this initiative as an opportunity to
reinforce our shared developmental objectives."[5]

An ambitious schedule was set out. A weather satellite would be
built and launched in 2012. An Earth observation satellite would
follow in 2014.[6] While this led to great expectations among
observers in South Africa, India and Brazil, the 2011 IBSA

Tshwane Declaration merely noted that India had agreed to host an IBSA satellite technical meeting to discuss the satellite project.

With the Sixth IBSA Summit postponed and no new date in sight, plans for the IBSA satellites have mostly been forgotten. Brazil preferred to cooperate with China. The two countries have developed and launched three Earth resources satellites already to benefit nations that do not have their own satellites to monitor natural resources, agricultural zones and urban development.[7] In 2012, Premier Wen and President Rousseff announced that the two countries would make concerted efforts to pursue the launch of Satellite 03 of the China-Brazil Earth Resource Satellite series in 2013 and Satellite 04 in 2014.[8]

Notes

[1] Keith Campbell, "South African Technology Key to Ibsa Satellite Programme," *Engineering News*, 30 April 2010, www.engineeringn ews.co.za/article/south-african-technology-key-to-india-brazil-south-africa-satellite-programme-2010-04-30.

[2] Ibid.

[3] Ibid.

[4] Press Trust of India, "IBSA to Develop Satellites, Cooperate on Global Issues," *The Hindu*, 16 April 2010, www.thehindu.com/news/national/ibsa-to-develop-satellites-cooperate-on-global-issues/article398622.ece.

[5] "Joint Satellite Launch Mooted at IBSA Summit," *Geospatial World*, 19 April 2010, geospatialworld.net/News/View.aspx?ID=17346_Article.

[6] Ibid. Earth observation satellites are satellites specifically designed to observe Earth from orbit, similar to spy satellites but intended for non-military uses such as environmental monitoring, meteorology and map making.

[7] Gabriel Marcella, "China's Military Activity in Latin America," *Americas Quarterly* (Winter 2012), americasquarterly.org/Marcella.

[8] Deng Shasha, "China, Brazil Issue Joint Statement on Strengthening Partnership," *Xinhua News*, 22 June 2012, news.xinhuanet.com/english/china/2012-06/22/c_131669821.htm.

Box 2.16 Foreign ministers meeting

Place: New York, United States
Date: 11 February 2011
Participants: India's Minister of External Affairs S.M. Krishna, Brazil's Minister of External Relations Antonio de Aguiar

Patriota, and Minister of International Relations and Cooperation
of South Africa Maite Nkoana-Mashabane
Results: Joint Statement of 2011 IBSA Ministerial Meeting

The presence of all IBSA countries as non-permanent members in the
UN Security Council clearly strengthened the political dimension of
the IBSA encounters. During the meeting of foreign ministers in New
York in February 2011, India and South Africa expressed support for
the debate promoted by Brazil, as president of the Security Council for
the month of February, on the interdependence between development
and security and its importance for sustainable peace. At the meeting,
India, Brazil and South Africa voiced their commitment to increase
IBSA consultations and coordination, both in New York and in capitals, on issues on the agenda of the Security Council. They also agreed
to resume discussions and coordination on Security Council issues
during the VII Ministerial IBSA Joint Commission in New Delhi on
7–8 March 2011.[55]

Box 2.17 Seventh meeting of the Trilateral Commission

Place: New Delhi, India
Date: 8 March 2011
Participants: India's Minister of External Affairs S.M. Krishna,
Brazil's Minister of Foreign Relations Antonio Patriota, and
Minister of International Relations and Cooperation of South
Africa Ambassador Maite Nkoana-Mashabane
Results: Seventh IBSA Trilateral Ministerial Commission
Meeting Communiqué

Box 2.18 Foreign ministers meeting at the 66th UN General Assembly

Place: New York, United States
Date: 24 September 2011
Participants: India's Minister of External Affairs S.M. Krishna,
Brazil's Minister of Foreign Relations Antonio Patriota, and
Minister of International Relations and Cooperation of South
Africa Ambassador Maite Nkoana-Mashabane

Box 2.19 Fifth IBSA Summit

Place: Pretoria, South Africa
Date: 18 October 2011
Participants: President of South Africa Jacob Zuma, Prime Minister of India Manmohan Singh, and President of Brazil Dilma Rousseff
Results: Fifth IBSA Summit Declaration

Ahead of the Fifth IBSA Summit, international nongovernmental organizations (NGOs) for the first time sought to exert public pressure on the three governments, in a sign that their meeting was thought to be important in the eyes of the international community. "Leaders of the three countries should use their two-day Heads of State and Government Dialogue Forum ... to categorically demand that the Syrian government end its widespread and systematic attacks on antigovernment protesters and activists. Syria should also grant access to UN investigators and human rights monitors," Human Rights Watch (HRW) wrote.[56] The organization also criticized the IBSA countries for their recent voting behavior in the UNSC, arguing that "by abstaining, India, Brazil, and South Africa have failed the Syrian people and emboldened the Syrian government in its path of violence against them. Their proclaimed distrust of the Western motives shouldn't blind them into siding with an abusive government. Syria's current behavior repudiates the very democratic ideals to which IBSA countries are committed."[57]

Possibly as a reaction to outside pressure or in an attempt to differentiate the IBSA grouping from the BRICS (now with South Africa), the Fifth IBSA Summit Declaration included more references to human rights and democracy than any previous document. In the first paragraph, "the leaders underscored the importance of the principles, norms and values underpinning the IBSA Dialogue Forum, i.e. participatory democracy, respect for human rights, and the Rule of Law."[58]

Paragraph 2 is equally noteworthy, clearly positioning the IBSA countries in the pro-democracy camp:

> This Summit took place at a critical time globally, when the world economy is faced with serious challenges and where democracy is being sought after in areas such as the Middle East and North Africa. The Leaders highlighted that the basic pillar of IBSA is the shared vision of the three countries that democracy and development

are mutually reinforcing and key to sustainable peace and stability. The Leaders posited that the entrenched democratic values shared by the three countries to the good of their peoples and are willing to share, if requested, the democratic and inclusive development model of their societies with countries in transition to democracy.[59]

In a direct reference to the recent selection of Christine Lagarde as the IMF's new managing director, which had underlined Europe's continued control of the process of selection of the institution's leadership, the IBSA leaders argue that:

> The Heads and senior leadership of all international institutions should be appointed through an open, transparent and merit-based process beginning with the selection of the next President of the World Bank in 2012. The Leaders underscored the importance of strictly adhering to the commitments already agreed in other fora, such as in the G20, including the development agenda.[60]

While the IBSA leaders did not accuse the Syrian government directly, they still included the topic, and expressed:

> their grave concern at the current situation in Syria and condemned the persistent violence. They expressed their belief that the only solution to the current crisis is through a Syrian-led all-inclusive, transparent, peaceful political process aimed at effectively addressing the legitimate aspirations and concerns of the population and at protecting unarmed civilians. The leaders welcomed IBSA's joint initiatives on Syria. They further called for an immediate end to violence, and respect for human rights and international humanitarian law. The Leaders decided to consider the possibility of undertaking a visit to Syria by an IBSA delegation in an effort to expedite the implementation of reforms promised by the Syrian Government.[61]

The Tshwane Declaration was thus by far the most extensive and profound IBSA declaration. Aware of scheduling issues in the following year, leaders decided to wait for two years until they would meet again. Yet despite the many issues dealt with in the declaration, most observers remained critical. In an editorial entitled "IBSA has Little to Show for Itself After 8 Years," South Africa's *The Star* wrote that there was "growing impatience that the high-profile forum is not delivering concrete benefits to its three members."[62] The author pointed out that promises of the IBSA satellite program had not made any real progress, and that the free trade agreement between the three seemed increasingly elusive.

2012–14: slowing the pace

> In the absence of a new mission it is not clear how long IBSA will survive.
>
> (al-Doyaili, Freytag and Draper[63])

In the context of a much reported Fourth BRICS Summit in Delhi and the absence of an IBSA Leaders Summit, the main debate around IBSA in the international media dealt with the question of whether it should merge with the BRICS grouping or not.[64] While foreign policy makers vigorously denied that such a debate was taking place internally, it also showed that they had not communicated the importance of IBSA's institutional structure (namely, the 16 working groups, nongovernmental forums and IBSA Fund) sufficiently.[65]

In November 2012, the leaders of India, Brazil and South Africa issued an "IBSA Statement on the Conflict in Gaza," in which they expressed "their strongest condemnation of the ongoing violence between Israel and Palestine, that threatens the peace and security of the region." The IBSA countries "deeply regret the loss of human lives and express their concern over the disproportionate and excessive use of force." Taking a clear political stance,[66] they stressed the:

> urgent need to lift the blockade on Gaza, which continues to worsen the already dire socio-economic and humanitarian situation in Gaza. The IBSA countries express their strong support to the mediation efforts of the Government of Egypt, the League of Arab States and the UN Secretary-General aimed at achieving a negotiated ceasefire. The IBSA countries believe that only diplomacy and dialogue will lead to the resolution of the current crisis, which makes it even more urgent to resume direct talks between Israel and Palestine, leading to a comprehensive solution to the Palestinian Question i.e. the achievement of a two-state solution. In view of the upcoming UN General Assembly discussion on the Question of Palestine, India, Brazil and South Africa express their support for Palestine's request to be accorded Observer State status in the United Nations system.[67]

Skeptics continued to dominate the discussion prior to the Sixth IBSA Summit in Delhi. Al-Doyaili *et al.* wrote:

At the time of its formation IBSA was widely regarded as representing a novel form of South-South cooperation, transcending older models rooted in the logic of North-South confrontation in the post-colonial, Cold War world. However, now, as the respective countries prepare for their tenth anniversary summit in India, the forum seems to face a growing sense of irrelevance, perhaps even an existential crisis. There has been a proliferation of other forums, notably BRICS and the G20, which means that IBSA needs to differentiate itself if it is to endure.[68]

Until early June 2013, the general expectation was that the Sixth IBSA Summit would take place in Delhi in June.[69] Yet at very short notice, the IBSA summit was canceled. While Brazilian policy makers pointed to South Africa's President Zuma, who had preferred not to travel to India due to former President Nelson Mandela's poor health at the time, Indian and South African policy makers said that Brazil's President Rousseff had been unwilling to travel to India due to a series of internal challenges.[70] Attempts by the Indian government to reschedule the meeting (it proposed 9 and 14 July) failed because by mid-June, large-scale protests had broken out in Brazil's major cities, forcing Rousseff to stay at home. In the Indian media and among policy makers, this led to speculations that Brazil no longer regarded the IBSA grouping as a priority.[71]

Until March 2014, five IBSA Summits of Heads of State and Government had been held, with the sixth, scheduled for June 2013, having been postponed without providing a new date. The foreign ministers of the IBSA countries have also met approximately once a year at meetings of the Trilateral Joint Commission. Furthermore, informal meetings between IBSA Heads of State and Government or IBSA foreign ministers have frequently been held at the margins of meetings of international forums such as the UNGA.

Partly due to the growing importance of the BRICS grouping, several observers questioned to what extent it would be viable to keep IBSA separate from BRICS in the long term. As Sean Woolfrey writes:

> Ten years on ... the commitment of the IBSA governments to the IBSA Forum appears to have waned somewhat. This was in evidence when the Sixth IBSA Summit of Heads of State and Government, which was to have been held in New Delhi in June 2013 and which would have commemorated the tenth anniversary of the establishment of the IBSA Forum, was postponed at short notice due to scheduling issues.[72]

Box 2.20 Meeting of IBSA foreign ministers on the sidelines of the 68th UN General Assembly

Place: New York, United States
Date: 25 September 2013
Participants: India's Minister of External Affairs Salman Khurshid, Brazil's Minister of External Relations Luiz Alberto Figueiredo Machado, and Minister of International Relations and Cooperation of South Africa Maite Nkoana-Mashabane
Results: IBSA 2013 Joint Communiqué

Contrasting such doubts, IBSA's foreign ministers met on the sidelines of the 68th UN General Assembly in New York and, on the occasion of the tenth anniversary of the Brasília Declaration in 2003, they "noted with satisfaction the progress on the consolidation of the IBSA Dialogue Forum."[73] Furthermore, they felt the necessity to "reaffirm their commitment for further strengthening the trilateral cooperation and recognized the renewed relevance of IBSA."[74] This underlines the effort to relaunch IBSA after very few IBSA-related meetings had taken place in 2012. For the first time since the existence of the grouping, IBSA foreign ministers had not had an official meeting, pointing to a lull in intra-IBSA relations in 2012. The rest of the declaration repeated the usual themes of the IBSA Fund, the need for UNSC and IMF reform.

Conclusion

Detailing the diplomatic history of the IBSA grouping, it becomes evident that after years of excitement, enthusiasm among policy makers for the grouping weakened markedly in 2012, when only a reduced number of meetings took place. The lull continued in 2013, when the IBSA summit was postponed without defining a new date. Since then, the public debates about IBSA have largely been dominated by the question of whether the grouping could survive the coming years, particularly considering that Brazil's President Rousseff shows only little interest in IBSA and foreign policy in more general terms. This new situation, however, cannot entirely eclipse the years of 2004–11, when the three governments undertook a remarkable effort to bring policy makers, bureaucrats and civil society from the three countries together with the aim of establishing long-term ties and identifying common denominators.

Notes

1 "India, Brazil, South Africa Join Forces," *Asia Times*, 15 March 2005, atimes.com/atimes/South_Asia/GC15Df04.html.
2 Ruchita Beri, "IBSA Dialogue Forum: An Assessment," *Strategic Analysis* 32, no. 5 (2008): 809–31.
3 Interview with Indian foreign policy maker, New Delhi, April 2010.
4 William Cortezia and Ajay Panicker, "An Alternative for Brazil and India," *The Hindu*, 10 February 2004, www.hindu.com/2004/02/10/stories/2004021000711000.htm.
5 Not all of the Focal Point meetings led to a final document. Fundação Alexandre de Gusmão (FUNAG), ed., *III Conferência Nacional de Política Externa e Política Internacional "O Brasil no mundo que vem aí"—III CNPEPI—Seminário IBAS*, ed. Fundação Alexandre de Gusmão (FUNAG) (Brasília, Brazil: FUNAG, 2008).
6 John Cherian, "The India, Brazil and South Africa Trilateral Cooperation Forum has Helped the Three Democracies in Trade and International Politics," *The Hindu*, 2006, www.hindu.com/thehindu/thscrip/print.pl?file=20061006006601300.htm&date=fl2319/&prd=fline.
7 India-Brazil-South Africa Dialogue Forum (IBSA), "New Delhi Agenda for Co-operation and Joint Communiqué on IBSA," 5 March 2004, www.dfa.gov.za/docs/2004/ibsa0305.htm.
8 India-Brazil-South Africa Dialogue Forum (IBSA), "Plan of Action," 5 March 2004, www.dfa.gov.za/docs/2004/ibsa0305a.htm, para. 12. See also: targeted trilateral trade of $10 billion by 2007 (from $4.5 billion in 2003).
9 From India-Brazil-South Africa Dialogue Forum (IBSA), "Joint Working Group (JWG) on Education—Introduction," ibsa.nic.in/intro_education.htm.
10 "Mbeki or Zuma: Who Travels the Most?" *Mail & Guardian*, 18 February 2014, mg.co.za/data/2014-02-18-abroad-all-the-presidents-acumen; Chris Landsberg, "South Africa's Foreign Policy Under Thabo Mbeki and Jacob Zuma," *Inroads Journal*, www.inroadsjournal.ca/transformation-continuity-and-diffusion-south-africas-foreign-policy-under-thabo-mbeki-and-jacob-zuma/.
11 India-Brazil-South Africa Dialogue Forum (IBSA), "Cape Town Ministerial Communiqué," 11 March 2005, www.itamaraty.gov.br/temas-mais-informacoes/saiba-mais-ibas/documentos-emitidos-pelos-chefes-de-estado-e-de/2nd-ibsa-ministerial-meeting-communique.
12 Ibid.
13 *Statement by H.E. Ambassador Celso Amorim, Minister of External Relations of the Federative Republic of Brazil, at the Opening of the General Debate of the 60th Session of the United Nations General Assembly*, 17 September 2005.
14 "Curb Your Enthusiasm," *The Economist*, 9 June 2005, www.economist.com/node/4064932.
15 Interviews with Brazilian, Indian and South African foreign policy makers, 2011, 2012 and 2013.
16 India-Brazil-South Africa Dialogue Forum (IBSA), "Rio de Janeiro Ministerial Communiqué," 30 March 2006, www.dfa.gov.za/docs/2006/ibsa0331.htm.

17 Felipe Seligman, "Brazil, India and South Africa Optimistic About Future Ties," *IPS News*, 13 September 2006, www.ipsnews.net/2006/09/trade-brazil-india-and-south-africa-optimistic-about-future-ties/.
18 Daniel Kurtz-Phelan, "What is IBSA Anyway?" *Americas Quarterly*, Spring 2013, www.americasquarterly.org/content/what-ibsa-anyway.
19 Seligman, "Brazil, India and South Africa Optimistic About Future Ties."
20 *Remarks by the President of South Africa, Thabo Mbeki, during the India-Brazil-South Africa (IBSA) Meeting of Heads of State and Government with CEO's, Brasilia, Brazil*, 13 September 2006, www.sahistory.org.za/archive/remarks-president-south-africa-thabo-mbeki-during-india-brazil-so uth-africa-ibsa-meeting-hea.
21 BuaNews, "Ibsa Tax Heads Consolidate Cooperation," *Engineering News*, 22 November 2006, www.engineeringnews.co.za/article/ibsa-tax-heads-cons olidate-cooperation-2006-11-22.
22 T.K. Arun, "India Grabs Opportunities in Brazil," *The Economic Times*, 14 September 2006, articles.economictimes.indiatimes.com/2006-09-14/news/27458216_1_india-brazil-south-africa-ibsa-pharma-industry.
23 Siddharth Varadarajan, "India Pitches for Greater IBSA, BRIC Role," *The Hindu*, 15 April 2010, www.thehindu.com/opinion/columns/siddharth-vara darajan/india-pitches-for-greater-ibsa-bric-role/article398359.ece.
24 Hasan Suroor, "Brazilian President's Visit to 'Transform' Relations with India," *The Hindu*, 3 June 2007, www.thehindu.com/todays-paper/tp-inter national/brazilian-presidents-visit-to-transform-relations-with-india/article1 851169.ece.
25 Rashmee Roshan Lall, "Brazil Promises Special, but Not Exclusive Ties," *The Times of India*, 3 June 2007, articles.timesofindia.indiatimes.com/2007-06-03/europe/27987426_1_president-luiz-inacio-lula-special-relationship-china-u nfavourably.
26 "Brazil Emerges India's Largest Latin American Trade Partner," *The Hindu*, 5 June 2007, www.thehindu.com/todays-paper/tp-business/brazil-emerges-indias-largest-latin-american-trade-partner/article1852036.ece.
27 Siddharth Varadarajan, "Brazil for IBSA Link to Mercosur, SACU," *The Hindu*, 17 July 2007, www.thehindu.com/todays-paper/brazil-for-ibsa-link-to-mercosur-sacu/article1874300.ece.
28 V.S. Chandrasekar, "IBSA Should Achieve Trade Target of $30 billion by 2012: PM," *Rediff Business*, 17 October 2012, www.rediff.com/money/report/ibsa/20071017.htm.
29 Celean Jacobson, "Trade Talks Overshadow India, Brazil, SA Meeting," *Mail & Guardian*, 17 October 2007, mg.co.za/article/2007-10-17-trade-talks-overshadow-india-brazil-sa-meeting.
30 "PM Manmohan Singh to Visit Nigeria, South Africa," *The Times of India*, 13 October 2003, articles.timesofindia.indiatimes.com/2007-10-13/india/27985784_1_south-africa-ibsa-visit.
31 Interviews with Brazilian, South African and Indian foreign policy makers, Brasília, Pretoria and Delhi, 2010–13.
32 Sandeep Dikshit, "In the World Economy, There Must be Freedom for People and Ideas to Move," *The Hindu*, 26 October 2007, www.thehindu. com/todays-paper/tp-opinion/in-the-world-economy-there-must-be-freedom-for-people-and-ideas-to-move/article1936550.ece.
33 Ibid.

34 Celso Amorim, "Os Brics e a Reorganização do Mundo," *Folha de S. Paulo*, 8 June 2008, www.itamaraty.gov.br/sala-de-imprensa/discursos-artigos-entrevi stas-e-outras-comunicacoes/ministro-estado-relacoes-exteriores/86355815846-a rtigo-do-ministro-das-relacoes-exteriores.

35 Narasimhan Ravi, "India, Brazil to Elevate Relations to Strategic Partnership," *The Hindu*, 13 September 2006, www.hindu.com/2006/09/13/stories/2006091320471400.htm.

36 Indo-Asian News Service, "India Seeks Reforms in UN, G-8," *India Today*, 15 October 2008, alpha.intoday.in/story/India+seeks+reforms+in +UN,+G-8/1/17680.html.

37 India-Brazil-South Africa Dialogue Forum (IBSA), "2008 New Delhi IBSA Summit Declaration," 15 October 2008, www.itamaraty.gov.br/temas-mais-informacoes/temas-mais-informacoes/saiba-mais-ibas/documentos-emitidos-pelos-chefes-de-estado-e-de/3rd-ibsa-summit-declaration/view.

38 Interviews with Indian and South African policy makers and former policy makers, 2011–13.

39 Interviews with Indian and Brazilian business representatives, 2012, New Delhi and São Paulo.

40 *Opening Address by Dmitry Medvedev at Restricted Format Meeting of BRIC Leaders*, 16 June 2009, archive.kremlin.ru/eng/speeches/2009/06/16/2230_type82914_217934.shtml.

41 "BRICs, Emerging Markets and the World Economy: Not Just Straw Men," *The Economist*, 18 June 2009, www.economist.com/node/13871969.

42 Interview with Celso Amorim, Rio de Janeiro, April 2013; interviews with Brazilian and Indian diplomats, 2013.

43 India-Brazil-South Africa Dialogue Forum (IBSA), "6th Trilateral Commission Meeting Ministerial Communiqué," 1 September 2009, www.ibsa-trilateral.org/images/stories/documents/comuneques/6th_IBSA_Ministerial_Meeting_Com munique_Brasilia_2009.pdf, para. 3.

44 IBSA, "6th Trilateral Commission Meeting Ministerial Communiqué," para. 12.

45 IBSA, "6th Trilateral Commission Meeting Ministerial Communiqué.

46 Bruce Gilley, "Look to Brasilia, Not Beijing," *The Wall Street Journal*, 8 April 2009, online.wsj.com/news/articles/SB123912571625797593.

47 This allowed South Africa's President Zuma to stay on for the BRIC Summit and lobby for South Africa's inclusion, which occurred in late 2010. Oliver Stuenkel, "South Africa's BRICS Membership: A Win-Win Situation?" *African Journal of Political Science and International Relations* 7, no. 7 (2013): 310–19.

48 Varadarajan, "India Pitches for Greater IBSA, BRIC Role."

49 Press Trust of India, "Manmohan Arrives in Brazil for BRIC, IBSA Summits," *The Hindu*, 15 April 2010, www.thehindu.com/news/national/article397647.ece.

50 India-Brazil-South Africa Dialogue Forum (IBSA), "4th Summit of Heads of State Brasília Declaration," www.itamaraty.gov.br/temas-mais-informac oes/saiba-mais-ibas/documentos-emitidos-pelos-chefes-de-estado-e-de/4th-i bsa-summit-declaration.

51 Mario Osava, "IBSA—Closer Social Connections, Not Just Gov't Ties," *Global Issues*, 16 April 2010, www.globalissues.org/news/2010/04/16/5252.

52 Alexandra A. Arkhangelskaya, "India, Brazil and South Africa Dialogue Forum: A Bridge Between Three Continents Challenges," Achievements and Policy Options, *The Nordic Africa Institute*, 1.

53 Varadarajan, "India Pitches for Greater IBSA, BRIC Role."

54 India-Brazil-South Africa Dialogue Forum (IBSA), "IBSA Ministerial Meeting at General Debate of UNGA 65," 25 September 2010, www.itamaraty.gov.br/sala-de-imprensa/notas-a-imprensa/reuniao-ministerial-do-ibas-a-margem-do-debate-geral-da-65a-assembleia-geral-das-nacoes-unidas-2013-nova-york-25-de-setembro-de-2010.

55 India-Brazil-South Africa Dialogue Forum (IBSA), "IBSA Ministerial Meeting—Joint Statement," 11 February 2011, www.itamaraty.gov.br/sala-de-imprensa/notas-a-imprensa/reuniao-ministerial-do-ibas-declaracao-conjunta-nova-york-11-de-fevereiro-de-2011.

56 "IBSA: Push Syria to End Bloodshed," Human Rights Watch, 16 October 2011, www.hrw.org/news/2011/10/16/ibsa-push-syria-end-bloodshed.

57 Ibid.

58 IBSA, "IBSA Ministerial Meeting—Joint Statement."

59 Ibid.

60 Ibid., para. 14.

61 2011 IBSA Declaration, para. 82.

62 Peter Fabricius, "IBSA has Little to Show for Itself After 8 Years," *The Star*, 19 October 2011, www.iol.co.za/the-star/ibsa-has-little-to-show-for-itself-after-8-years-1.1159939.

63 Sarah al-Doyaili, Andreas Freytag and Peter Draper, "IBSA: Fading out or Forging a Common Vision?" *South African Journal of International Affairs* 20, no. 2 (2013): 297–310, 301.

64 See, for example: John Fraser, "Q&A: Will the BRICS Bury IBSA?" *Inter Press Service*, December 2012, www.ipsnews.net/2012/12/qa-will-the-brics-bury-ibsa/; Ian Taylor, "Has the BRICS Killed IBSA?" *South African Foreign Policy Initiative*, 15 August 2012, thediplomat.com/2012/08/keep-the-brics-and-ibsa-seperate/; and Saliem Fakir, "BRICS and IBSA: Friend and Foe Alike," *The South African Civil Society Information Service*, 3 July 2012, sacsis.org.za/site/article/1350.

65 Interviews with Indian, Brazilian and South African foreign policy makers, 2012 and 2013.

66 M.K. Bhadrakumar, "IBSA Steals a March on BRICS," *Russia & India Report*, 22 December 2012, indrus.in/articles/2012/12/22/ibsa_steals_a_march_on_brics_21215.html.

67 India-Brazil-South Africa Dialogue Forum (IBSA), "Statement Issued by the IBSA Member-States on the Situation Between Israel and Palestine," 22 November 2012, ibsa.nic.in/situation_ip.htm.

68 Al-Doyaili *et al.*, "IBSA: Fading out or Forging a Common Vision?" 297.

69 "India to Host IBSA Summit in June," *The Hindu*, 26 April 2013, www.the-hindu.com/news/national/india-to-host-ibsa-summit-in-june/article4657311.ece.

70 Interviews with Indian, Brazilian and South African foreign policy makers, 2013.

71 Charu Sudan Kasturi, "Brazil Clouds Tri-Meet Future," *The Telegraph*, 10 July 2013, www.telegraphindia.com/1130711/jsp/nation/story_17104373.jsp#.UwjhzV5RHpB.

72 D. Gibson, "Not Worth Divorce," *Financial Mail*, 30 May 2013, www.fm. co.za/opinion/2013/05/30/not-worth-divorce. In Sean Woolfrey, "The IBSA Dialogue Forum Ten Years On: Examining IBSA Cooperation on Trade," *Tralac Trade Brief* No. S13TB05/2013, August 2013, 4.
73 India-Brazil-South Africa Dialogue Forum (IBSA), "IBSA Joint Communiqué on the Margins of 68th Session of the United Nations General Assembly," 25 September 2013, www.un.int/india/2013/pmi66.pdf.
74 Ibid.

3   IBSA's institutional structure

- **IBSA working groups**
- **IBSA nongovernmental forums**
- **The IBSA Fund**
- **Conclusion**

This chapter presents the IBSA Forum's institutional structure, principally made up of its working groups and nongovernmental forums. While the international media usually focuses on the forum's meetings of state leaders, an assessment of the IBSA grouping cannot be complete without understanding the 16 working groups that have been created over the past decade. In addition, the IBSA Fund, a development initiative, needs to be taken into consideration when analyzing the importance of IBSA.

IBSA working groups

One of IBSA's main features is its weak institutionalization and the absence of legally binding agreements. Rather than having a secretariat or an organizational structure,[1] the consultations take place among heads of state and/or government (Summit),[2] ministers (Trilateral Joint Commission)[3] and senior officials (Focal Point).[4] Further down the scale, there are interactions between government officials who are part of the working groups, as well as academics, business leaders and civil society.[5]

While the IBSA countries share similar interests and aspirations with regard to global governance, they also face common challenges relating to poverty, inequality and shortages of technical expertise in certain areas. In order to address these and other challenges, India, Brazil and South Africa have used the IBSA Forum to share expertise and experiences of successful policies and programs with one another. This pillar of "technical" or "sectoral" cooperation between the IBSA countries involves efforts to facilitate closer engagement between specialists from the three countries and the development of concrete projects for collaboration. To facilitate this process, IBSA foreign ministers identified five broad areas at the Brasília meeting in 2003: trade, investment, tourism, defense, and science and technology (including IT and energy).[6] A considerable proliferation of areas has since occurred, covering a large segment of public policies. Sixteen IBSA working groups have been established since 2004, focusing on a range of issue areas including revenue administration,[7] culture and energy. Why did the three governments create so many working groups?

Al-Doyaili, Freytag and Draper explain that "a common interest in development challenges constitutes a core component of the 'dialogue' aspect of the IBSA Dialogue forum, and the three countries realised they had much to learn from each other about their unique approaches to addressing development challenges."[8]

The main goal of the IBSA working groups is to facilitate trilateral cooperation through dialogue, knowledge sharing for capacity building. The reasoning behind them is that ideas for further cooperation in areas IBSA leaders had not thought of would emerge out of these regular encounters. Their governance structure makes them quite independent from the cabinets of India, Brazil and South Africa. Each working group contains representatives of all three countries—members are either diplomats or public officials based at the relevant ministries. Several working groups whose activities are related to civil society are regularly in contact with representatives of IBSA's nongovernmental forums such as the IBSA Business Forum, which is coordinated by the Brazilian National Confederation of Industries (CNI in its Portuguese abbreviation).

In some working groups there are subgroups that focus on a more specific topic. The Working Group on Agriculture, for example, contains a subgroup for animal health, for agro processing and for research. The Working Group on Education contains a subgroup that deals with cooperation in sports and between the diplomats' schools attached to each Foreign Ministry. The Working Group on Science and Technology contains a subgroup on Antarctica-related research.

At first sight, the sheer number and broad themes of the IBSA working groups and seven nongovernmental forums is impressive, and proof that the IBSA Forum is far more complex than the majority of observers believe. Most analysts merely focus on summits attended by foreign ministers or heads of state. According to those policy makers involved in the set-up of IBSA's institutional structure, the driving

Table 3.1 Number of meetings of the IBSA working groups (since 2003)

Working group	Year of creation	Number of meetings (until February 2014)
Agriculture	2005	4
Culture	2005	4
Defense	2004	4
Education	2005	3
Energy	2004	5
Environment	2007	3
Health	2004	2
Human settlements	2007	5
Information society	2004	4
Public administration	2005	6
Science and technology	2004	6
Social development	2005	2
Tax and revenue administration	2007	7
Tourism	2007	3
Trade and investment	2004	6
Transport and infrastructure	2005	4

Source: Author's research

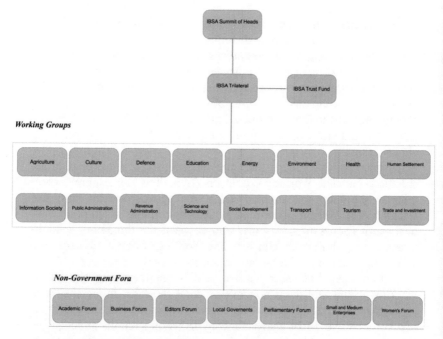

Figure 3.1 IBSA's institutional structure
(Folashadé Soule-Kohndou, "The India-Brazil-South Africa Forum a Decade on: Mismatched Partners or the Rise of the South?" *Global Economic Governance Programme Working Paper 2013/88*, University of Oxford, November 2013)

motivation was the firm belief that bringing experts from different fields together could cause mutual learning and improve public policy in a number of areas—particularly regarding social and economic development.[9] Indeed, a broad array of ministries in all three countries is actively involved in the IBSA working groups. In the case of Brazil, for example, the Ministries of Planning, Economy, Agriculture, Fishery, Cities, Science and Technology, Development, Culture, Mines and Energy, Environment, Health, Social Development, Tourism and Defense participate in the groups. As the Ministry of Foreign Affairs coordinates five working groups itself, aside from the summits and trilateral commissions, virtually all the important ministries in the three countries are to some degree engaged in the IBSA process. This involvement reflected a larger trend of internationalization of federal governments. Under Brazil's President Lula, for example, all 23 ministries at the time (except the Foreign Ministry itself) created international secretariats or similar structures to develop an international structure. An additional eight secretariats with the status of ministries also created such structures. Engaging internationally through the IBSA network was, for several of those newly established offices a first test of international cooperation that did not involve the Foreign Ministry as an intermediary.[10]

In the following sections, each working group will be briefly described.

Agriculture

The Working Group on Agriculture, created in 2005, faces a particular challenge because Brazil's and India's agricultural sectors, and agriculture-related positions during trade negotiations, differ substantially. Brazil's agriculture is the world's most productive, while India is home to millions of highly unproductive and vulnerable farmers. While Brazil seeks to ease agricultural trade barriers, protecting its farmers is a question of national security in India.

In theory, Brazil's impressive success in boosting agricultural productivity over the past decades provides a great opportunity for South Africa and India to learn. Workshops and seminars have been organized periodically since 2008. That year, the Brazilian government organized a seminar on animal genetics, yet South Africa failed to send a representative. Further workshops, such as a planned one on the avian flu, did not take place due to scheduling issues.[11]

In 2008, workshops had been planned on several issues including genetic improvement of cattle, integrated fruit production and phytosanitary certification; cotton, vineyard and soybean production and value addition, among others; and tools and techniques for scenario building to advance a collaborative study on "The future of Agriculture in India, Brazil and South Africa (IBSA) with special reference to smallholder farmers."[12] Yet neither the workshop nor the collaborative study has led to tangible action.

While regular meetings have been held successfully, creating joint projects has been a challenge due to the different positions mentioned above. Six years after its creation, there are therefore no joint projects yet, other than the exchange of information. Policy makers interviewed about this working group furthermore pointed out that there existed many other agricultural forums and platforms to discuss very similar themes with similar actors, and that the need for an additional grouping was very limited.[13] Such was the lack of interest that in one country, the representative of the Ministry of Agriculture said he had not been following the activities of the IBSA working group for years.

This suggests that, at least in this particular case, the creation of an IBSA working group did not respond to an existing demand, and has failed to be accepted by the relevant actors. In addition, the example shows that whenever issues of national interest are at stake, finding compromise within the IBSA grouping becomes a lot harder.

Culture

Created in 2005, the Working Group on Culture has perhaps produced the most visible results for citizens in India, Brazil and South Africa. Dance, cinema and gastronomy festivals have been organized since 2007 to enhance knowledge of each other's cultures. The First IBSA Music and Dance Festival was held in Salvador, Brazil, in October 2007. Promoted by the Ministry of External Relations, with the support of the Secretariat of Culture of the State of Bahia, the festival consisted of two workshops and two free performances by groups of the three countries. Brazil was represented by the Afropopbrasileiro Movement, which brings together several social cultural entities of Bahia. India brought to Brazil the Sadhya Dance Company, which staged a choreography based on *Mahabharata*, a famous Hindu poem. South Africa presented the Group Phambili Marimba and Brass Ensemble from Cape Town. In 2008, the IBSA Food Festival took place in Delhi parallel to the Third IBSA Summit,[14] generating some visibility in the Indian media.[15]

In this aspect, there is an overlap with the Working Group on Tourism, which also organized several festivals to promote cross-cultural understanding. In addition, the working group plans to organize seminars about the conservation of cultural heritage and about indigenous knowledge systems. There are several projects being developed that translate Brazilian and South African books into regional Indian languages.

Yet participants of the IBSA Working Group on Culture all bemoaned that budgetary constraints made more serious engagement very difficult. Since the Food Festival in Delhi in 2008, no large-scale cultural events have taken place as a result of the IBSA working group. Interestingly enough, the country where the Brazilian government spent most on cultural diplomacy in 2012 was China.

Defense

What is the potential for military cooperation among India, Brazil and South Africa? Bhatia argues that:

> On the face of it, defense cooperation may seem to lack potential; but the reality is different. IBSA does not face a common conventional threat, but it has been developing shared threat perceptions, especially in the region around South Africa, the geographical center of the IBSA world. This explains its growing interest in augmenting cooperation among the three Navies.[16]

The Working Group on Defense, created in 2004, deals primarily with nuclear issues (the Working Group on Energy, by contrast, works mostly on alternative types of energy). Cooperation in the area of defense between South Africa and Brazil is more advanced due to a joint project to develop a short-range missile.[17]

In addition, contrary to general expectations, and largely without much attention in each country's domestic public debates, a process called IBSAMAR was instituted to enhance cooperation between the three navies. IBSAMAR I took place on 5–16 May 2008 off the coast near Durban, South Africa. An Initial Planning Conference (IPC) for Exercise IBSAMAR II was held in Mumbai, India, over the period of 12–16 October 2009.[18] IBSAMAR II had 11 ships participating from the navies of India, Brazil and South Africa. As the *Times of India* commented then, "the trilateral naval war games, IBSAMAR, will be part of the strategic initiative launched under the IBSA framework to bring together the maritime forces of three dynamic democracies and economies from three continents under one umbrella."[19] During the exercise, the three navies conducted anti-air and anti-submarine warfare simulations, visit-board-search-seizure operations and anti-piracy drills. In October 2012, IBSAMAR III was held in the international waters off the South African navy's main naval base at Simon's Town. India played a leading role, and it included a disaster exercise simulating a military incursion into a small coastal community that required the involvement of security personnel, firefighters and medical teams.

Joint military exercises are thus one area in which intra-IBSA cooperation is more advanced than intra-BRICS.[20] According to Flemes, "the low level of institutionalization is not limiting military-to-military cooperation in terms of common war games and personnel exchange, but it might pose an obstacle to IBSA playing a stronger political role in global security affairs."[21]

A more ambitious agenda for defense cooperation has not been put into action so far, partly because all three ministries of defense are engaged in their own process of restructuring, and because budget cuts (in Brazil's case) have made it difficult to assume additional responsibilities and engage in new projects. The 2004 New Delhi Plan of Action had identified a rather ambitious program for strengthening security cooperation, including joint peacekeeping, training and military exchange, cooperation in the area of combating narcotics trafficking and in the arms industry. Yet aside from a few specific projects, most plans have not been implemented. Intra-IBSA cooperation in the realm of security thus does not yet contribute to global security in any meaningful way.

Still, IBSAMAR is a notable, albeit initial, step towards connecting India, Brazil and South Africa in an area where cooperation between countries in the global South remains rare. As Celso Amorim argued, "I don't think that a group of sociologists meeting in a room causes such attention, but a group of boats assembling with their flags causes attention."[22]

Education

The Working Group on Education, created in 2004,[23] has been coordinated by each country's Ministry of Education, yet Ministries of Sport have also played a key role. In July 2007, a first academic seminar was organized together with the working group meeting, during which broad themes of scientific cooperation were defined: social inclusion, global governance and trade and investment. In addition, engineering, mathematics, computer science, biotechnology, agriculture, sustainable development and higher education were included in the list. Efforts to ease bureaucratic obstacles to academic cooperation have been ongoing since then, but have made only slow progress. Recognizing diplomas in other IBSA countries remains a complex and highly bureaucratic process, which makes it difficult for graduates from other countries to apply for positions. This is generally regarded as a powerful barrier that keeps intra-IBSA migration low. Financial support for exchange programs remains relatively scarce. As a consequence, the number of intra-BRICS academic exchanges remains far lower than those each IBSA country has with developed countries, such as the United Kingdom, France, the United States or even China.

In addition, exchanges began among the countries' diplomatic academies. Their directors met in 2007 and 2008 and decided to institutionalize the practice, which allows young diplomats to establish contacts with their respective counterparts early in their careers.

However, members of the working group admitted that while many ideas had been developed during the meetings, few of them have been implemented so far.

Energy

Since its creation in 2004, few working groups have met as frequently as the one on energy, which can partly be explained by India's great interest in the topic. Contrary to Brazil, which has ample fossil and renewable sources of energy, India is a major energy importer. As a consequence, the country has often played a leading role in this working group, frequently presenting new proposals and sharing ideas. During the working group's meeting in 2008, for example, India made a presentation about the advantages of biodiesel and other renewable energies. A year later, India proposed a memorandum of understanding about the promotion of biofuels, and firms from the country expressed interest in producing sugar cane-based ethanol, as is common in Brazil. For this purpose, a subgroup on biofuels has been created. The Indian representatives also proposed the realization of a seminar about biofuels and food security, and debates about carbon trading and clean development.

Environment

Created in 2007,[24] it took until September 2008 for the Working Group on the Environment to meet for the first time, due to a lack of consensus about whether the group should focus on climate change or on other types of environmental degradation, such as deforestation. Since the group has started operating later than the others, there has not been any tangible progress yet.

Health

The Working Group on Health has been among the most frequently mentioned during interviews with policy makers, partly because the three IBSA countries had already extensively cooperated on the matter prior to the creation of the grouping. The main issues the group focuses on are traditional medicine, laboratory services, HIV/AIDS, tuberculosis, malaria and screening of medicine quality. Rather than focusing on research and development of drugs, which is dealt with by the Working Group on Science and Technology, the Working Group on Health works on prevention, control and distribution of medicines.

Members of the working group include representatives from several different ministries in all countries, ranging from the Foreign Ministries to the Ministries of Health. Several agencies such as, in Brazil's case, the National Health Surveillance Agency (ANVISA) and the Oswaldo Cruz Foundation (Fiocruz), also take part in the consultations. In this sense, the IBSA grouping not only brought health experts from the three countries together, but also improved communication between the Foreign Ministries and their respective Ministries of Health, contributing to the Foreign Ministries' integration with the rest of the government.

The working group organizes workshops about food security and how to control epidemics, which are coordinated by ANVISA. As part of this recently created network, health experts from India and South Africa are expected to begin regular visits to laboratories.

While the interaction envisaged by this working group is often cited by those supportive of the IBSA grouping, actual participants admit privately that little progress has been made since the group's inception.[25] One of the problems noted by participants is that each country's respective policies are at times too complex to be explained properly during the fairly short meetings, and that they do not have adequate time and incentives truly to understand other member countries' approaches.

At the same time, cooperation at the World Health Organization (WHO) between India, Brazil and South Africa continues to be frequent and productive, and the working group has proven a useful platform to develop common positions. This reflects a dual purpose of the working groups which was not necessarily planned when the groupings were set up. In addition to exchanging technological knowledge, countries learned early about each other's stance on health-related issues and had the opportunity to coordinate their voting behavior in multilateral forums.

Human settlements

All three IBSA members' societies face severe problems regarding human settlements. Slums pose a challenge in all major urban centers in Brazil and South Africa, and large-scale urbanization in India is set to complicate settlement challenges further in India's cities. Created only in 2007,[26] the Working Group on Human Settlements provided policy makers from the IBSA countries with a platform to interact and exchange on their respective approaches and policy responses regarding human settlements development. A meeting hosted by the World Bank and Cities Alliances in 2011 brought together local- and provincial-level practitioners from the IBSA countries to discuss and share lessons on national programs to implement slum upgrading policies, land tenure security and financing instruments for slum upgrading interventions at scale.

In 2012, the working group, with support from the World Bank Institute, convened a high-level workshop among national policy makers, city managers, urban practitioners, academics and slum dwellers' organizations.[27] In 2013, in the IBSA Working Group on Human Settlements (WGHS) workshops in Pretoria, Cape Town and Durban, a number of academics, policy makers, NGOs and professionals active in the field of informal settlement upgrading were invited to share information and experiences. They focused on their cross-country initiatives and partnerships to identify key issues and ideas about how the IBSA WGHS can support stakeholders' interests.[28]

These examples show that socialization in the IBSA working group allows for establishing learning networks between policy makers from the three countries and for capacity building through knowledge sharing, a main feature of South-South cooperation.[29] Brazil's Ministry for Cities has played the leading role in this working group, and the Indian government organized a seminar on "The challenge of the slums" in 2010.

Information society

As one of the earliest outfits within the IBSA framework, created in 2004, the IBSA Working Group on Information Society works on issues such as digital inclusion. It is also responsible for the grouping's website, www.ibsa-trilateral.com. This website has been roundly criticized among academics and civil society representatives for its failure to provide up-to-date information. Similar to the Working Group on Social Development, Brazil has assumed leadership on the topic of social inclusion, which has been one of the hallmarks of the country's federal government. Both poor rural and urban areas have been connected to the internet in Brazil over the past years. In addition, the subgroup on "electronic government" has been coordinated by the Brazilian government.

South Africa, for its part, has been responsible for an IBSA website on information technology and communication, which is meant to allow municipalities and local government to exchange best practices and establish a common framework for an "electronic government." Finally, India is responsible for working on the sub-theme "information society."

Public administration

The Working Group on Public Administration, created in 2005, has organized a series of seminars on a range of topics related to public management. In 2008, for example, Brazil's National School of Public Administration (ENAP) organized a seminar on South-South practices in public management in public sector training schools and public services. Aside from ENAP, South Africa's Public Administration Leadership and Management Academy (Palama) and India's Administrative Staff College of India (ASCI) participated.

In addition, the Working Group on Public Administration created an IBSA Virtual Center of Excellence on Governance and Public Administration, which aims to facilitate the exchange of knowledge in the area of public administration and governance.[30]

Science and technology

Created in 2004, the Working Group on Science and Technology has met frequently. This is largely due to its broad focus and the importance of the topic in the three governments' overall strategies. Subgroups work on issues as diverse as research and development of new medicines, the environment and Antarctica-related research. In addition, subgroups deal with topics such as biotechnology and biosecurity. The working group thus partly overlaps with the work of many other working groups, including health and energy. Given the independent nature of each working group, limiting the overlap has been a challenge.

The broad political support by the member countries' governments explains why its activities have proliferated. Immediately after its inception in 2004, priorities were defined, and the grouping featured prominently when IBSA's foreign ministers signed, during their second meeting in 2005, the Rio Declaration on Science and Technology. A year later, the three ministers of science and technology met in Angra dos Reis (Brazil), where they decided to set up a fund to support trilateral cooperation in the field of science and technology. Yet the fund's small size—US$3 million in total—raises the question in how far each government's commitment exceeds mere symbolism.

Still, the group members interviewed expressed confidence that the group is highly productive, pointing to results in space research, nanotechnology, and the financial benefits for almost 300 researchers and 33 projects.

In 2008, the working group added Arctic-related research to its portfolio. Since 2009, Brazil and South Africa have opened their respective research stations to researchers from IBSA countries. In the same year, Brazil organized an "IBSA Antarctica Forum." It is here in particular where an overlap exists with the IBSA Working Group on the Environment, which also deals with the South Pole's role in climate change.

In 2011, the working group convened in Pretoria for the eighth time. After a pause in 2012 (just like most other working groups), meetings continued in 2013 with the ninth encounter in New Delhi, in late May. In 2014, the tenth meeting will take place in Brazil.

Social development issues

Created in 2005, the Working Group on Social Development Issues focuses on anti-poverty strategies, social security and microfinance. Discussions revolve around best practices used internally as well as common voting behavior in international forums.

It organized regular encounters to present each country's experience in areas such as sustainable development including Social Fuel Stamp (Brazil), Expanded Public Works Programme (South Africa) and National Rural Employment Guarantee (NREGA) (India). Other examples are conditional monetary cash transfers including the Integrated Child Development Services Scheme (India), Child Support Grant (South Africa) and Bolsa Familia (Brazil). In the same way, government experts learned about food security programs, including Fome Zero (meaning "zero hunger," Brazil), Nutrition Programs (South Africa), and the Targeted Public Distribution System (TPDS) and National Program of Nutritional Support to Primary Education (India).

Since inequality and poverty remain one of the key challenges all three IBSA members are facing, this working group has received considerable attention and is deemed, by policy makers, an important one, even though it has convened less frequently than other working groups. Brazil, in particular, has made the promotion of its Bolsa Familia abroad a pillar of its stronger engagement in the global South, advising and partly financing similar projects in other countries such as Bolivia.[31]

Tax and revenue administration

The Working Group on Tax and Revenue Administration seeks to share best practices. A first meeting took place in late 2006 between the three countries' leaders of the revenue administration agencies.[32] There, participants identified common positions and hopes about a network of information exchange to strengthen already existing cooperation.[33] They also agreed to boost trade and economic development while also seeking to thwart smuggling, drug trafficking, fraud and tax avoidance in the three nations. As a consequence, the grouping launched a virtual platform called the IBSA Center for Exchange on Tax Information to promote the discussion about identifying and avoiding abusive tax schemes.[34] This platform complements existing mechanisms and virtual spaces created by the Organisation for Economic Co-operation and Development (OECD).

Such policies of alignment may also contribute to reducing non-tariff trade barriers, and hence the working group's overall purpose somewhat overlaps with the Working Group on Trade and Investment.

Tourism

Created in 2007, the Working Group on Tourism, since its inception, has had to deal with competition from the already existing Working Group on Transport, created two years earlier. Intra-IBSA tourism remains extremely limited, even though the number of Brazilians traveling to South Africa has increased somewhat over the past years. While the number of foreign tourists going to South Africa already stands at 9.2 million, Brazil and India remain fringe destinations, with only 5.67 and 6.58 million tourists in 2012, respectively.[35] Nationals from all IBSA countries still have a strong preference to travel to Europe or the United States.[36] Since the grouping's inception, seminars for tour operators have been organized, as well as cinema screenings and gastronomy festivals. Several marketing campaigns have been planned for 2014, but it is too early to gauge their impact.

Trade and investment

Also created in 2004, the Working Group on Trade and Investment is concerned with a broad range of issues. First of all, the grouping is responsible for trade deals between the three blocs (MERCOSUR, SACU and India), which will be discussed in detail below. Second, it is to promote foreign intra-IBSA investment, as well as trade in more general terms. In all countries, not only the Foreign Ministries are involved, but also Ministries of Development and Foreign Trade.

Given the low probability of a larger trade agreement any time soon, reducing trade barriers (most of which are not related to tariffs) is one of the working group's key tasks. Considering that one of IBSA's main objectives is to strengthen economic South-South ties, the working group on trade and investment is often said to be one of the most important elements of the entire IBSA Forum.

Another important aspect of the grouping has been an initiative to help small and medium-sized companies to increase intra-IBSA trade and investment. This process involves South Africa's Small Enterprise Development Agency, India's National Small Industry Cooperation and the Brazilian Micro and Small Business Support Service (SEBRAE), which operate within a specific subgroup.

Transport

Insufficient transport links are a major impediment to stronger ties between India, Brazil and South Africa. Improving these ties—both maritime and air—is thus the key objective of the IBSA Working Group on Transport, created in 2005. Several analysts have pointed out that improving transport links could have a greater impact on trade than an actual reduction in tariffs.[37] The working plan presented by the group includes a series of projects, including greater cooperation between shipping companies, shipyards and ports. Similar ideas have been articulated between airlines. Even a decade after IBSA's inception, there is still no direct commercial flight between Brazil and India.

Impact evaluation

How can we evaluate all these activities? Official statements continuously point out that the working groups have been great success stories. Yet at the same time, there is no doubt that several working groups have produced relatively little during the past years. For example, the working groups on the environment and on tourism have met less frequently, but policy makers are currently planning the launch of a large-scale tourism campaign in 2014 to increase intra-IBSA tourism.[38]

Immediate problems with less productive working groups are related to scheduling issues, geographical distance and language barriers. An additional problem is that the working groups have no binding agreements on their output, so members must come up with their own projects. Most importantly, however, some working groups work in areas that are not a policy priority, and, as a consequence, they have no separate funds. IBSA's activities are financed by the budget of line ministries and are not provided by the cabinets of Foreign Ministries of each IBSA country—as a consequence, several working groups receive very little funding.

In a detailed study on the structure of IBSA working groups, Faria, Nogueira and Lopes report difficulties regarding proper and timely coordination between the working groups. According to them, this is due to the large number of entities and differing expectations and priorities regarding each group's outcome. They point out that in some cases, such as the Working Group on Culture, no specific person has been designated within the respective ministries, a situation that naturally makes rapid and efficient communication difficult. In order to deal with this problem, a proposal is being studied that would organize the groups into three large clusters, each of which would be managed, on a rotating basis, by one country. According to a Brazilian proposal, such clusters would be divided in the following way: social topics, which would include the working groups on public administration, human settlements, culture, social development, education and health; economic topics, which would include the working groups on tax and revenue administration, trade and investment, transport, tourism, and information society; and topics related to natural resources, including the working groups on agriculture, science and technology, defense, energy and the environment. A full evaluation of the grouping's impact follows in Chapter 4.

While in 2008 Brazilian diplomats still wrote about the possibility of increasing the number of working groups,[39] during the ministerial meeting of the Trilateral Commission in January 2011 in New Delhi, participants debated the option of closing underperforming working groups, but in the end discarded the option as this may send a negative signal about the grouping to the international community. Since then, internal discussions have taken place regularly about how to revive some of the working groups.[40]

IBSA nongovernmental forums

The idea of nongovernmental forums was born out of the preoccupation that the IBSA grouping would become a top-heavy, elite-driven project with little impact on the three countries' societies.[41] In fact, only a small elite in India, Brazil and South Africa had ever heard of the IBSA grouping, and mutual ignorance of each other's societies remained widespread. As a consequence, in 2006, together with the first presidential IBSA Summit in Brasília, an academic seminar and a business forum took place to strengthen ties between academics and businessmen and -women.

Since then, they have become a key part of the IBSA grouping's institutional structure, and leaders continually mention the importance in connecting their societies. As Prime Minister Singh has pointed out several times, IBSA was supposed to be a "peoples project."[42] The Indian leader said in his opening remarks of the Third IBSA Summit in New Delhi in 2007 that "the Dialogues held during the last two days by the Business, Academic, Editors and Women's Forums have been enriching and have contributed to making IBSA a truly people's movement."[43] In the leaders' 2007 Tshwane Declaration, they:

> Welcomed and fully supported the launch of the Women's Forum which strengthens participation of women in IBSA and recognized the fundamental contribution of women in the social, cultural and economic development of India, Brazil and South Africa. They reaffirmed their commitment to the promotion of gender equality and women's rights.[44]

During the Fourth IBSA Summit in 2010 in Brasília, six forums were held in parallel, bringing together women, researchers, journalists, parliamentarians, local governments and small businesses, indicating that this is "a project that belongs to our societies," as Brazilian President Lula put it.[45]

Table 3.2 Number of meetings of nongovernmental forums (since 2003)

Nongovernmental forums	Year of creation	Number of meetings (until 2013)
Academic forum	2006	3
Business forum	2006	2
Editors forum	2010	2
Local governance forum	2010	2
Parliamentarians forum	2007	2
Small, micro and medium enterprises forum	2010	3
Women's forum	2007	3

Source: Author's research

IBSA Academic Forum

As one of the most important nongovernmental forums, the IBSA Academic Forum has, since its inception in 2006, regularly brought together academics and researchers from the three countries to discuss their work. Interviews with involved academics show that these meetings tend to bring together individuals who otherwise would not have been able to meet, given that the South African, Indian and Brazilian research communities are largely disconnected.[46] The forum has also used small academic grants for trilateral cooperation projects in the field of global governance, sustainable development, biotechnology, social transformation and engineering.

In this sense, the IBSA Forum is, among academics of the three countries, seen as a useful exercise to broaden research networks and possibly commence joint research projects, particularly on topics that are of interest to scholars in the three countries, such as inequality, global governance or education. However, eight years after the first forum, there is only very limited evidence of growing joint publications by South African, Indian and Brazilian scholars in internationally recognized peer-reviewed academic journals. At the same time, scholars interviewed in the three countries affirm that the IBSA Forum has led to greater interest in each other's regions. Considering the rather insular nature of each country's academic communities, this certainly counts as a success.

IBSA Business Forum and IBSA Small and Medium Enterprise Forum

Similar to the Academic Forum, the IBSA Business Forum and the Small and Medium Enterprise Forum have yielded some tangible results. While there was little or no formal dialogue before, business has now become an active and visible gathering on the sidelines at IBSA summits.[47] The Business Forum has taken place during every summit since 2011, while the Small and Medium Enterprise Forum has existed since 2010. At the same time, interviews with business leaders show that despite such activities, most private sector actors in Brazil, India and South Africa do not consider investing or trading with other IBSA nations a priority.[48] Low intra-IBSA trade and investment data confirm this impression.

IBSA Editors Forum

"Our countries should not continue to receive news about each other via New York or London, but directly," said the Brazilian ambassador to South Africa, José Vicente Pimentel, at the first Editors Forum, where Brazil's Deputy Minister for Communication, Ottoni Fernandes, proposed cooperation between public television broadcasters across IBSA.[49] This underlying narrative was at the heart of debates between participants of the IBSA Editors Forum in 2010. More than 20 media editors and senior journalists participated in the forum. The event ended with proposals including that IBSA add an official working group on communication, create a website for information about IBSA and establish a program to generate interest among journalists in these new developments.

The Editors Forum met again during the 2011 IBSA Summit in Delhi. There, government representatives again expressed that the media had been too slow to highlight the growing importance of South-South ties. According to them, a "change of mind-set in newsrooms" was necessary to focus on developing countries and their potential.[50]

Speaking at the 2011 meeting, which was co-hosted by the South African National Editors' Forum (SANEF) and the Inter Press Service (IPS) Africa with support from the Government Communication and Information Services (GCIS) and the World Bank, GCIS CEO Jimmy Manyi said the focus should be more on developmental issues and the South-South agenda: "We ... urge the editors to focus on the IBSA agenda, because it is the future. These countries have a lot of untapped resources ... therefore the media should be playing more of a promotional role ... rather than consuming other people's news we need to focus more on our agenda."[51] One participant noted that there was a "need for the story of the south to be told by reporters using sources from the south—promoting the idea of a database of experts who could be accessed by reporters from the IBSA countries."[52] "India, Brazil and South Africa have emerged as confident leaders in South-South cooperation. Yet, even as new maps of political and economic relations have emerged, the flow of information remains focused on the north," added another speaker.[53]

It is of course highly questionable how far a government-driven process can or should affect independent media in India, Brazil and South Africa. There may be truth to the claim that "journalists have failed to keep up with this process and with the economic and geopolitical changes taking place in the world today that are bringing about a shift in power relations"[54]—yet it has also led to a situation in which journalists favorable of the IBSA and BRICS concept are generally seen as pro-government. This is the case particularly in Brazil, where the concept of South-South cooperation is strongly tied to the ruling Workers' Party (PT).

Still, the organization of a meeting that helped media in the three countries to gain a greater understanding of each other has been welcomed by most participants, several of whom had not been in contact with colleagues from other IBSA countries.[55] Given the postponement of the summit in 2013, the Editors Forum has not met since 2011.

IBSA Local Government Forum

The IBSA Local Government Forum has existed since 2010, when it took place parallel to the Fourth IBSA Summit in Brasília. In 2011, an IBSA Local Government meeting for knowledge sharing on climate change response took place. However, meetings so far have been rare and very small, without producing any tangible results.

IBSA Parliamentary Forum

The IBSA Parliamentary Forum has existed since 2007. Its main task is to oversee the implementation of decisions adopted at the IBSA Summit of heads of state and government and ministerial meetings.[56]

IBSA Women's Forum

The IBSA Women's Forum seeks to promote the empowerment of women and the elimination of violence against them.[57] This forum guides and coordinates the efforts of both governmental and non-governmental organizations in the IBSA countries working in the fields of women and child development.

After meeting for the first time in 2007,[58] the Women's Forum reconvened a year later, when a memorandum was prepared and was soon after signed in New Delhi by state leaders, on cooperation in the field of women's development and gender equality programs.[59]

In 2010, during the meeting in Brasília, the group launched a book, *Elaborating an Inclusive Macroeconomic Structure: A South-South Feminist Approach*, the result of a 2008 seminar with representatives from all three countries.[60]

The Women's Forum met again in 2011, when they signed a resolution in which they proposed that part of the IBSA Trust Fund should be set aside for women's development projects.[61]

The IBSA Women's Forum met again in 2013 in Delhi.[62] There they signed a resolution that urged governments to do more to end violence against women and girls; to work towards economic empowerment of women, especially rural and marginalized women; to promote gender responsive budgeting, and equitable and sustainable development.[63] Stating that ending violence against women must be the goal for a more equitable society, India's Union Minister for Women and Child Development Krishna Tirath said: "The 'Stop Rape Campaign' of South Africa is particularly appreciable for its intrinsic value in gender sensitizing school children. Also, social programs, such as Bolsa Familia of Brazil, have popularized the model for effective delivery of financial benefits to poor families."[64]

Indeed, several analysts have pointed out that India, Brazil and South Africa all face severe challenges regarding violence against women. As Kornegay writes:

> In India ... a "Red Brigade" womens' [sic] movement might be studied as a possible model of local grassroots anti-violence mobilization (offsetting corrupt and slow to transform law enforcement systems and patriarchal conservatism which many women as well as men are steeped in). This is why there may be a case to be revisited for transforming IBSA's gender forum into a sectoral working group given the endemic crisis in violence against women experienced in all three countries.[65]

The IBSA Fund

In one of the most commented-on decisions in the history of the trilateral grouping, IBSA has established the IBSA Facility Fund for Alleviation of Poverty and Hunger, through which development projects are executed with their funding in fellow developing countries. It was created in 2004 and became operational in 2006.[66] An annual sum of $1 million has been contributed by each IBSA member country since then.

According to the IBSA governments, the Trust Fund operates through a demand-driven approach. Governments of developing countries requesting support from this fund initiate discussions with Focal Points appointed among IBSA countries' officers around the world. These Focal Points then submit proposals to the IBSA board of directors for review.[67] If a proposal receives a favorable review, the UN Development Programme's (UNDP) Special Unit for South-South Cooperation, which acts as the fund manager and board of directors' secretariat, initiates contact with a potential executing agency to advance a project formulation, and to facilitate the project's implementation.

IBSA projects are executed through partnerships with UNDP, national institutions or local governments. Important concerns of IBSA partners in the design of their projects include capacity building among projects' beneficiaries, built-in project sustainability and knowledge sharing among Southern experts and institutions.

Despite its small size, the IBSA Fund received the 2010 Millennium Development Goals (MDGs) Award for South-South Cooperation[68] from the NGO "Millennium Development Goals Awards Committee," an organization that focuses on the MDGs. In 2012 the fund earned the "South-South and Triangular Cooperation Champions Award," given by the UN, for its innovative strategy in the field of triangular cooperation.[69]

The IBSA Fund has financed projects in Haiti, Guinea-Bissau, Cape Verde, Burundi, Palestine, Cambodia, Laos and Sierra Leone. Until today, a series of small projects in developing countries in Latin America, Africa and Asia have been implemented. For example, in Burundi, the IBSA Fund supported, until 2012, a project to increase the government's capacity to combat HIV/AIDS. In Cape Verde, a public health center was reformed and modernized in 2008. In Guinea-Bissau, an agricultural project was implemented until 2007. In a second phase, operationalized by 2011, the project was expanded.[70] In Haiti, a waste collection project was supported in Port-au-Prince, finalized in 2011. A sports complex has been completed and inaugurated in 2011 in Ramallah under the IBSA Fund.[71] In 2012, the refurbishment of a hospital in Gaza began.[72]

At the time of writing, projects were being financed in Cape Verde (desalinization to increase access to drinking water and provide water for agriculture), Cambodia (medical services for children and adolescents with special needs), Guinea-Bissau (farming, solar energy), Laos (irrigation), Palestine (support for a hospital, center for people with special needs), Sierra Leone (leadership training), and Vietnam (agriculture).

While such cooperation is notable, one must admit that the amounts involved remain small compared to existing development institutions.[73] While policy makers officially hail the IBSA Fund as a centerpiece of the grouping, former diplomats concede that a lack of political will is the only way to explain why the fund remains so small—in particular when considering that all IBSA members spend far larger amounts on bilateral development and humanitarian aid. Rajiv Bhatia, who served as India's high commissioner to South Africa in 2006–09, commented that "IBSA assistance is too limited, with each member-state contributing just $1 million annually. Surely, they can afford to be more generous. If IBSA truly wants to make a difference, it should step up its assistance, expedite its decision-making and undertake more projects."[74]

Governments point out in response that the IBSA Fund is meant to develop "new paradigms" and can thus be successful even while maintaining its small size. Yet several development experts who are not involved in the IBSA Fund point out that unless the fund's size increases, it is virtually impossible to judge its scalability—i.e. how far others can learn from and copy the IBSA Fund's strategy.[75]

As a consequence, several observers have called on the fund to be expanded if it is to be taken seriously. Lyal White argues that if countries were to commit more financial resources, the fund could become IBSA's "flagship and its interface with the developing world." He recommends that a greater part of Brazilian, Indian and South African bilateral aid should be incorporated into an enlarged IBSA development fund.[76]

In addition, civil society organizations have criticized the IBSA Fund for its lack of transparency. Laura Waisbich of Conectas, a Brazilian human rights NGO, argues:

> Apart from the annual report which retrospectively gives broad details of projects undertaken by the IBSA Fund, there is very little information on IBSA projects. The website dedicated to the Fund shields any information of relevance, with passwords. An interested citizen has no access to information on—the selection process of projects, the projected timeline, details of sub-contractors, impact assessment reports, target beneficiaries, overall project assessment, etc.[77]

Waisbich writes about a conversation with Vrinda Choraria, from the Delhi-based Commonwealth Human Rights Initiative, who had argued that "this lack of information on the Fund is frustrating as even a recent exercise of filing formal requests under the respective information laws, by organizations based in the three countries elicited no relevant information ... It is perplexing that a Fund that the three countries promote as a symbol of cooperation and assistance should be shrouded in such secrecy."

Finally, she reports that an information request to the UN Office for South-South Cooperation in UNDP, which manages the IBSA Fund, under its information disclosure policy, did not provide the information that was sought.[78]

The incapacity of civil society to monitor and assess the impact of IBSA Fund projects reduces the buy-in of NGOs and public opinion makers, which directly affects the grouping's image in India's, Brazil's and South Africa's civil society. On the IBSA Fund's website, a project description affirms that a project in Guinea-Bissau was "received positively in the local official press"[79]—yet inviting independent NGOs to visit and evaluate the projects would certainly enhance trust in the IBSA Fund.

The IBSA Fund—one of the IBSA grouping's few elements that has produced tangible results—is a great idea which may not only alleviate poverty, but also enhance the debate about innovative ways of poverty reduction and South-South cooperation in general. Yet in order to make a serious contribution in the global debate, IBSA governments should dramatically enhance financial support, and make the fund's operation more transparent.

Conclusion

While IBSA's institutional structure is indeed limited, the working groups and nongovernmental forums show the three governments' efforts to bring their administrations and societies closer to each other. As will be analyzed in the next chapter, success has been mixed. Despite attempts to foster people-to-people ties, most IBSA-related meetings retain a distinctive official and state-driven nature.

Notes

1 While there is no official secretariat, diplomats say there is a so-called informal secretariat, managed by a different foreign ministry each year, which is responsible for all ministerial meetings and presidential summits.

2 Five IBSA Summits have been held so far: the first IBSA Summit in Brasília on 13 September 2006; the second in South Africa on 17 October 2007; the third in New Delhi on 15 October 2008; the fourth in Brasília on 15 April 2010; and the fifth in Pretoria on 18 October 2011.

3 The Brasília Declaration established a Trilateral Commission at the level of foreign ministers. The commission meets regularly; the first meeting of the Trilateral Commission was held in New Delhi on 4–5 March 2004. The seventh meeting of the commission was also held in New Delhi on 8 March 2011; the eighth meeting was due in South Africa. In addition, foreign ministers meet regularly before every IBSA Summit as well as on the sidelines of the UNGA in New York.

4 Senior officials from the foreign offices of the three countries dealing with IBSA are the designated Focal Points; Secretary (West), assisted by Joint Secretary (MER), Ministry of External Affairs, is the IBSA Focal Point for India. Focal Points meet once a year for a stand-alone meeting and also meet prior to the Trilateral Commission.

5 Alexandra A. Arkhangelskaya, "India, Brazil and South Africa Dialogue Forum: A Bridge Between Three Continents Challenges," *Achievements and Policy Options*, The Nordic Africa Institute, 1.

6 Rajiv Bhatia, "IBSA: Talking Shop or Powerhouse?" *The Hindu*, 12 October 2010, www.thehindu.com/opinion/lead/article825414.ece.

7 Sean Woolfrey, "The IBSA Dialogue Forum Ten Years On: Examining IBSA Cooperation on Trade," *Tralac Trade Brief* No. S13TB05/2013, August 2013, 6.
8 Sarah al-Doyaili, Andreas Freytag and Peter Draper, "IBSA: Fading out or Forging a Common Vision?" *South African Journal of International Affairs* 20, no. 2 (2013): 297–310, 300.
9 Interview with Indian, Brazilian and South African foreign policy makers, 2012 and 2013.
10 Carlos Aurélio Pimenta de Faria, Joana Laura Marinho Nogueira and Dawisson Belém Lopes, "Coordenação Intragovernamental para a Implementação da Política Externa Brasileira: O Caso do Fórum IBAS," *DADOS—Revista de Ciências Sociais, Rio de Janeiro* 55, no. 1 (2012): 173–220, 212.
11 Ibid.
12 India-Brazil-South Africa Dialogue Forum (IBSA), "5th IBSA Ministerial Meeting Communiqué," www.itamaraty.gov.br/temas-mais-informacoes/temas-mais-informacoes/saiba-mais-ibas/documentos-emitidos-pelos-chefes-de-estado-c-de/5th-ibsa-ministerial-meeting-communique/view, para. 42.
13 Interview with Brazilian and South African policy makers, Brasília and Pretoria, 2013.
14 Shobhan Saxena, "Dumpukht Diplomacy," *The Times of India*, articles.timesofindia.indiatimes.com/2008-10-19/special-report/27914612_1_food-festival-diplomacy-delhi-hotel.
15 Himanshu Bhagat, "Chakalaka or Churrasco?" *Live Mint*, www.livemint.com/Leisure/j80VceB2Tr39y3o6pnzNmM/Chakalaka-or-Churrasco.html.
16 Bhatia, "IBSA: Talking Shop or Powerhouse?"
17 "South Africa, Brazil Developing A-Darter SRAAM," *Defense Industry Daily*, 16 December 2012, www.defenseindustrydaily.com/south-africa-brazil-to-develop-adarter-sraam-03286/.
18 "Análise COMDEFESA: Integração Sul-Americana em Defesa: Perspectivas e Desafios," *FIESP*, 2 February 2010, www.fiesp.com.br/indices-pesquisas-e-publicacoes/integracao-sul-americana-em-defesa-perspectivas-e-desafios.
19 Times News Network, "Navies of India, Brazil, SA to Conduct Wargames," *The Times of India*, 12 August 2010, articles.timesofindia.indiatimes.com/2010-08-12/india/28283833_1_wargames-navies-ins-ganga.
20 "Global Insider: IBSA Countries Take Tentative Steps Toward Defense Cooperation," *World Politics Review*, 21 December 2012, www.worldpoliticsreview.com/trend-lines/12567/global-insider-ibsa-countries-take-tentative-steps-toward-defense-cooperation.
21 Ibid.
22 "IBSA Naval Exercise No Precursor to Treaty," *Thai Indian*, 13 May 2008; in Hal Brands, "Dilemmas of Brazilian Grand Strategy," Strategic Studies Institute Monograph.
23 India-Brazil-South Africa Dialogue Forum (IBSA), "Joint Working Group (JWG) on Education—Introduction," ibsa.nic.in/intro_education.htm.
24 BuaNews, "IBSA Leaders Committed to Uplifting Poor Countries," *The Skills Portal*, 22 October 2007, www.skillsportal.co.za/page/features/economy/655403-IBSA-leaders-committed-to-uplifting-poor-countries#.UuqN4D1dVKo.
25 Interviews with policy makers from Brazil, India and South Africa, July 2012.
26 BuaNews, "IBSA Leaders Committed to Uplifting Poor Countries."

27 "India, Brazil and South Africa Address the Challenge of Slums," *The World Bank*, 22 March 2012, wbi.worldbank.org/wbi/stories/india-brazil-and-south-africa-ibsa-addressing-challenge-slums.

28 "IBSA Working Group on Human Settlement," *South African Cities Network*, www.sacities.net/what-we-do/programmes-areas/sustainable/urban-sus tainability/urban-environment-management-programme/69-themes/strategy/ 986-ibsa-working-group-on-human-settlement.

29 Folashadé Soule-Kohndou, "The India-Brazil-South Africa Forum a Decade on: Mismatched Partners or the Rise of the South?" *Global Economic Governance Programme Working Paper* 2013/88, University of Oxford, November 2013, 14.

30 IBSA Virtual Centre for Excellence on Governance and Public Administration, *Home*, ibsa.cgg.gov.in; "DAR& pg Launches India-Brazil-South Africa Web Portal," *Governance Knowledge Centre*, 11 January 2011, indiagovernance.gov.in/news.php?id=542.

31 Súsan Faria, "Bolívia Terá Programa Similar ao Bolsa Família," *Ministério do Desenvolvimento Social e Combate à Fome*, www.mds.gov.br/saladeim prensa/noticias/2009/janeiro/bolivia-tera-programa-similar-ao-bolsa-familia.

32 BuaNews, "Ibsa Tax Heads Consolidate Cooperation."

33 Marcos Aurelio Valadão, "Brazil, India and South Africa Reaffirm Tax and Customs Cooperation," *Inter-American Center of Tax Administrations*, www.ciat.org/index.php/en/news/archived-news/news/1308-brasil-india-y-sudafrica-reafirman-cooperacion-fiscal-y-aduanera.html.

34 India-Brazil-South Africa Dialogue Forum (IBSA), *About IBSA CETI*, www.ibsaceti.org/IBSACeti.aspx.

35 "Estudo da Demanda Turística Internacional," *Fundação Instituto de Pesquisas Econômicas*, Ministry of Tourism, Government of Brazil, 2013, www. copa2014.gov.br/sites/default/files/08282013_estudo_demanda_turistica.pdf; "India Tourism Statistics at a Glance," *Ministry of Tourism*, Government of India, July 2013, tourism.gov.in/writereaddata/CMSPagePicture/file/ marketresearch/Ministry%20of%20tourism%20English%202013.pdf; "President Jacob Zuma Announces Impressive Growth of 10.2 percent in International Tourist Visitors to South Africa in 2012," Department of Tourism, Republic of South Africa, 25 April 2013, www.tourism.gov.za/AboutNDT/ Ministry/News/Pages/Zuma-announces-impressive-Tourism-Stats.aspx.

36 .Faria *et al.*, "Coordenação Intragovernamental para a Implementação da Política Externa Brasileira," 208; nationals from all IBSA countries still have a strong preference to travel to Europe or the United States.

37 Woolfrey, "The IBSA Dialogue Forum Ten Years On," 20

38 Interview with Brazilian, South African and Indian policy makers, December 2013.

39 At the time, the Brazilian diplomat envisioned adding groups to work on the following issues: gender/women, small businesses, cooperation between unions, prison systems, public works/infrastructure, forest issues, disarmament and non-proliferation and intellectual property. In Gilberto F.G. de Moura, "O Diálogo Índia, Brasil, África do Sul—IBAS: Balanço e Perspectivas," in *III Conferência Nacional de Política Externa e Política Internacional "O Brasil no mundo que vem aí"—III CNPEPI—Seminário IBAS*, ed. Fundação Alexandre de Gusmão (FUNAG) (Brasília, Brazil: FUNAG, 2008), 157–31.

40 Soule-Kohndou, "The India-Brazil-South Africa Forum a Decade on," 21. Since then, internal discussions regularly take place about how to revive some of the working groups.

41 Interviews with policy makers in Pretoria, Brasília and New Delhi, 2012, 2013.

42 Priya Chacko, "IBSA in the Foreign Policy of a Rising India," in *Contemporary India and South Africa: Legacies, Identities, Dilemmas*, ed. Sujata Patel and Tina Uys (New Delhi, India: Routledge, 2012).

43 *Manhoman Singh's Opening Remarks at the 3rd IBSA Summit Meeting*, 15 October 2008, pmindia.gov.in/speech-details.php?nodeid=706.

44 India-Brazil-South Africa Dialogue Forum (IBSA), "Tshwane IBSA Summit Declaration," 17 October 2007, www.dfa.gov.za/docs/2007/ibsa1018.htm.

45 Mario Osava, "IBSA—Closer Social Connections, Not Just Gov't Ties," *Inter Press Service*, 16 April 2010, www.ipsnews.net/2010/04/ibsa-closer-social-connections-not-just-govt-ties/.

46 Phone interviews with academics from India, Brazil and South Africa, 2012.

47 Lyal White, "IBSA Six Years On: Co-operation in a New Global Order," *SAIIA Emerging Powers Programme Policy Briefing* 8, November 2009, 3.

48 Interviews with business representatives, São Paulo, 2012 and 2013.

49 Osava, "IBSA—Closer Social Connections, Not Just Gov't Ties."

50 "Editors Agree to Intensify IBSA Coverage," *The Skills Portal*, www.skillsport al.co.za/page/features/1066220-Editors-agree-to-intensify-IBSA-coverage.

51 Ibid.

52 "IBSA Editors Build Networks," *IBSA News*, 21 October 2011, www.ibsanews.com/ibsa-editors-build-networks/.

53 "SANEF, IPS Co-host IBSA Editors' Forum," *BizCommunity*, 17 October 2011, www.bizcommunity.com/Article/196/15/65713.html.

54 Osava, "IBSA—Closer Social Connections, Not Just Gov't Ties."

55 Telephone interviews with participants, 2012.

56 India-Brazil-South Africa Dialogue Forum (IBSA), "Joint Declaration of the IBSA Parliamentary Forum," Brasília, 14 April 2010, ibsa.nic.in/parli amentary_forum.htm.

57 India-Brazil-South Africa Dialogue Forum (IBSA), "Parliamentary Forum—Women's Forum Introduction," www.ibsa.nic.in/intro_womensforum.htm.

58 "2nd IBSA Summit Programme and Logistical Information," www.dirco.gov.za/docs/2007/ibsa1015.htm.

59 "IBSA Meet on Women's Issues," *The Hindu*, www.hindu.com/2008/10/15/stories/2008101552371400.htm.

60 Osava, "IBSA—Closer Social Connections, Not Just Gov't Ties."

61 IBSA, "Parliamentary Forum—Womens Forum Introduction."

62 "Stakeholders' Consultations of IBSA Women's Forum 2013 (Inaugural Session)," www.wcd.nic.in/icdsimg/ibsaforumdtd10052013.pdf.

63 "5th IBSA Women's Forum Resolution was Approved by India, Brazil and South Africa," *Jagran Josh*, 16 May 2013, www.jagranjosh.com/current-affairs/5th-ibsa-womens-forum-resolution-was-approved-by-india-brazil-and-south-africa-1368706262-1.

64 "Krishna Tirath Signs IBSA Resolution to Empower Women," *The Hindu*, 17 May 2013, www.thehindu.com/news/cities/Delhi/krishna-tirath-signs-ibs a-resolution-to-empower-women/article4723799.ece.

65 "Francis A. Kornegay, Jr, "Long-Term Visioning for BRICS—and IBSA?" *Institute for Global Dialogue*, www.igd.org.za/home/4601-long-term-visioning-for-brics-and-ibsa.
66 "IBSA Fund," *UN Office for South-South Cooperation*, tcdc2.undp.org/ibsa/. The IBSA Fund website contains information about current and past projects.
67 The IBSA Fund Board of Directors comprises the ambassadors, permanent representatives and deputy permanent representatives, of India, Brazil and South Africa to the United Nations in New York.
68 "India, Brazil, South Africa Fund Receives UN Award," *India Post News Service*, 22 September 2010, www.indiapost.com/india-brazil-south-africa-fund-receives-un-award/.
69 The award was given by the "Millennium Development Goals Awards Committee," a nongovernmental organization that seeks to raise awareness of the MDGs and to publicize the efforts undertaken by governments, multilateral organizations, nongovernmental organizations and individuals who have worked toward achieving the MDGs. "Fundo IBAS Recebe o Prêmio "Millennium Development Goals," *Brazilian Ministry of Foreign Affairs*, 21 September 2010, www.itamaraty.gov.br/sala-de-imprensa/notas-a-imprensa/fundo-ibas-recebe-o-premio-201cmillennium-development-goals201d.
70 "IBSA-Guinea Bissau—Boosting Food Self-Sufficiency," *The South-South Opportunity Case Stories*, www.impactalliance.org/ev_en.php?ID=49219_201&id2=DO_TOPIC.
71 "Press Release—The Governments of India, Brazil and South Africa (IBSA), Through UNDP Inaugurate the First Project in the Middle East—a Sports Centre in Ramallah," *United Nations Development Programme (UNDP)*, unispal.un.org/UNISPAL.NSF/0/D0AA80386B580361 8525794F00521844#sthash.BUP5RtEY.dpuf.
72 "Press Release—The Governments of India, Brazil and South Africa (IBSA), through UNDP Launch the Rehabilitation Phase of the Palestinian Red Crescent Society Hospital in Gaza," *United Nations Development Programme (UNDP)*, unispal.un.org/UNISPAL.NSF/0/5F1A62555243E AC7852579EB00685996#sthash.WVywEnNc.dpuf.
73 "Fundo Ibas Ajuda Países Pobres," *Folha de S. Paulo*, 16 April 2010, www1.folha.uol.com.br/fsp/dinheiro/fi1604201008.htm.
74 Bhatia, "IBSA: Talking Shop or Powerhouse?"
75 Phone interviews conducted with development experts from Switzerland and the United States, January 2013.
76 White, "IBSA Six Years On."
77 Laura Waisbich, "IBSA 10 Years On," Conectas Human Rights, www.conectas.org/en/actions/foreign-policy/news/6470-ibsa-10-years-on.
78 Ibid.
79 "IBSA Fund," UN Office for South-South Cooperation, tcdc2.undp.org/ibsa/.

4   Does IBSA matter?

- **Autonomy through diversification**
- **Socialization**
- **Increasing leverage**
- **India, Brazil, South Africa and the regional leadership dilemma**
- **The BRICS challenge**
- **Conclusion**

Considering the three motivations described in Chapter 1 that led to the creation of IBSA in 2003, and considering its achievements described in Chapters 2 and 3, how far has the grouping fulfilled expectations during the first decade of its existence? This chapter takes up the three main motivations and critically assesses whether the group has achieved its aims. It will also address one of the grouping's main dilemmas, namely its members' contested regional leadership claim. Finally, it will analyze how far the rise of the BRICS grouping—which includes Russia and China—has affected the IBSA outfit:

> IBSA is more than a talking shop; it strives to be an influential powerhouse. In order to get there, it needs to work harder, implement its decisions faster, and involve civil society more.
> (Rajiv Bhatia, India's high commissioner to South Africa, 2006–09[1])

> Mostly ... statements of intent have remained unfulfilled.
> (al-Doyaili, Freytag and Draper[2])

Autonomy through diversification

The attempt to reduce the dependence on traditional trading partners such as the United States and the European Union can be regarded, as mentioned above, as one of the IBSA grouping's key goals. In order to diversify trade partnerships, the group established—among other steps—an IBSA Working Group on Trade and Investment. In addition an IBSA Action Plan on Trade Facilitation for Standards was signed in 2006, a Technical Regulations and Conformity Assessment conducted, and an IBSA Business Forum was created. Efforts have also been made under the IBSA Forum to use existing preferential trade agreements (PTAs) between the three IBSA countries as steps towards the creation of a trilateral free trade agreement (TFTA) involving all three countries, although little progress has been made on this front, as will be described in detail in the next chapter.

Strong growth in intra-IBSA trade is generally seen as proof of the IBSA grouping's success. In the decade after 2003, trade between the three grew more slowly than during the 10 years preceding the creation of IBSA, yet this can largely be explained by the fact that growth during the 1990s occurred from a very low base. Between 2003 and 2012, intra-IBSA imports grew by 22.7 percent a year, while total IBSA imports increased by 20.3 percent annually. The share of intra-IBSA imports in total IBSA imports grew slightly, from 2.6 percent in 2003 to 3.1 percent in 2012. Intra-IBSA exports grew 26.9 percent annually between 2003 and 2012, while total IBSA exports increased by 15.9 percent a year. Intra-IBSA exports increased from 1.6 percent of total IBSA exports in 2003 to 3.7 percent of total IBSA exports in 2012 (see Table 4.1 and Figure 4.1).[3]

While these data seem promising, Soule-Kohndou shows that the attempt to diversify trade relations substantially over the past decade has only been partially successful:

> To what extent has IBSA resulted in economic diversification? Trade flows since the creation of IBSA in 2003 significantly increased between the three countries: intra-IBSA trade grew from $2.5bn in 2003 to $21bn in 2012. The targets set during the summits and ministerial meetings to reach $10bn by 2004, and $15bn by 2010 were all reached. However in terms of percentage of their total exports, IBSA trade remains marginal, although it gradually increased compared to the pre-IBSA period (1995–2002). In 2012, India's trade to Brazil and South Africa only represented 3.8 percent of its total trade, and Brazil's trade to South Africa and India represented 3.0 percent of its total trade. For South Africa, trade towards India and Brazil was more significant, at 6.7 percent in 2012.[4]

Intra-IBSA trade was not only relatively insignificant, but also concentrated in a small number of products. Some 50 percent of Brazil's exports to India, for example, are oil, 15 percent are copper and 13 percent are chicken.[5]

A comparison with China also helps provide additional perspective. Despite the absence of a formal agreement between China and the IBSA countries, IBSA-China trade grew much more rapidly than intra-IBSA trade during the first decade of the IBSA Forum's existence. Furthermore, it did so from a much higher base. While the share of intra-IBSA imports in total IBSA imports increased from 2.6 percent in 2003 to 3.1 percent in 2012, the share of imports from China in total IBSA imports increased from 5.2 percent to 12.6 percent over the same period of time. In the same way, while the share of intra-IBSA exports in total IBSA exports increased from 1.6 percent in 2003 to 3.7 percent in 2012, the share of exports to China in total IBSA exports grew from 4.8 percent to 9.5 percent during the same time.[6]

Sean Woolfrey questions the impact the IBSA Forum has had on trade, pointing out that:

> Rapidly growing IBSA-China trade and the fact that the share of IBSA trade conducted with traditional partners such as the EU, the US and Japan has decreased significantly over the past decade, suggests that rapidly growing intra-IBSA trade may in fact reflect a broader shift in global trading patterns whereby an increasing

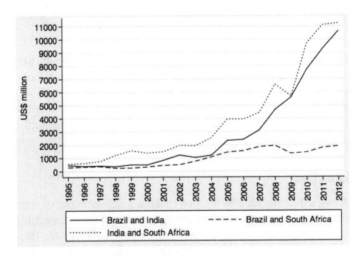

Figure 4.1 Intra-IBSA trade flow (1995–2012)
(UNCTAD statistical database (UNCTAD STAT), unctad.org/en/pages/Statistics. aspx)

Table 4.1 Intra-IBSA trade flow (1995–2012)

Year	Trade flow—IBSA (US$ million)	Annual growth
1995	1,312,009	
1996	1,349,880	2.88%
1997	1,545,895	14.52%
1998	1,836,899	18.82%
1999	2,332,189	26.96%
2000	2,213,466	-5.09%
2001	2,774,919	25.36%
2002	3,694,825	33.15%
2003	3,741,669	1.26%
2004	4,846,935	29.53%
2005	7,745,746	59.80%
2006	7,914,179	2.17%
2007	9,422,402	19.05%
2008	13,199,178	40.08%
2009	12,633,206	-4.28%
2010	18,831,201	49.06%
2011	22,176,605	17.76%
2012	23,739,515	7.04%

Source: (UNCTAD statistical database (UNCTAD STAT), unctad.org/en/pages/Statistics.aspx)

proportion of developing country trade is being conducted with other developing and emerging countries, often at the expense of "traditional" trading partners in the developed world.[7]

While often used as the best example of IBSA's positive impact, it is thus questionable how far the grouping's institutionalization has in fact caused trade ties to increase. Most likely, growth in intra-IBSA trade seems to be a result of several factors, including trade liberalization during the 1990s and a global trend towards more South-South trade (see Figures 4.2–4.4).

Socialization

It is easy to mock the idea of meetings for the sake of meetings. But they can create webs of mutual trust and even friendship that leaders can draw on in a crisis—and conversations over late-night drinks can do more to draw countries together than all the diplomats in the world.

(*The Economist*[8])

How far has the IBSA grouping helped bring India, Brazil and South Africa together? How far has it succeeded in promoting multi-level socialization between actors who barely interacted two decades ago? Have the working groups produced tangible results that allow the three countries to learn from each other?

In theory, IBSA is an extremely useful vehicle to close the gap that existed and continues to exist between the three countries' governments. As many observers argue, India, Brazil and South Africa face many similar internal challenges—ranging from socioeconomic inequality and low levels of public education to rapid urbanization—so exchanging views and experiences could be a productive exercise for policy makers.

For example, the IBSA Small, Micro and Medium Enterprises Forum in collaboration with the IBSA Working Group (WG) on Trade and Investment launched an online platform (called "IBSA B2B"), which shares investment opportunities, contacts, events, trade statistics, and best practice among the three IBSA countries. It is difficult to prove, however, whether the initiative has produced any tangible results.[9] While the website has been active throughout 2013, it is notable that no South African businessperson has yet registered. This suggests that the initiative has failed to have any impact in South Africa's business community.

During extensive interviews with public officials who participated in the IBSA working groups, many of those placed in ministries other than the Foreign Ministry voiced profound frustration with their group's inefficiency. Several complained that the diplomats responsible for the IBSA grouping usually carried little weight within their respective ministries.[10] An often-mentioned complaint was that there was no overall guidance or strategic incentive to make the working groups function properly. "We received absolutely no institutional support from our Foreign Ministry, which rarely acknowledged the progress reports we used to send," one said.[11]

Working group performance thus entirely depends on the personal disposition of members. Interest in the topic, naturally, differs from country to country. As a consequence, some working group members complained that their counterparts in the other countries failed to reciprocate their enthusiasm for making the group work. Members of numerous groups complained that it sometimes took months to obtain a response to emails or phone calls, and that other countries at times failed to communicate that the person in charge had changed. One reported she had "at least five different interlocutors over the course of two years." In two cases, interviewees accused counterparts of "lack of

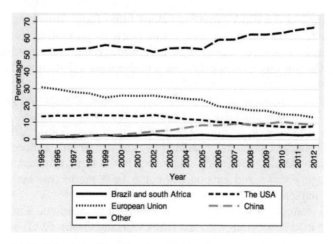

Figure 4.2 India's trade diversification (2003–12)
(UNCTAD statistical database (UNCTAD STAT), unctad.org/en/pages/Statistics.
aspx)

professionalism" and complained to their respective Foreign Ministries. Another said that over several months, the working group's activities came to a standstill because one country's lead member was busy fighting off corruption charges. The large time difference, in particular between India and Brazil was mentioned many times as an additional

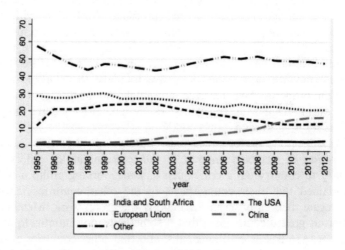

Figure 4.3 Brazil's trade diversification (2003–12)
(UNCTAD statistical database (UNCTAD STAT), unctad.org/en/pages/Statistics.
aspx)

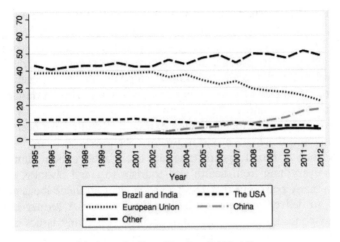

Figure 4.4 South Africa's trade diversification (2003–12)
(UNCTAD statistical database (UNCTAD STAT), unctad.org/en/pages/Statistics.
aspx)

complicating factor.[12] Finally, working group members pointed out
that one obstacle over the past years was that counterparts often
lacked the authority to take any decisions, which severely slowed down
cooperation.

Evidence that the IBSA grouping generated trust between the three
governments is that, according to policy makers, it was Brazil's and
India's experience in working together with South Africa in the context
of the IBSA framework that made South Africa's inclusion into the
BRICS seem a relatively safe choice.[13] Flemes argues that "sectoral
cooperation will form a sound base for trilateral diplomacy in world
affairs"[14]—yet it remains difficult to find tangible examples to substantiate
his claim.

In the same way, civil society in the three countries could make use
of a space to exchange expertise in areas in which they face similar
challenges. IBSA offers a platform for media, academia, women's
organizations and business representatives to engage and share best
practices. The Indian government has probably been most active in
promoting societal links between the three, but efforts are still negligible when compared to China's strategy—for example, there are now
many more Confucius Institutes across all IBSA countries than anything
comparable by the Brazilian, Indian or South African governments.

The majority of observers are critical of IBSA's usefulness when it
comes to its capacity to produce mutual learning. Skeptics have argued

that national interests diverge too much for the three to agree on what matters,[15] and that the grouping is a largely irrelevant "gathering of friends."[16] Some policy makers privately concede that the working groups have yet to produce any tangible results, because they lack high-level political support.[17] White is emphatic in his criticism, and argues that "outside of government and even within certain ministries, criticism of IBSA and its working groups is unanimous: these groups have proved more complicated than expected. Results have been slow in coming and there is a need for greater coherence and focus."[18]

With such a broad agenda and an overloaded action plan that includes everything from health and tourism to small business development, many point out that IBSA lacks a clear strategic focus and is unlikely to deliver concrete results any time soon.[19] A former Indian diplomat concedes that rather than focusing on many issues at the same time, the grouping should have concentrated on a few to obtain tangible results.[20] In the same way, Daniel Flemes writes that the grouping's perspectives will depend on its ability to focus on specific areas of cooperation.[21]

This multi-issue focus often generated expectations that the grouping proved unable to fulfill. For example, while some had hoped for a breakthrough on the project to launch a joint space satellite in 2011, the Tshwane Declaration of that year merely noted that India had agreed to host more meetings to debate the matter.

A practical problem is that the IBSA website has been neglected, making it very difficult for outsiders to obtain recent information about the grouping's activities. This is true for both the summits and the working groups, which rarely publish anything about their activities.[22] In a similar way, David Fig is highly critical when analyzing intra-IBSA cooperation, pointing out that tangible results are rare.[23]

In addition, many analysts had an overly romanticized vision of South-South cooperation which did not seem to take into account that, as is the case with any other group of countries, economic (and often political) relations are primarily marked by competition.[24] Why, a critical observer may ask, should a Brazilian company voluntarily share knowledge with an Indian or a South African company? Interviews with leading business representatives in all three countries made clear that from a private sector perspective, there is no fundamental qualitative difference between North-South and South-South cooperation.[25] Put differently, the private sector, which is seen as so essential by policy makers in establishing stronger South-South ties, does not share the belief in a common Southern identity that would justify treating Southern competitors differently from Northern ones.

In at times overly simplistic analyses, policy analysts often exaggerated the potential for cooperation, often due to a lack of knowledge of the three economies. In 2006, Nagesh Kumar argued that "Air India can learn from the great successes of South African Airways and Varig Airways"[26]—the latter of which had already filed for bankruptcy protection at the time, and was no longer operating independently.[27] In the same text, he also argued that "Goa, a well-known Indian beach resort with large Portuguese population could be of substantial interest to Brazilians"—even though the vast majority of Goans today speak no Portuguese. In addition, given the geographic distance between Brazil and India, tourism between the two countries is unlikely ever to reach significant numbers.

In the same way, notions of what the IBSA grouping was capable of were often exaggerated, particularly during the time of high growth around 2010. Lyal White expresses his hope that " ... with an emphasis on alternatives for rapid economic growth—IBSA does suggest alternatives to the currently accepted economic orthodoxy, debunking some of the approaches to development advocated by credit lending agencies and countries of the North for the developing world."[28] Yet there is little evidence that policy makers from India, Brazil and South Africa ever intended or would have been capable of providing alternative models of development—even though, as suggested above, their rhetoric seemed to suggest that South-South cooperation was fundamentally different from traditional trade relations. Unrealistic expectations may thus influence the way observers assess whether the IBSA grouping has been a success or a failure.

Chris Landsberg concludes that "while IBSA can boast clear positions on a host of strategic issues, these have to date taken the form more of declarations, statements and pronouncements rather than strategies, tactics and plans of action."[29] Many analyses written about IBSA are therefore of aspirational nature and point to the great potential of the grouping.

Responding to criticism that IBSA has produced little during its first decade, policy makers usually argue that due to its nature as a "forum," IBSA is primarily meant to establish a dialogue rather than concrete results. In the same way, Zélia Campbell writes that IBSA's main goal is merely to create a platform to "induce a climate whereby three culturally so different countries can get to know each other and, in the process, develop an atmosphere of mutual trust." If this were the grouping's sole objective, it would indeed be difficult to assess whether IBSA had been successful or not.[30]

As Paulo Sotero points out, IBSA, as an alliance of three highly diverse democratic societies, "might best be viewed as a laboratory for exploring the future of democracy and international cooperation in the Global South."[31] Indeed, there are few groupings that provide any blueprint regarding where IBSA may be headed in the future.

Increasing leverage

How far have IBSA countries been able to increase their leverage in international forums as a consequence of the grouping they formed?

Refilwe Mokoena writes that when the IBSA countries first engaged in 2003, "it rapidly became clear that the three countries shared common views on a range of global challenges and that working together in multilateral forums, especially the UN and the World Trade Organization (WTO), they could further their collective aims."[32] As Manmohan Singh said, IBSA was based on a "common political identity," and its members came from different continents, but that they shared "similar world views and aspirations."[33]

It seems certain that their cooperation has, in several instances, allowed them to play a leadership role, such as in Cancún in 2003. Their close coordination at the time allowed IBSA to be instrumental in the creation of the G20+ and NAMA. By strengthening ties between three major developing countries in the global South, IBSA has thus improved their joint capacity to influence global negotiations. Yet even when assessing Cancún alone, some observers are skeptical about IBSA's impact. Sean Woolfrey notes that acting together:

> has undoubtedly increased the bargaining power of the IBSA countries at the WTO, and India and Brazil, in particular, have graduated to the inner-circle of Doha Round trade negotiations. These gains have not, however, translated into significant progress in terms of achieving the particular objectives the IBSA countries have been pursuing at the Doha Round, such as restrictions on developed-world agricultural subsidies, greater market access for developing-country agricultural products, flexibilities for developing countries in terms of market-access commitments on industrial goods and institutional reform of the WTO itself. If anything, the increased bargaining power achieved by IBSA and other large developing countries has contributed to the current deadlock at the Doha Round and a waning interest in trade multilateralism. As the likes of the EU and the US continue to turn their attention towards bilateral and regional trade deals as a way to achieve their trade-related objectives, the prospects for substantial progress at the

multilateral level will diminish, and many of the goals of the IBSA countries will remain unfulfilled.[34]

Woolfrey may be right that WTO negotiations hardly progressed in 2003, partly due to developing countries' better capacity to organize themselves under IBSA leadership. Yet diplomats from Brazil, India and South Africa rightly responded that deadlock was necessary in order to rebalance a negotiation process that was dominated by developed countries' positions.[35] It seems clear that after the negotiations in Cancún, the three IBSA members have been able to improve dramatically their individual positions in the international trade hierarchy.[36] It was largely due to their performance in 2003 that Brazil and India were asked to be part of the G5 preparation group a year later (with the EU, the United States and Australia), which would form a crucial element of the WTO negotiations. Two years later, at the G8 Summit in Germany, the three IBSA countries (as well as China and Mexico) were invited to institutionalize their dialogue with the group through the so-called Heiligendamm or Outreach 5 process.[37]

These developments are strongly indicative of the fact that IBSA's multilateral activism enhanced the notion in capitals around the world that emerging powers needed to be better represented in the principal institutions. The invitation of emerging powers to the G5 and Outreach 5 reflects a growing acceptance by established powers that it is necessary to reform existing bodies.

How far has the IBSA Forum provided leaders with additional visibility on the international stage, possibly increasing their chance of turning into international agenda setters? Several observers write that IBSA summits have gained growing media coverage over the past years,[38] although they concede that this visibility is largely limited to other developing countries. Whenever major newspapers such as The *New York Times, El País* or *Le Monde* covered IBSA, they highlighted aspects of cooperation and specific projects such as the IBSA satellite project.[39] Most importantly, however, the IBSA grouping is—contrary to the BRICS group—usually described as a group of "vibrant" democracies, which has a highly positive connotation.[40]

While the summits may thus generate a satisfactory response in the media, it is unclear how far this international recognition increases their bargaining power in international forums. The most important positive impact is possibly the fact that IBSA countries are seen in a less threatening, more benign light, given that they usually stress their democratic credentials during the IBSA encounters.

India, Brazil, South Africa and the regional leadership dilemma

While policy makers from other developing countries admitted that IBSA's role had been exemplary in Cancún, they largely rejected the grouping's capacity to "represent" the developing world.[41] In fact, IBSA countries attempted to consider other developing countries' preferences throughout the process. The São Paulo Round of the Global System of Trade Preferences among Developing Countries, for example, was supported by IBSA. Yet in other instances, the three countries did not represent others' interests. For example, net food importers like the majority of least developed countries (LDCs) were not interested in the reduction of agricultural subsidies in Europe and the United States which kept prices low.[42]

This limitation has direct consequences for India's, Brazil's and South Africa's interest in obtaining support for a permanent seat on the UN Security Council. While all three countries share the same goal, they do not campaign together: India and Brazil have been explicit regarding their mutual support for each other's candidacy for permanent membership as members of the G4 (with Germany and Japan). India and Brazil invited South Africa to join the group, but the government in Pretoria decided to abide by African Union guidelines, preventing it from launching an open candidacy on its own.

Other developing countries' skepticism about the IBSA grouping's leadership points to an important limitation when discussing its potential. Brazil, India, and South Africa all share singularly complex relations with their respective regions, due to their preponderant economic and military position relative to other states.[43] Yet none of the three members' regional leadership project is uncontested, and in all three cases, there has been significant resistance in the past to their individual attempts to base their global ambitions on their regional hegemony. The creation of the so-called "Coffee Club," which includes countries such as Argentina and Pakistan, is a case in point: India, Brazil and South Africa may be seen as regional leaders from afar, but their neighbors are far from convinced or interested in bestowing them with the right to speak for their respective regions.[44] As Daniel Flemes argues, "for different reasons Pakistan opposes India's leadership, Argentina, Mexico and Venezuela undermine Brazil's regional power status, and Nigeria, Zimbabwe and other African states refuse to follow South Africa."[45] Mittelman asks:

> How is Nigeria, for instance, to regard South African leadership in global coalitions? Far more populous, larger in area and richer in

energy resources than is South Africa, though not as technologically developed or as prosperous on a per capita basis, Nigeria is
an obvious candidate for a prominent role in continental leadership. Is Pretoria entitled, and does it presume, to represent
Abuja, or Africans in other countries, on a global stage? The
point is that in choosing one among other regional actors, the risk
lies in repeating a pattern of exclusivity to which colonialism
and imperialism subjected the now emerging market powers
themselves.[46]

It seems clear that the key to building a sustainable partnership
between India, Brazil and South Africa is for these countries to invest
in consolidating their leadership role in South Asia, South America
and Southern Africa, respectively. The paradox, interestingly enough,
is that, while the United States has welcomed the regional leadership
role of IBSA members, their neighbors are uncertain about the actual
intentions of New Delhi, Brasília, and Pretoria.

The BRICS challenge

> IBSA has a personality of its own. It is three separate continents,
> three democracies. BRIC is a conception devised by Goldman
> Sachs.
>
> (Manmohan Singh[47])

> When BRICS speaks, its views are bound to receive much greater
> notice than those of IBSA. If IBSA does not become stronger, it
> will become irrelevant.
>
> (Rajiv Bhatia[48])

On 14 April 2011, the Third BRICS Summit began in China's southern resort city of Sanya. After two successful summits in Yekaterinburg
in 2009 and Brasília in 2010, this third summit in China marked the
definitive establishment of the BRICS grouping as an important part
of South-South cooperation. Most importantly, however, South Africa
participated for the first time as the fifth member of the group, whose
name thus officially changed from "BRIC" to "BRICS." By inviting a
country that the creator of the term, Jim O'Neill, had not initially
included (and the inclusion of which he severely criticized),[49] policy
makers in emerging powers assumed ownership of the grouping.[50] The
BRICS were now primarily a political construct, no longer a mere
investment category devised by an economist at Goldman Sachs.[51]

After significant diplomatic efforts, South Africa's inclusion in the BRICS grouping in late 2010, several months prior to the third summit, can be regarded as one of South Africa's principal foreign policy achievements in recent years. A crucial factor of success was that Brazilian and Indian policy makers had been well aware of South Africa's position after having frequently cooperated since 2003 in the IBSA framework.[52]

Far from being a mere additional member of an already mature structure, South Africa's inclusion has fundamentally altered the nature of the BRICS grouping, turning it into a more global alliance with a stronger capacity to speak on behalf of the emerging world.[53] South Africa's inclusion also underlined the BRIC countries' long-term commitment to strengthening their presence in Africa, and as an effort to depict the grouping as Africa's partner in the larger context of South-South cooperation.

Much more than IBSA, the BRICS grouping powerfully symbolized a narrative that seemed distant in the 1990s but appeared to make sense in the 2000s: a momentous shift of power from the United States and Europe towards emerging powers such as China, India and Brazil was taking place, making the world less Western and more ideologically diverse.[54] Economic liberalization in emerging market economies began to pay off, resulting in consistently higher growth rates than in the developed world. In contrast, the United States' hitherto unlimited power seemed to reach its limits in costly and potentially ill-conceived military engagements in Iraq and Afghanistan and a challenging "war on terror," which seemed to reduce US legitimacy, opening a window of opportunity for emerging countries to gain greater visibility.[55] At a remarkable speed, unipolarity turned into a mere transition phase on the way towards a multipolar age. As Randall Schweller and Xiayou Pu argued, "unipolarity, which seemed strangely durable only a few years ago, appears today as a 'passing moment'." They continue that the United States "is no longer a hyperpower towering over potential contenders. The rest of the world is catching up."[56]

Finally, globalization and a growing interconnectedness also played an important role. The increased prominence of global challenges, ranging from climate change and failed states, to poverty reduction and nuclear proliferation, contributed to a growing consensus that emerging countries such as Brazil, India and China were indispensable in the effort to develop meaningful solutions.[57] Global summits could no longer claim legitimacy and inclusiveness without inviting Brazil, Russia, India and China. The transition from the G8 to the G20 is one of the most powerful symbols of this shift towards a more multipolar order. Aside from making up 43.3 percent of the global population and a quarter of the Earth's territory, the BRICs had been responsible for 36.3 percent of world GDP growth in purchasing power parity (PPP) terms (or 27.8 percent in US dollars) during the first decade of the century.[58]

The BRIC acronym both captured and further enhanced these sentiments and proved a useful shorthand for a complex scenario marked by the redistribution of global power,[59] the emergence of non-established actors and the advent of a "Post-American World"[60] or a "Post-Western World."[61]

This raises an important question about the continued usefulness of IBSA. Now that all IBSA members are also part of BRICS, why not simply merge IBSA into BRICS? As Taylor argues, "the raison d'être of the BRICS initiative is identical to IBSA's," asking whether "BRICS has killed IBSA"—a question he answers affirmatively.[62]

At the Fourth BRICS Summit, in New Delhi in 2012, several delegates and observers noted how much the BRICS grouping had evolved: the agenda now included not only first-order geostrategic issues such as the global distribution of power and institutional responsibility and questions of war and peace, but also developmental and social questions such as education, universal health care and the environment—many issues that had previously been discussed between India, Brazil and South Africa at the yearly IBSA summits. From a Chinese point of view, the "IBSA-ization" of the BRICS summits was desirable as it might at some point lead to the merger of the two groupings. Such a move could eliminate IBSA, an attractive and potentially meaningful outfit which had deliberately chosen not to invite China.

As the BRICS grouping further institutionalizes, the two forums present similar tendencies and institutional settings. A BRICS working group on experts of agriculture was created in 2010 while the IBSA Working Group on Agriculture has existed since 2004.

In April 2012, BRICS finance ministers and central bank governors met in Washington, DC, and agreed to develop a cooperative approach on issues relating to international taxation, transfer pricing, exchange of information, and tax evasion and avoidance. Compared to other areas, tax cooperation is thus rather recent. At the first meeting, in January 2013, the heads of revenue deliberated on issues of mutual concern related to tax administration, international taxation, transfer pricing, cross-border tax evasion and tax dispute resolution mechanisms.[63] This initiative is very similar to the IBSA Working Group on Tax and Revenue Administration, created in 2007. A BRICS meeting of senior budget officials also took place in January 2013 and discussions on mutual cooperation in the field of tax policy and tax administration are ongoing. The BRICS meeting of senior officials in Science and Technology also took place in 2010, while the IBSA Working Group on Science and Technology is among the first IBSA WG created in 2004.

This tendency poses the risk of overlapping and redundant activities in the IBSA and BRICS forums, and poses a challenge for the different officials across governments dealing with these two forums' issues.

The discussion about the possibility of merging the two groupings gained momentum among policy analysts in June 2013, when the IBSA summit in New Delhi was postponed. While diplomats from India, Brazil and South Africa emphatically state that they seek to keep the two groupings separate, some privately concede that doing so would be unnecessary. A former Indian diplomat privately pointed out that organizing two separate stand-alone summits was simply too burdensome on policy makers, who already "spend too much time on the plane."[64] If IBSA meetings are to continue, he argues, they should take place on the margins of already existing meetings, such as BRICS, the G20, or the UN General Assembly.

Defenders of the IBSA grouping argue that while IBSA's visibility in international affairs pales against that of the yearly BRICS summits, the three IBSA members have identified themselves as partners because they share a set of fundamental notions about global order. As emerging countries that are not yet fully integrated in today's international structures, all IBSA countries consider the current order to be unjust and in need of reform. While the degree of rejection of some institutions differs—for example, India is far more hostile towards the Non-Proliferation Treaty (NPT) than Brazil—all three agree that they deserve more institutional responsibility, including permanent seats on the UN Security Council. On this front, they clearly diverge from China and Russia, both of which are relatively established players—a position best symbolized by their status as veto-wielding permanent members of the UN Security Council and recognized nuclear powers in the NPT.

In addition, all three IBSA members are multiparty democracies and are thus able to debate freely how to implement difficult reforms necessary to boost growth in a messy and complex political context. These matters cannot be discussed openly at BRICS summits. In the same way, issues related to human rights and civil society are not mentioned when the BRICS meet.

China is likely to push for IBSA to be replaced by BRICS. Most diplomats interviewed said that Brazil, India and South Africa should resist such a move, even when there are clear overlaps between the debates at BRICS and IBSA summits. China's absence is precisely what makes IBSA an interesting platform for debating global challenges in a different context, and also speaks frankly about challenges that cannot be addressed at BRICS summits, including the question of how to deal with the rise of China.[65]

While the BRICS grouping gained much more visibility on a global scale[66] (not least due to China's membership), some policy makers argue that shared democratic experience could give IBSA greater long-term potential. "Our heart is not in BRICS, but with IBSA. Common values matter," a former top Indian official said privately. As mentioned above, Indian Prime Minister Singh has noted that "IBSA has a personality of its own ... BRICS is a conception devised by Goldman Sachs." When the suggestion arose that China would lead an effort to subsume IBSA into the expanded BRICS, he replied "We should preserve the common principles and values we stand for."[67]

Yet how important is the fact that India, Brazil and South Africa are democracies for their capacity to build a useful platform, and what is the theoretical foundation of their assertions?

Liberalist theory makes a series of arguments about democracies' behavior in international politics.[68] Democracies are less likely to fight wars against each other, they are more likely to conclude trade agreements, and they are more likely to cooperate in general and seek membership in international organizations.[69] For example, as Mansfield, Milner and Rosendorff argue, the probability of states cooperating on trade policy strongly depends on their regime type. The more democratic a state, the more likely it will be to conclude trade agreements. According to their analysis, "the superior ability of elections in democracies to constrain leaders prompts democratic rulers to be more cooperative internationally than their non-democratic counterparts."[70] Autocratic leaders, on the other hand, do not face regular worries about re-election, so they have fewer incentives to relinquish policy autonomy and sign trade agreements, making them less likely than democratic leaders to seek commercial cooperation.[71]

Why are democracies more likely to engage in a democratic, rule-based and open international system, or form networks of cooperation? According to Kant, it should be one of liberal states' foreign policy goals to preserve, strengthen and expand the pacific union[72] or, as Doyle has put it, to build a "steady worldwide pressure for a liberal peace."[73] Ikenberry argues that elites who work in the context of democratic domestic state structures try to engage in an international order that is congenial with their domestic system—hence, they seek to cooperate with others.[74] Democracies will prefer to exist in the midst of an international system imbued with democratic values, strengthening the importance of democratic polity on a global scale. The "stickiness" of interlocking institutions is thus greater between democratic regimes than between non-democratic regimes, because democracies' promises are more reassuring. The decentralization and openness of democratic states provides opportunities for all states to consult and make representations directly, thus strengthening their willingness to make serious commitments.[75]

In the case of South-South cooperation, all this suggests that IBSA should be far more willing and able to strengthen cooperation than any other grouping that includes non-democratic regimes such as China. Applied to the case of the BRICS, one would expect that, due to the presence of two non-democratic regimes, cooperation is significantly more difficult than between a grouping that is entirely democratic.

Yet, intra-BRICS cooperation is far more sophisticated than is generally assumed by outside observers. Furthermore, in almost none of the areas of cooperation is there a strong sense that differing regime type hinders multi-level engagement. This shows that one of the BRICS critics' main claims about why the BRICS countries cannot cooperate is flawed. Many argue that IBSA would be a far more viable platform for cooperation, largely since India, Brazil and South Africa all have democratic regimes.[76] Yet contrary to such expectations, cooperation in the context of the IBSA grouping is not necessarily more advanced and diverse than in the context of BRICS.

Policy makers from IBSA countries often agree that intra-BRICS cooperation is as viable as intra-IBSA cooperation. In 2007, Lula dismissed comments of Brazil's under secretary-general of political affairs, Roberto Jaguaribe, who contrasted China unfavorably with India and said "It's inevitable for Brazil to have a special relationship with India (instead of China)." "No," the Brazilian president said when asked if Brazil wanted a special and exclusive relationship with India, which would cut out China. "Today, it is important to talk to China. You cannot take China out of the picture. As in all pictures China will be present. A country of 1.3 billion; 9.5 per cent growth rate per year; an extraordinary share of world trade ... but a good partnership with one country (China) does not mean one cannot have a strategic partnership with another (India)."[77]

There are only two issue areas where intra-IBSA cooperation is indeed more advanced than intra-BRICS cooperation: poverty alleviation and joint military exercises. First of all, IBSA has established the IBSA Facility Fund for Alleviation of Poverty and Hunger, through which development projects are executed with IBSA funding in fellow developing countries. While this is notable, the amounts involved remain small compared to existing development institutions, and the proposed BRICS Development Bank would dwarf the IBSA Fund.

The second notable area of intra-IBSA cooperation is IBSAMAR. Yet the main reason for more sophisticated intra-IBSA cooperation in this particular field may simply be that coordinating military exercises between five countries is logistically more challenging than between three countries. An additional reason may be that due to Russia's and China's might and somewhat antagonistic stance towards the United States, BRICS member countries did not want to appear as a grouping with a military connotation. Finally, while IBSAMAR is certainly notable, its strategic importance should not be overestimated.

In fact, 10 years after the creation of the grouping, intra-IBSA cooperation is not more profound than intra-BRICS cooperation. The fact that the BRICS grouping consists of three democracies and two autocracies is thus far no obstacle to greater rapprochement, and intra-BRICS cooperation is by now far more sophisticated than that of all-democracy groupings such as IBSA. After five years of growing ties between the BRICS, little would suggest that a democratic China or Russia would lead to an acceleration or significant increase of joint activities. Rather, economic and strategic interests seem to play a more important role—cooperation in the fields of trade, agriculture and health care, for example, may be driven by the genuine belief that cooperation within the BRICS brings tangible benefits at virtually no cost—largely because BRICS is not institutionalized enough at this stage to impose any binding rules on its members.

Table 4.2 Democracy and institutional agreement

Characteristic	Implication
Transparency	Reduces surprises
	Generates higher confidence
	information
Decentralized policy process	Policy viscosity
	Opportunities for enforcement
Open and decentralized system	Access and voice opportunities
	Transnational and transgovernmental
	connecting points

Source: G.J. Ikenberry, *After Victory: Institutions, Strategic Restraint, and the Rebuilding of Order after Major Wars* (Princeton, N.J.: Princeton University Press, 2001)

Conclusion

To summarize, we can argue that despite IBSA's innovative design, most of the grouping's potential remains unfulfilled. This is not to say that its goals are misguided. There seems to be little doubt that promoting South-South cooperation has significant benefits for all those involved. The question, however, is how far the IBSA grouping has helped countries achieve this aim. Trade between the three member countries has increased, as has mutual knowledge, yet it is unclear to what extent this can be attributed to the creation of the IBSA grouping. As a consequence, the majority of observers are critical when it comes to evaluating the usefulness of the IBSA grouping. The risk that the BRICS grouping will eventually eclipse and replace IBSA is thus set to remain.

Notes

1 Rajiv Bhatia, "IBSA: Talking Shop or Powerhouse?" *The Hindu*, 12 October 2010, www.thehindu.com/opinion/lead/article825414.ece
2 Sarah al-Doyaili, Andreas Freytag and Peter Draper, "IBSA: Fading out or Forging a Common Vision?" *South African Journal of International Affairs* 20, no. 2 (2013): 297–310, 301.
3 UNCTAD, *Handbook of Statistics 2009.*
4 Folashadé Soule-Kohndou, "The India-Brazil-South Africa Forum a Decade on: Mismatched Partners or the Rise of the South?" *Global Economic Governance Programme Working Paper* 2013/88, University of Oxford, November 2013, 10.
5 Adriana Schor, "Cooperação Sul-Sul e IBAS: Mais Comércio na Política," *Centro de Estudos e Negociações Internacionais*, 11 October 2013, caeni.com.br/blog/?p=419.
6 Sean Woolfrey, "The IBSA Dialogue Forum Ten Years On: Examining IBSA Cooperation on Trade," *Tralac Trade Brief* No. S13TB05/2013, August 2013, 14.
7 Ibid., 15.
8 "America and China: The Summit," *The Economist*, 6 July 2013, www.economist.com/news/leaders/21579003-barack-obama-and-xi-jinping-have-chance-recast-centurys-most-important-bilateral.
9 Ibid., 13.
10 Interviews with public officials in Pretoria, Brasília and New Delhi, 2012, 2013 and 2014.
11 Ibid.
12 Ibid.
13 Interviews with Indian and Brazilian diplomats, May and June 2012.
14 Daniel Flemes, "India-Brazil-South Africa (IBSA) in the New Global Order: Interests, Strategies and Values of the Emerging Coalition," *International Studies* 46, no. 4 (2009): 401–21, 403.

15 Sanusha Naidu, "A Pragmatic Voice of the South or a Vending Machine of Competing and Diffused Interests," *Policy Studies Bulletin of CPS* 8, no. 2 (2006): 17–19.

16 Lyal White, "IBSA Six Years On: Co-operation in a New Global Order," *SAIIA Emerging Powers Programme Policy Briefing* 8, November 2009.

17 Phone interviews with former and current policy makers from India, Brazil and South Africa, 2011, 2012 and 2013.

18 White, "IBSA Six Years On," 3.

19 Lyal White, "IBSA: A State of the Art," in *South African Yearbook of International Affairs 2003/4* (Johannesburg: South African Institute of International Affairs, 2004), 8.

20 Phone interview with former Indian diplomat, December 2013.

21 Daniel Flemes, "Emerging Middle Powers' Soft Balancing Strategy: State and Perspectives of the IBSA Dialogue Forum," *GIGA Working Papers* 57 (2007).

22 Al-Doyaili, Freytag and Draper also mention this problem. In al-Doyaili *et al.*, "IBSA: Fading out or Forging a Common Vision?" 301.

23 David Fig, "Scientific, Agricultural and Environmental Collaboration in the IBSA Dialogue Forum, 2003–10," in *Contemporary India and South Africa: Legacies, Identities and Dilemmas*, ed. S. Patel and T. Uys (New Delhi, India: Routledge, 2012).

24 Schor, "Cooperação Sul-Sul e IBAS: Mais Comércio na Política."

25 Interviews with business representatives, São Paulo, Johannesburg, Mumbai, 2011, 2012 and 2013.

26 Nagesh Kumar, "Sectoral Cooperation within IBSA: Some Explorations in South-South Cooperation," *Policy Studies Bulletin of CPS* 8, no. 2 (2006): 8–11.

27 Prabir De made a similar suggestion a year earlier: Prabir De, "Trade in IBSA Economic Cooperation: The Role of Transportation Linkages," *RIS Discussion Papers 104*, East Asian Bureau of Economic Research, December 2005, 19.

28 White, "IBSA: A State of the Art."

29 Chris Landsberg, "IBSA's Political Origins, Significance and Challenges," *Policy Studies Bulletin of CPS* 8, no. 2 (2006): 4–7, 5.

30 Zélia Campbell, "IBSA: Overview and Perspectives," in *III Conferência Nacional de Política Externa e Política Internacional "O Brasil no mundo que vem ai"—III CNPEPI—Seminário IBAS*, ed. Fundação Alexandre de Gusmão (FUNAG) (Brasília, Brazil: FUNAG, 2008), 155–72.

31 Paulo Sotero, "Emerging Powers: India, Brazil and South Africa (IBSA) and the Future of South-South Cooperation," Special Report, Woodrow Wilson International Center for Scholars, August 2009, 2.

32 Refilwe Mokoena, "South-South Co-operation: The Case for IBSA," *South African Journal of International Affairs* 14, no. 2 (2007): 125–45, 125.

33 Suzanne Gratius, "IBSA: An International Actor and Partner for the EU?" *FRIDE Activity Brief*, July 2008.

34 Woolfrey, "The IBSA Dialogue Forum Ten Years On," 19–20.

35 Interviews with Brazilian, Indian and South African policy makers, 2011 and 2012.

36 Daniel Flemes, "Network Powers: Strategies of Change in the Multipolar System," *Third World Quarterly* 34, no. 6 (2013): 1016–36, 1021.

37 Lesley Masters, "The G8 and the Heiligendamm Dialogue Process: Institutionalising the 'Outreach 5'," *Global Insight 85*, Institute for Global Dialogue, November 2008, 1–7, 3.

38 Soule-Kohndou, "The India-Brazil-South Africa Forum a Decade on," 18.

39 Ibid.

40 Thalif Deen, "South-South Cooperation Revs Up," *Al Jazeera*, 22 August 2011, www.aljazeera.com/indepth/features/2011/08/201182284856866748.html.

41 Interviews with policy makers from Argentina, Uruguay and Costa Rica, 2013.

42 Flemes, "Emerging Middle Powers' Soft Balancing Strategy," 12.

43 Chris Alden and Marco Antonio Vieira, "The New Diplomacy of the South: South Africa, Brazil, India and Trilateralism," *Third World Quarterly* 26, no. 7 (2005): 1077–95, 1080.

44 Ian Taylor, "Has the BRICS Killed IBSA?" *South African Foreign Policy Initiative*, 15 August 2012, thediplomat.com/2012/08/keep-the-brics-and-ibsa-seperate/.

45 Flemes, "Emerging Middle Powers' Soft Balancing Strategy," 7.

46 James H. Mittelman, "Global Bricolage: Emerging Market Powers and Polycentric Governance," *Third World Quarterly* 34, no. 1 (2013): 23–37, 30.

47 Indrani Bagchi, "PM Against Merger of IBSA, BRIC Blocs," *The Times of India*, 17 April 2010, articles.timesofindia.indiatimes.com/2010-04-17/india/28133294_1_bric-countries-ibsa-populations-and-diverse-societies.

48 Rajiv Bhatia, "BRICS Set to Outshine IBSA?" *The Hindu*, 2 May 2011, www.thehindu.com/opinion/lead/brics-set-to-outshine-ibsa/article1978593.ece.

49 Sébastien Hervieu, "South Africa Gains Entry to Bric Club," *The Guardian*, 19 April 2011, www.theguardian.com/world/2011/apr/19/south-africa-joins-bric-club.

50 Oliver Stuenkel, "Keep BRICS and IBSA Separate," *The Diplomat*, 13 August 2012, thediplomat.com/2012/08/keep-the-brics-and-ibsa-seperate/.

51 Oliver Stuenkel, "South Africa's BRICS Membership: A Win-Win Situation?" *African Journal of Political Science and International Relations* 7, no. 7 (2013): 310–19.

52 Mokoena, "South-South Co-operation."

53 Candice Moore, "BRICS Partnership: A Case of South-South Cooperation? Exploring the Roles of South Africa and Africa," *Institute for Global Dialogue*, 9 July 2012, www.igd.org.za/home/206-brics-partnership-a-case-of-south-south-cooperation-exploring-the-roles-of-south-africa-and-africa.

54 Randall Schweller, "Emerging Powers in an Age of Disorder," *Global Governance* 17, no. 3 (2011): 285–97, 285.

55 In fact, Jim O'Neill describes the terrorist attacks on 11 September 2011, as the key event that caused him to develop a grouping that symbolized "globalization" was not about Americanization. Beth Kowitt, "For Mr. BRIC, Nation Meeting a Milestone," *CNN Money*, 17 June 2009, money.cnn.com/2009/06/17/news/economy/goldman_sachs_jim_oneill_interview.fortune/.

56 Randall Schweller and Xiaoyu Pu, "After Unipolarity: China's Visions of International Order in an Era of U.S. Decline," *International Security* 36, no. 1 (2011): 41–72, 41.

57 Andrew Hurrell, "Hegemony, Liberalism and Global Order: What Space for Would-be Powers?" *International Affairs* 82, no. 1 (2006): 1–19, 3.

58 D. Wilson, A. Kelston and S. Ahmed, "Is this the 'BRICs Decade'?" *BRICs Monthly*, Goldman Sachs Global Economics, Commodities and Strategy Research, No: 10/03 (20 May 2010): 3.

59 Philip Stephens, "A Story of Brics Without Mortar", *Financial Times*, 24 November 2011, www.ft.com/intl/cms/s/0/352e96e8-15f2-11e1-a691-00144f eabdc0.html.

60 Fareed Zakaria, *The Post-American World* (New York: W.W. Norton & Company, 2008).

61 Simon Serfaty, "Moving into a Post-Western World," *The Washington Quarterly* 34, no. 2 (2011): 7–23.

62 Taylor, "Has the BRICS Killed IBSA?"

63 Oliver Stuenkel, "Understanding Intra-BRICS Cooperation: The Case of Tax Administration," *Post-Western World*, 3 June 2013, www.postwestern world.com/2013/06/03/understanding-intra-brics-cooperation-the-case-of-ta x-administration/.

64 Interview with former Indian diplomat, December 2013.

65 Rajeev Sharma, "BRIC vs IBSA = China vs India?" *The Diplomat*, 2 March 2011, thediplomat.com/2011/03/bric-vs-ibsa-china-vs-india/.

66 Taylor, "Has the BRICS Killed IBSA?"

67 Daniel Kurtz-Phelan, "What is IBSA Anyway?" *Americas Quarterly*, Spring 2013, www.americasquarterly.org/content/what-ibsa-anyway.

68 Edward D. Mansfield, Helen V. Milner and B. Peter Rosendorff, "Why Democracies Cooperate More: Electoral Control and International Trade Agreements," *International Organization* 56, no. 3 (2002): 477–513; Fernando Henrique Cardoso, "An Age of Citizenship," *Foreign Policy* 119 (2000): 40–43.

69 Bruce Russett and William Antholis, "Do Democracies Fight Each Other? Evidence from the Peloponnesian War," *Journal of Peace Research* 29, no. 4 (1992): 415–34.

70 Mansfield *et al.*, "Why Democracies Cooperate More," 478.

71 Thinking along similar lines, several thinkers, including Kant, have pointed out that liberal democracies are inherently peaceful because politically empowered citizens are, contrary to autocratic monarchs, unwilling to bear the cost of war. Montesquieu, Paine and Schumpeter have argued that capitalism and trade leads to rationality and makes war less likely. In addition, Doyle points out that regular elections in liberal democracies cause frequent changes of leadership. That reduces the chance that personal animosities between heads of state cause long-term friction. See M.W. Doyle, "Liberalism and World Politics," *The American Political Science Review* 80, no. 4 (1986): 1151–69. Weart argues that tolerance and compromise are central aspects of democratic culture, so diplomats from democratic countries will seek to find negotiated agreements rather than engage in conflict. See S.R. Weart, *Never at War: Why Democracies Will Not Fight One Another* (New Haven, Conn.: Yale University Press, 1998).

72 Immanuel Kant, *To Perpetual Peace: A Philosophical Sketch* (Indianapolis, Ind.: Hackett Publishing, 2003).

73 M.W. Doyle, "Kant, Liberal Legacies, and Foreign Affairs, Part 2," *Philosophy and Public Affairs* 12, no. 4 (1983): 323–53.

74 John Ikenberry, "The Intertwining of Domestic and International Politics," *Polity* 29, no. 2 (1996): 293–98.
75 John Ikenberry, *After Victory. Institutions, Strategic Restraint, and the Rebuilding of Order After Major Wars* (Princeton, N.J.: Princeton University Press, 2001).
76 Sandeep Dikshit, "IBSA Needs to Step up Pace on Trade Within the Grouping and Security," *The Hindu*, 18 October 2011, www.thehindu.com/news/national/article2546692.ece.
77 Rashmee Roshan Lall, "Brazil Promises Special, but Not Exclusive Ties," *The Times of India*, 3 June 2007, articles.timesofindia.indiatimes.com/2007-06-03/europe/27987426_1_president-luiz-inacio-lula-special-relationship-china-unfavourably.

5 The politics of South-South cooperation
Towards a new paradigm?

- **Behind the hype**
- **The IBSA free trade agreement (FTA): lack of political will?**
- **Protectionist measures**
- **Conclusion**

> The centre of global economic gravity is heading South.
>
> (Stephen King[1])

Is South-South trade different from North-South trade? Can South-South cooperation live up to the high expectations generated by the notion of solidarity and the special responsibility that this puts on them? This chapter shows that while policy makers from developing countries such as Brazil, India and South Africa regularly stress the qualitative superiority of trade between countries located in the global South, there is very little empirical evidence to support this claim. This does not mean that it would be wrong to focus on strengthening South-South trade—quite the contrary. Yet South-South trade does not seem to generate greater benefits than North-South trade, or be more likely to be less equitable or less exploitative. Finally, largely due to a lack of political will, attempts to sign a free trade agreement between them have hardly progressed over the past 10 years.

A lot of the rhetoric around the IBSA grouping praises the virtues of South-South cooperation, yet the term remains little understood. On what principles and paradigms, in comparison to existing structures, is South-South cooperation based? These questions have gained growing importance since the end of the Cold War, when emerging powers in the global South began to try to diversify their partnerships. Since then, an important element of their diversification strategy has focused on strengthening ties with other developing countries. These are important questions as it is South-South trade that is poised to grow most over the coming decades, fundamentally altering global trade dynamics. Emerging powers will thus increasingly be able to influence global discussions about trade, and their views regarding South-South cooperation will matter more than ever.

While developing countries have articulated their desire for greater cooperation since the Bandung conference in 1955 as they sought to promote economic and cultural cooperation on the basis of mutual interest and respect, it is quite clear that the challenge that today's rising powers pose to global governance is of a qualitatively different nature to that of previous Third World political movements, such as the Non-Aligned Movement or the G-77,[2] and their efforts in the 1970s to set an agenda for an NIEO. There is thus a fundamental difference between historical and contemporary South-South cooperation (SSC) regarding their relationship with and attitude to West-led international economic institutions. Emerging powers in the global South share the fact that their recent growth owes much to their extensive and increasing international engagement, rather than to any partial withdrawal or "de-linkage" from the global economy.[3] Recent attempts to institutionalize South-South cooperation, such as the IBSA and BRICS grouping, should therefore not be understood as a revival of Third Worldism. After all, none of their declarations questions the foundational underpinnings of liberal economic globalization. At the same time, the assumption that the less advanced economies could progress by de-linking from the advanced economies remains valid for some proponents.[4]

The past two decades have seen a surge in South-South economic cooperation—including trade, investment, development assistance and other financial flows.[5] Since 2008–09, developing countries have exported more to other developing countries than to developed countries.[6] Brazil's trade with Africa increased between 2000 and 2012 from US$4 billion to $28 billion. Some 58 percent of Brazil's trade is with the global South, 22 percent of it with other Latin American countries; thus, 36 percent is intercontinental Southern trade. This percentage is expected to increase, exceeding trade with the developed world by a multiple of eight in the next 40 years.[7] Intercontinental South-South trade could easily account for more than half of all Brazil's trade by 2050.[8] Brazil has now 37 embassies on the African continent, more than the United Kingdom. China has turned into Africa's most important trading partner. China has also become Brazil's, South Africa's and India's most important trading partner over the past years, in a clear signal that South-South trade was growing at consistently higher rates than North-South trade. Trade between Africa and the BRICS has grown so fast that it now even exceeds intra-BRICS trade.[9] The value of exports from developing countries to other developing countries ("South-South" trade) now exceeds exports from poor countries to rich ones ("North-South" trade).[10] By comparison, in 1985, South-South trade only accounted or 7 percent of overall trade.[11] Furthermore, China, India and Brazil are also increasingly active as so-called "emerging donors," both in Africa and in their respective neighborhoods, and the past years have witnessed an unprecedented growth of what can be called "South-South aid."[12]

This chapter seeks to answer the question of whether and how South-South cooperation qualitatively differs from North-South cooperation, and whether these differences can be translated into clear norms and rules. After all, it is this assumption of qualitative superiority that seems to motivate many official statements during IBSA meetings.

SSC is usually defined as collaboration between developing countries in the political, economic, cultural, social and environmental spheres. Participating countries share resources, expertise, knowledge and skills to further each other's development. Despite these broad descriptions, South-South trade lies at the heart of South-South cooperation. It is also the most tangible aspect and the easiest to assess systematically. Therefore, this chapter uses South-South trade as a substitute for South-South cooperation in more general terms.

Many analyses of South-South cooperation are based on the implicit and somewhat vague assumption that trade between Southern states would be less exploitative than that between the South and the North, and the belief that economic interactions between states of the South would be more responsive to the development needs of the South. The idea of South-South cooperation evokes a positive image of solidarity between developing countries through the exchange of resources, technology, and knowledge. As Philip Nel writes:

> South-South solidarity (SSS) implies a mutual attitude of affective empathy flowing from a shared experience that involves common hardship of one sort or another, the collective pursuit of a common good, and the recognition and observance of reciprocal moral duties, including respect for national sovereignty, fundamental equality and mutual benefit. In this meaning it is mainly used as a qualifier for South-South Cooperation (SSC).

He cites the Nairobi Outcome Document of the 2009 High-level United Nations Conference on South-South Cooperation, which operationalizes this "morally demanding understanding of solidarity" as follows:

> We recognize the importance and different history and particularities of South-South cooperation, and we reaffirm our view of South-South cooperation as a manifestation of solidarity among peoples and countries of the South that contributes to their national well-being, national and collective self-reliance and the attainment of internationally agreed development goals, including the Millennium Development Goals. South-South cooperation and its agenda have to be set by countries of the South and should continue to be guided by the principles of respect for national sovereignty, national ownership and independence, equality, non-conditionality, non-interference in domestic affairs and mutual benefit.[13]

According to that narrative, SSC aims to discover and exploit the principle of "complementarity" in production, consumption, trade, investment, and technological and development cooperation.[14] These processes may in turn generate forward and backward linkages, which eventually may produce positive synergies across Southern economies. For Brazil's former Foreign Minister Celso Amorim, "South-South cooperation is a diplomatic strategy, which originates from an authentic desire to exercise solidarity toward poorer countries."[15] In a similar way, India has recently also "attached more weight to solidarity with fellow developing countries."[16]

These assumptions have tangible consequences. For example, in WTO circles and discussions, South-South trade is often viewed as invariably positive—not to be disturbed and certainly to be enhanced. Any measure that might lessen the flow of South-South trade is viewed negatively, almost to be avoided at all costs.[17] As a consequence, there is strong enthusiasm for South-South cooperation, leading to its inclusion in many countries' foreign policy agendas, in the strategic planning of various organizations, and in the research agendas of some scholars.

However, this narrative is not entirely uncontested. For example, critics of the assumption that South-South cooperation is always beneficial for all those involved have pointed to what they call the BRICS' "Scramble for Africa," indicating that South-South cooperation is increasingly similar to North-South trade as emerging powers are transforming themselves into major poles of the global economy, and as disparities within the global South increase.[18] As Bond argues, like the meeting in Berlin in 1884–85, the Fifth BRICS Summit that took place in March 2013 in Durban, South Africa—during which the BRICS decided to create their own development bank—sought to "carve up Africa," unburdened by "Western" concerns about democracy and human rights.[19] Mittelman writes that:

> The use of Chinese nationals to build infrastructure, and exports of cheap clothing, have supplanted local labour, provoking the ire of trade unions in recipient countries, precipitating discourses about re-colonisation and sparking violent protests. Research on this topic traces the linkages to outbreaks of conflict, as over the supply of resources, particularly oil, the impact of new investors on the petro-states in Africa, questions of human rights standards, and competition among the emerging market powers.[20]

It seems clear that South-South cooperation cannot be de-linked from power and politics—especially since we are witnessing an increasing hierarchization of the global South. It is thus perhaps unsurprising that the most recent models of South-South cooperation are not occurring in the context of large groupings such as the G77, but small outfits such as IBSA and BRICS, made up of some of those countries with the most successful economic trajectory over the past decades. The question about the supposedly different quality of SSC is not new. Prior to the Second BRIC Summit in Brasília, in 2010, Rathin Roy, head of IPC-IG, a joint project between UNDP and the Brazilian government to promote South-South cooperation, asked:

> Will the rise of the emerging economies portend just a broadening of the "great game," the only result being a little more elbow room for developing countries in their engagement with the G-20 economies? Or will the global South seize this opportunity to forge a new and more inclusive paradigm that secures faster and more sustainable development for all citizens? ... Can we look forward to exciting paradigm shifts in the discourses on global trade, aid, development cooperation and the rhetoric of best practice? Will emergent regional and global plurilateral groupings afford new avenues for effective development cooperation?[21]

In order to answer these questions, which have gained growing importance over the past years, this chapter will look at the characteristics of new arrangements that can be classified as South-South cooperation and compare them, as far as possible, with existing institutions.

Behind the hype

As detailed in the previous chapter, trade between IBSA countries has grown sharply over the past two decades, in particular when compared to overall growth in global trade. South-South trade today accounts for one quarter of global trade, compared to only a fraction of the total after the end of the Cold War.[22] This increase in South-South trade is often cited by those who defend the IBSA grouping's track record.[23] This direct causation, of course, is difficult to prove. Yet even if we assume that IBSA led to an increase in South-South trade, it is necessary to grasp the asymmetries of global trade relations between developing countries.

Most importantly, the greatest part of South-South trade takes place within Asia and does not involve developing countries in Africa or Latin America. Only 20 percent of South-South trade involves a non-Asian country (6 percent Africa and 10 percent Latin America). African exports to Asia (principally to China) tripled from 2007 to 2011, but it only remains Africa's third biggest export market, behind the European Union and the United States.[24]

In addition, more than 60 percent of Africa's exports to Asia are made up of primary goods, while imports are made up of manufactured goods.[25]

This suggests that a key characteristic of North-South trade that is so often criticized—namely, its unequal terms of trade—largely applies to South-South trade as well. As Nel argues:

> Economic history shows that, unless economies are moving up the value chain, they will be stuck in the rut of trading on commodities that simply provide diminishing returns in the medium to long term. Unless an economy is engaged in activities that deliver increasing returns over time (as found in manufacturing production), then that economy is not developing ... [26]

In addition, intra-IBSA solidarity could not prevent the outbreak of major trade disputes between the three either, with the recent Brazil-South African "chicken wars" being the most visible.

The IBSA free trade agreement (FTA): lack of political will?

One of perhaps the most commented ways in which the three IBSA members have attempted to promote trade between them has been through a trade agreement. Since the grouping's inception, discussions about liberalizing trade have been present at virtually all meetings of heads of government and foreign ministers. Yet given Brazil's MER-COSUR membership and South Africa's SACU membership, both countries need to articulate and negotiate particular trade agreements as part of their regional blocs—a goal that was established during the IBSA Summit in 2004.[27] As policy makers pointed out to underline the potential importance of such an agreement, an integrated market between India, SACU and MERCOSUR would have a population of over 1.2 billion people, with a GDP of more than \$1.2 trillion.[28]

Indeed, initial steps have been taken over the past decade. A preferential trade agreement (PTA) between India and SACU began after a meeting between the Indian and South African trade ministers in 2000 in New Delhi. A framework agreement was reached four years later, including a small number of tariff concessions. Since then, negotiations towards a complete PTA have not made any meaningful progress. According to policy makers interviewed, the existence of the IBSA grouping has had no tangible impact on the discussions.[29]

MERCOSUR and SACU, on the other hand, finalized a PTA in late 2004, a little more than a year after the creation of IBSA. A revised PTA was adopted four years later, increasing the number of preferences to some degree, yet still covering only a relatively small number of product categories. As of early 2014, the SACU-MERCOSUR PTA is still awaiting ratification by several member states.

MERCOSUR and India, meanwhile signed a Framework Agreement in June 2003 to increase economic ties, promoting bilateral trade and creating the conditions for the establishment of a full FTA. At the time, a more limited PTA was agreed upon.[30] This led to the signing of a PTA in New Delhi in January 2004, as a first step towards the creation of an FTA. The India-MERCOSUR PTA, which came into effect only in June 2009, grants preferential access to a very limited number of product categories and contains provisions on measures such as trade remedies and technical barriers to trade. The agreement grants tariff concessions of between 10 and 100 percent on 452 Indian product categories for import into MERCOSUR, and on 450 MERCOSUR product categories for import into India—hence, it only affects a fraction of overall trade between the two parties.

Regarding the IBSA grouping as a whole, little progress has been made towards an all-encompassing agreement for the past 10 years. During interviews, several policy makers from the three countries involved assured that talks continue and that it is normal for trade negotiations to take many years. They argue that Brazil and South Africa, in particular, face the arduous task of going back and forth between their South African and Indian contacts and the other MER-COSUR members, a process that severely hampers the speed of negotiations.[31] In addition, some analysts have pointed out that despite having similar roles, which are derived from their status as middle powers, the IBSA countries have developed different strategies concerning their trade policy.[32]

Yet other negotiators involved privately admit that given the limited scope and complexity of the proposed agreement, it would have been possible to proceed much faster. They mostly focus on cooperation and engagement, and do not involve a comprehensive institutional framework for governing bilateral trade. "What is the point of the IBSA Forum if they cannot accelerate the trade negotiations?" a former policy maker asked during the interview, saying that regular meetings of representatives of SACU, MERCOSUR and India have been organized by the IBSA Forum.[33] Indeed, it is quite remarkable that despite frequent praise for South-South cooperation, the majority of South Africa's trade agreements are with developed countries.

In the same way, Sean Woolfrey writes:

> The fact that the entry into force of these PTAs has taken so long suggests a lack of political will—something that perhaps could and should have been addressed under the IBSA Forum—and does not augur well for attempts to establish a far more ambitious India-Mercosur-SACU FTA. It must surely be seen as a disappointment that, more than eight years after being put on the IBSA agenda, the goal of an India-Mercosur-SACU FTA is not significantly closer to being realised ... The minimal scope of these FTAs and the significant time it has taken for their conclusion suggest the influence of protectionist interests and a lack of political will to push for more substantial progress.[34]

It is also questionable whether a trade agreement would have any discernible impact, given that the major barriers to trade between Brazil, South Africa and India are not necessarily high tariffs, but poor transport connections and a lack of trade complementarity between the three countries.[35] Flemes writes that "India, Brazil and South Africa are not natural trading partners and the limits to commercial exchanges between them should be recognized." Arguing that a trade agreement will be difficult to achieve, he points out that "a more realistic approach could be directed towards trade facilitation and the improvement of transport and infrastructure links between the three players."[36] White argued that better connectivity, removal of double taxation, homogeneous business practices and visa exemption are more urgent and likely to be more far-reaching than an IBSA-wide FTA.[37]

Protectionist measures

The rise of protectionist measures between the IBSA countries is another strong indicator that South-South trade is qualitatively very similar to North-South trade. Contrary to what one would expect, the regular meetings between the three countries have not reduced protectionist measures much. Most visibly, in 2012, Brazil challenges South Africa's decision at the WTO to use anti-dumping measures against Brazilian poultry meat. The South African International Trade Administration Commission (ITAC) had decided, after a complaint by the South African Poultry Association (SAPA) to take the step after a drawn-out investigation between 2008 and 2010. After analyzing the results of the investigation, the South African government imposed a duty of 62.9 percent on Brazilian whole chickens and 46.5 percent on boneless cuts from Brazil. However, after several discussions, including in the IBSA meetings, a final decision by the Department of Trade and Industry (DTI) rejected ITAC's recommendation that definitive anti-dumping be imposed.[38]

In early 2013, a similar row ensued after South Africa blocked frozen boneless buffalo meat imports from India. These examples show that despite the rhetoric of South-South solidarity, competition remains one of the key characteristics of their economic relations.

Conclusion

This chapter sought to assess whether South-South cooperation can live up to the high expectations generated by the notion of solidarity and the special responsibility that this puts on them. The analysis shows that while policy makers from developing countries such as Brazil, India and South Africa frequently mention the qualitative superiority of trade between countries located in the global South, there is little empirical evidence to support this claim. As mentioned above, this does not mean that it would be wrong to focus on strengthening South-South trade—quite the contrary. Growing economic ties between India, Brazil and South Africa are most likely to have a positive impact on all three economies. Yet it would be wrong to expect South-South trade to generate greater benefits than trade with countries in the North, or be more likely to be less equitable or less exploitative.

In a similar vein, Nel argues that:

> SSC has, as yet, not realised the high expectations that many have had of it since the advent of the postcolonial epoch. Initially narrowly focused on technical cooperation and tinged with a strong anti-North sentiment, during the past two decades its development focus and geographical scope have been broadened and institutions such as UNCTAD have increasingly reflected such developments. While it is still often promoted as constituting an exploitation-free alternative to international interaction, SSC is today more generally accepted as a complement to and not as a substitute for North-South exchanges. Bodies as wide-ranging as the IMF, OECD, the UN, the Commonwealth and the Non-Aligned Movement have come to embrace it as a core instrument for promoting economic growth in developing countries, in general, and in the group of 48 LDCs, in particular. But this form of solidarity is evacuated of most meaningful content, other than the fetishisation of growth and trade.[39]

This mismatch between rhetoric and reality carries profound risks. While policy makers from economically strong countries in the global South may use a language favorable of South-South trade, it may generate unreasonable expectations abroad that can lead to a public backlash at some point. In fact, it may be precisely what happened when China's economic ties with African countries grew over the past decade. Initially welcomed as a long-awaited alternative to Western trade partners, China's growing presence has led to unease in many countries across the African continent.[40]

The major challenge for policy makers in IBSA countries will therefore be to convince other developing countries that India's, Brazil's and South Africa's economic rise is good for the rest of the global South as well, without exaggerated promises about the qualitative superiority of South-South cooperation.

Notes

1 Stephen King, "Time to Put the Southern Silk Road on the Map," *Financial Times*, 13 June 2011, www.ft.com/intl/cms/s/0/ed40e8f0-95f3-11e0-ba20-00144feab49a.html#axzz2nXHdoDLT.

2 For the South-South cooperation principles see: "Ministerial Declaration of the 33rd Annual Meeting of the Ministers of Foreign Affairs of the Member States of the Group of 77 and China," 25 September 2009, New York, para. 70.

3 Kevin Gray and Craig N. Murphy, "Introduction: Rising Powers and the Future of Global Governance," *Third World Quarterly* 34, no. 2 (2013): 183–93.

4 Candice Moore, "BRICS Partnership: A Case of South-South Cooperation? Exploring the Roles of South Africa and Africa," *Institute for Global Dialogue*, 9 July 2012, www.igd.org.za/home/206-brics-partnership-a-case-of-south-south-cooperation-exploring-the-roles-of-south-africa-and-africa.

5 Shikha Jha and Peter McCawley, "South-South Economic Linkages: An Overview," *ADB Economics Working Paper Series*, no. 270, August 2011.

6 Folashadé Soule-Kohndou, "The India-Brazil-South Africa Forum a Decade on: Mismatched Partners or the Rise of the South?" *Global Economic Governance Programme Working Paper* 2013/88, University of Oxford, November 2013, 4.

7 James H. Mittelman, "Global Bricolage: Emerging Market Powers and Polycentric Governance," *Third World Quarterly* 34, no. 1 (2013): 23–37, 25.

8 King, "Time to put the Southern Silk Road on the Map."

9 Jeremy Stevens and Simon Freemantle, "BRIC and Africa: BRICS Trade is Flourishing, and Africa Remains a Pivot," *Standard Bank*, 12 February 2013.

10 "O for a Beaker Full of the Warm South," *The Economist*, 19 January 2013, www.economist.com/news/finance-and-economics/21569747-poor-countries-other-poor-countries-matter-more-rich-ones-o-beaker.

11 UNCTAD, *Handbook of Statistics 2009*.

12 Fahimul Quadir, "Rising Donors and the New Narrative of 'South-South' Cooperation: What Prospects for Changing the Landscape of Development Assistance Programmes?" *Third World Quarterly* 34, no. 2 (2013): 321–38.

13 Philip Nel and Ian Taylor, "Bugger thy Neighbour? IBSA and South-South Solidarity," *Third World Quarterly* 34, no. 6 (2013): 1091–110, 1092.

14 Ibid., 1093.

15 C. Amorim, cited in Peter Dauvergne and Déborah B.L. Farias, "The Rise of Brazil as a Global Development Power," *Third World Quarterly* 33, no. 5 (2012): 903–17, 909. In Nel and Taylor, "Bugger thy Neighbour?" 1093.

16 C. Raja Mohan, "Balancing Interests and Values: India's Struggle with Democracy Promotion," *The Washington Quarterly* 30, no. 3 (2007): 99–115, 99. In Nel and Taylor, "Bugger thy Neighbour?" 1093.

17 Aileen Kwa, "The Challenges Confronting South-South Trade," in *South-South Cooperation: The Same Old Game or a New Paradigm?—Poverty in Focus 20*, ed. Rathin Roy and Melissa Andrade (Brasília, Brazil: International Policy Centre for Inclusive Growth, 2010), 9–10.

18 Paul Ladd, "Between a Rock and a Hard Place: LDCs in a G-20 World," in *South-South Cooperation: The Same Old Game or a New Paradigm?—Poverty in Focus 20*, ed. Rathin Roy and Melissa Andrade (Brasília, Brazil: International Policy Centre for Inclusive Growth, 2010), 5–6.

19 Gray and Murphy, "Introduction: Rising Powers and the Future of Global Governance."

20 Mittelman, "Global Bricolage," 25. See also: Pádraig Carmody, *The Rise of the BRICS in Africa: The Geopolitics of South-South Relations* (London: Zed Books Ltd, 2013).

21 Rathin Roy, "Introduction," in *South-South Cooperation: The Same Old Game or a New Paradigm?—Poverty in Focus 20*, ed. Rathin Roy and Melissa Andrade (Brasília, Brazil: International Policy Centre for Inclusive Growth, 2010), 2.

22 UNCTAD, *Handbook of Statistics 2013* (Geneva: United Nations, 2013), unctad.org/en/pages/PublicationWebflyer.aspx?publicationid=759.

23 Otaviano Canuto, "South-South Trade is the Answer," *World Bank Growth and Crisis Blog*, 11 May 2011, blogs.worldbank.org/growth/south-south-trade-answer.

24 Sumit Roy, "China and India, the 'Emerging Giants,' and African Economic Prospects," *Global Policy*, July 2012. In Nel and Taylor, "Bugger thy Neighbour?" 1093.

25 Ibid.

26 Nel and Taylor, "Bugger thy Neighbour?" 1094.

27 India-Brazil-South Africa Dialogue Forum (IBSA), "Plan of Action," 2004, www.dfa.gov.za/docs/2004/ibsa0305a.htm.

28 India-Brazil-South Africa Dialogue Forum (IBSA), "1st IBSA Summit Meeting: Joint Declaration," 2006, www.itamaraty.gov.br/temas-mais-informacoes/saiba-mais-ibas/documentos-emitidos-pelos-chefes-de-estado-e-de/1st-ibsa-summit-declaration/at_download/file.

29 Interview with Indian and South African policy makers in Pretoria and Delhi, 2012 and 2013.

30 "Framework Agreement Between the Mercosur and the Republic of India," June 2003, commerce.gov.in/trade/indiamercosur/framework.pdf.

31 Interviews with policy makers from South Africa, India and Brazil, in Pretoria, Delhi and Brasília, 2012 and 2013.

32 Paulo Sotero, "Emerging Powers: India, Brazil and South Africa (IBSA) and the Future of South-South Cooperation," Special Report, Woodrow Wilson International Center for Scholars, August 2009, 3.

33 Interview with former Indian policy maker in New Delhi, August 2012.

34 Sean Woolfrey, "The IBSA Dialogue Forum Ten Years On: Examining IBSA Cooperation on Trade," *Tralac Trade Brief* No. S13TB05/2013, August 2013, 19–20.

35 Ibid., 20.

36 Daniel Flemes, "Emerging Middle Powers' Soft Balancing Strategy: State and Perspectives of the IBSA Dialogue Forum," *GIGA Working Papers* 57 (2007), 24.

37 Lyal White, "IBSA Six Years On: Co-operation in a New Global Order," *SAIIA Emerging Powers Programme Policy Briefing* 8, November 2009, 1.

38 International Trade Administration Commission of South Africa (ITAC), "Final Decision in the Investigation into the Alleged Dumping of Frozen Meat of Fowls of the Species Gallus Domesticus, Whole Bird and Boneless Cuts Originating in or Imported from Brazil," Notice 173, 2013, www.itac.org.za/docs/Notice%20173%20of%202013.PDF. In Soule-Kohndou, "The India-Brazil-South Africa Forum a Decade on," 23.

39 Nel and Taylor, "Bugger thy Neighbour?" 1107.

40 Craig Timberg, "In Africa, China Trade Brings Growth, Unease," *The Washington Post*, 13 June 2006, www.washingtonpost.com/wp-dyn/content/article/2006/06/12/AR2006061201506.html.

6 IBSA
Rising democracy promoters?

- **Axis of virtue?**
- **Why promote democracy? The debate**
- **Brazil and democracy promotion**
- **The case of India**
- **The case of South Africa**
- **Conclusion**

> IBSA's common identity is based on values such as democracy, personal freedoms and human rights.
>
> (Daniel Flemes[1])

> IBAS is in favour of a multipolar world where democracy—political, social, cultural—prevails.
>
> (Celso Amorim[2])

> To forge a common vision, IBSA should ... seek to transcend the identification of common interests and their elevation into international forums, in favour of elaborating and deepening a common values framework.
>
> (Sarah al-Doyaili, Andreas Freytag and Peter Draper[3])

While the BRICS grouping has been perceived as a threat by some, IBSA is generally seen in a benign light: in the Western media, descriptions of the trilateral grouping generally include mention of the three countries' "vibrant democracies."[4] The importance of democracy has appeared in most official statements and declarations of IBSA meetings. For example, in September 2010, the IBSA foreign ministers made a point of writing in their communiqué that they "wished the Government and people of Brazil well with the presidential elections that will take place on 3 October 2010 and reiterated IBSA's commitment to democratic values."[5] This chapter analyzes the role democracy plays for each of the IBSA countries' foreign policy. Have they promoted democracy in their regions or abroad?

Axis of virtue?

The IBSA coalition is generally seen as an "axis of virtue,"[6] which is often thought to contribute to the promotion or defense of liberal global values. Analysts point out that India, Brazil and South Africa are among the key emerging powers whose citizens enjoy a human rights-abiding liberal democratic system. All three countries have been able to maintain such institutions and rights despite highly diverse populations, a lack of social inclusion and high rates of poverty. In a world where an increasing number of national leaders look to China as an economic and political model to copy, India, South Africa and Brazil provide powerful counter-examples that political freedom is no obstacle to economic growth.[7] In a statement that can equally be applied to all the IBSA countries, Manmohan Singh said that, "'[u]nlike China's rise, the rise of India does not cause any apprehensions' for '[t]he world takes a benign view of India. They want us to succeed'."[8]

As a consequence, there is an often-implicit expectation that the IBSA countries are keen on promoting democracy. Addressing the UN General Assembly in September 2010, US President Barack Obama appealed to rising democracies around the world to help spread the democratic message, declaring that "we need your voices to speak out," and reminding them that "part of the price of our own freedom is standing up for the freedom of others."[9]

After a very brief theoretical consideration of democracy promotion, this chapter analyzes how far regime type matters in the context of South-South cooperation and whether IBSA countries promote or defend democracy. Democracy promotion remains an area traditionally dominated by the United States and Europe on both policy and academic levels.[10] While all IBSA members are rising democracies[11] and thus seem, from a Western point of view, to be ideal candidates to assist the United States and Europe in promoting democracy in a "post-Western world,"[12] the IBSA grouping historically has been reluctant to embrace the idea, and there is no evidence of any jointly coordinated pro-democracy work between IBSA countries.[13] Yet do they promote democracy individually?

Why promote democracy? The debate

Political theorists usually explain states' desire to promote democracy[14] by variants of the democratic peace theory, which finds its origin in Immanuel Kant's vision of a "federation of republics."[15] Kant argued that the division of power would prevent leaders from launching wars without strongly reasoned arguments framed in terms of collective interests. According to the democratic peace proposition, established democracies not only have a normative claim to, but also a genuine strategic interest in, extending democracy around the globe.[16] A world of democracies would likely be more peaceful and better for trade and investment (as the rule of law is usually weaker in authoritarian regimes), providing the basis for international peace and mutually benefiting cooperation.[17] By mitigating the security dilemma, democracies thus enable the maximization of economic welfare through far-reaching interdependence.[18] In addition, proponents of democracy promotion argue that it is "the right thing to do," spreading universally conceived values and helping all human beings obtain political rights and representation.[19] The promotion and defense of democratic values, ideas and concepts is thus one of the most powerful legacies of liberal thought.

From a realist point of view, on the other hand, international norms are mainly seen as instruments for great powers to project their influence and advance their interests. Realists may agree that promoting democracy can be well intentioned, but argue that countries only promote democracy if this is aligned with other interests in the strategic or economic realms. They point out that the United States promotes democracy because democracies are more likely to trade with the United States and integrate into the US-led global system, thus becoming less likely to cause instability. Whenever democracy promotion collides with economic or geopolitical interests, democracy promotion will become a secondary issue.[20] Democracy promotion has thus been a US tool to legitimize its hegemony. As Pratap Mehta argues:

> Nations typically appeal to some form of philanthropy for external legitimation. The delicate trick in any imperial intervention is to make this philanthropy—be it saving the world, making it safe for democracy, or safeguarding socialism—coincide with the best and most enlightened expression of the national interest. An expansionary power needs an ideology that can connect its national interest to its philanthropic aims. And its philanthropic aims must represent an idea of international order that other nations can accept.[21]

According to this logic, democracies—no matter whether long established or recently democratized—will promote democracy themselves if doing so is aligned with their overall strategic and economic interests and if they are willing to adopt democracy promotion as a means to legitimize their growing influence.

Emphasizing the legality aspect of sovereign right, many thinkers are also critical of the practice, pointing out that it invariably violates another country's sovereignty and self-determination.[22] Foreign intervention of any kind, even benevolent advice, is thus generally considered an inappropriate intrusion into another's domestic affairs, something democracy promoters often overlook as they are seduced by a notion of "unity of goodness," according to which responsive institutions and all other desirable things flow from democracy.[23] In addition, excluding non-democratic regimes, such as by launching the idea of a "League of Democracies," creates an "insider vs. outsider" dynamic that sows mistrust and possibly even conflict, reducing the space for dialogue.[24] Concerns about the internal character of regimes may provoke resistance and endanger world order.[25] Accordingly, US foreign policy during the Cold War reflected American policy makers' conviction that it was safer to ally oneself "with elites one could trust rather than the masses whom one could not."[26]

Many critics of democracy promotion also describe democracy promotion as a continuation of colonialism.[27] From this perspective, Western democracy promotion can be understood as a new form of transnational control accompanying the rise of global capitalism. William Robinson describes it as "an effort to replace coercive means of social control with consensual ones in the South within a highly stratified international system, in which the United States plays a leadership role on behalf of an emergent transnational hegemonic configuration and a transnational elite.[28] In the general debate, critics describe the democracy promotion as incoherent, insincere and only thinly veiling economic interests. With frequency, they point to the West's reluctance to elevate the objective of democracy promotion above all other interests at all times. For example, critics ask why the Bush Administration did so little to promote democracy in autocratic Saudi Arabia, while targeting Venezuela with democracy assistance even though its president was elected democratically.[29] Who decides which country needs to democratize and which dictatorship is allowed to persist? An often used argument is that, seen from an historical perspective, rather than acting as a force of democratization, the principal political form that the United States has promoted is that of authoritarian regimes.[30]

Western democratic governments and organizations spend billions of dollars every year on democracy-related projects,[31] turning them into the dominant actors in the field of democracy promotion. Yet a notable shift of power is taking place towards countries that are more hesitant when it comes to systematic democracy promotion. Have India, Brazil and South Africa promoted democracy in the past? How do analysts and policy makers in emerging democracies—using the three countries as an example in this analysis—think about democracy promotion? How can we characterize their arguments in relation to the critiques cited above?

Brazil and democracy promotion

Brazil accounts for over half of South America's wealth, population, territory, and military budget, which suggests that it is relatively more powerful in its region than China, India and Germany are in their respective neighborhoods.[32] Yet despite this dominant position, it shied away from intervening in its neighbors' internal affairs prior to the 1990s. The preservation of national sovereignty and non-intervention have always been and remain key pillars of Brazil's foreign policy,[33] so any attempt to promote or defend self-determination and human rights abroad—a commitment enshrined in Brazil's 1989 Constitution[34]—stands in conflict with the principle of non-intervention.[35] The tension arising from these two opposing visions—respecting sovereignty and adopting a more assertive pro-democracy stance, particularly in the region—is one of the important dilemmas in Brazilian foreign policy of the past two decades.

In fact, particularly during the 1990s, Brazil abstained several times from promoting or defending democracy. In 1990, under President Fernando Collor de Mello (1990–92), Brazil blocked—largely due to economic interests—calls for a military intervention in Suriname after a military coup there. In 1992, it remained silent over a political crisis in Ecuador. In 1994, Brazil—then a member of the UNSC—abstained from UN Security Council Resolution 940 that authorized the use of force in Haiti with the goal to reinstate President Aristide, who had been removed from power in 1991 in a coup.[36]

However, contrary to what is often believed, Brazil has defended democracy abroad in many more instances, and over the past two decades, its views on intervention have become decidedly more flexible.[37] Even under indirectly elected President José Sarney (1985–89), the first president after democratization, Brazil supported the inclusion of a reference to democracy in a new preamble to the Organization of American States (OAS) Charter.[38] Under President Fernando Henrique Cardoso (1995–2002), Brazil intervened in neighboring Paraguay in 1996 to avoid a military coup there—working through MERCOSUR and the OAS to obtain higher leverage, and ultimately convincing

General Lino Oviedo not to stage a *coup d'état* against then President Juan Carlos Wasmosy.[39] The Brazilian president again played an important mediating role during political crises in Paraguay in 1999 and 2000.[40] When Alberto Fujimori falsified the election results in 2000, Brazil's President Cardoso refused to criticize the Peruvian president, and Brazil was the major obstacle to US and Canadian efforts to condemn Peru at the OAS General Assembly.[41] Yet, in an important gesture, President Cardoso stayed away from President Fujimori's inaugural ceremony, and a year later Brazil supported the Inter-American Democratic Charter, largely aimed at Fujimori, which includes the norm of democratic solidarity.[42]

Since the coup in Venezuela, Brazil has assumed a more assertive pro-democracy stance in the region. In 2002, Brazil actively engaged in Venezuela when a group sought illegally to oust Hugo Chávez, who was reinstated 48 hours later.[43] Looking back over the last decade, Santiso argues that Brazil has had an exemplary and fundamental role in strengthening democratic norms and clauses across the region.[44] In his memoirs, President Cardoso reflected on the issue by saying that "Brazil always defends democratic order."[45] Burges and Daudelin argue that "one can say that Brazil has been quite supportive of efforts to protect democracy in the Americas since 1990."[46] This tendency strengthened further in the twenty-first century. In 2003, President Lula (2003–10) swiftly engaged to resolve a constitutional crisis in Bolivia, and in 2005, he sent his foreign minister to Quito to deal with a crisis in Ecuador. In the same year, Brazil supported the OAS to assume a mediating role during a political crisis in Nicaragua, including financial support for the electoral monitoring for a municipal election there. In 2009, the international debate about how to deal with the coup in Honduras was very much a result of Brazil and the United States clashing over the terms of how best to defend democracy, rather than whether to defend it.[47]

Over the past two decades, Brazil has systematically built democratic references and clauses into the charters, protocols and declarations of the sub-regional institutions of which it is a member. The importance of democracy in the constitution and activities of the Rio Group, MERCOSUR and the more recent South American Community of Nations (UNASUL) can to a large extent be traced back to Brazil's activism.[48] At the same time, Brazil sought to ensure that the protection of democratic rule be calibrated with interventionism, combining the principle of non-intervention with that of "non-indifference."[49] The term's policy relevance remains contested, yet it symbolizes how much Brazil's thinking about sovereignty has evolved. For example, when explaining why Brazil opposed a US proposal to craft a mechanism within the OAS Democratic Charter that permits the group to intervene in nations to foster or strengthen democracy, then Foreign Minister Celso Amorim argued that "there needs to be a dialogue rather than an intervention," adding that "democracy cannot be imposed. It is born from dialogue."[50] It thus positions itself as an alternative and more moderate democracy defender in the hemisphere than the United States, and one which continuously calibrates its interest in defending democracy with its tradition of non-intervention.

Brazil's decision to lead the UN peacekeeping mission MINUSTAH in Haiti, starting in 2004, cannot be categorized as democracy promotion per se, yet the mission's larger goal did consist in bringing both economic and political stability to the Caribbean island, which has been the recipient of US democracy promotion for years.[51] In the same way, Brazil's ongoing involvement in Guinea-Bissau, member of the Community of Portuguese Language Countries (CPLP) proved yet another important moment for Brazil's role as a promoter of peace and democracy.[52] Brazil had provided some electoral assistance to Guinea-Bissau in 2004–05, and it continued to support efforts to stabilize the country by operating through the UN peace mission there.[53] During a CPLP meeting in 2011, Brazil signed a memorandum of understanding to implement a Project in Support of the Electoral Cycles of the Portuguese-speaking African Countries and Timor-Leste.[54] In addition, in the lead-up to the anticipated elections in April 2012, Brazil made further financial contributions to the UNDP basket fund in support of the National Electoral Commission for assistance in the execution of the election.[55]

Brazil's pro-democracy stance became most obvious in 2012, when President Dilma Rousseff—together with Uruguay's and Argentina's leadership—suspended Paraguay from MERCOSUR after the impeachment of Paraguay's President Fernando Lugo, which most governments in the region regarded as the equivalent of a *coup d'état* or a "parliamentary coup."[56] The Brazilian government thus set a clear precedent that anti-democratic tendencies in the region would cause a rapid and clear reaction from leaders in Brasília. President Rousseff's decision to work through MERCOSUR, rather than the OAS, is consistent with a growing preference to use local regional bodies, possibly in an effort to strengthen projection as a regional leader.

Yet there are also critical voices. Summarizing Brazilian foreign policy over the past two decades, Sean Burges argues that "Brazil has not behaved consistently in support of democratic norm enforcement"[57] and that decisive action to preserve democracy was "tepid,"[58] and Ted Piccone reasons that "when it comes to wielding ... influence in support of democracy in other countries ... Brazil has been ambivalent and often unpredictable"[59]—both evaluations made prior to Brazil's assertive stance in Paraguay in 2012. Still, despite this strategy, the term "democracy promotion" is not used either by Brazilian policy makers or by academics when referring to Brazil's Paraguay policy. In the same way, Brazil does not promote any activities comparable to those of large US or European NGOs whose activities range from political party development, electoral monitoring, supporting independent media and journalists, capacity building for state institutions, and training for judges, civic group leaders and legislators.

This brief analysis shows that Brazil is increasingly assertive in its region, and willing to intervene if political crises threaten democracy. Brazil is most likely to intervene during constitutional crises and political ruptures, and less so when procedural issues during elections may affect the outcome—as was the case during Hugo Chávez's re-election in 2012, when several commentators criticized Brazil's decision not to pressure the Venezuelan government to ensure fair elections.[60] Yet despite this distinction, it seems clear that the consolidation of democracy in the region has turned into one of Brazil's fundamental foreign policy goals.

This development must be seen in the context of Brazil's attempt to consolidate its regional leadership. In the 1980s, Brazilian foreign policy makers perceived the necessity to engage with its neighbors, principally its rival, Argentina, a trend that continued and strengthened throughout the 1990s. At the beginning of Fernando Henrique Cardoso's first term, the president began to articulate a vision that fundamentally diverged from Brazil's traditional perspective—a vision that identified "South America" as a top priority.[61] This trend has continued ever since, and was intensified under Cardoso's successor, Luiz Inácio Lula da Silva. Over the past years, as Brazil's economic rise has caught the world's attention, the region has firmly stood at the center of Brazil's foreign policy strategy.[62] This trend continues under Brazil's current administration, with a focus on reducing a growing fear in the region that Brazil could turn into a regional bully—over the past years, an anti-Brazilian sentiment has been on the rise in South America.[63]

Yet while Brazil may de facto defend democracy with frequency in the region, it rarely engages in the liberal rhetoric so common in Europe and the United States. It may be precisely because of Brazil's traditional mistrust of US attempts to promote freedom that Brazilian policy makers refrain from using similar arguments. Rather, Brazil can be said to defend and promote, above all else, political stability, a key ingredient of Brazil's interest in expanding its economic influence on the continent. Rather than merely the strength of its neighbors, their weakness is now a threat, as weak nations may not be able to provide basic levels of public order. For example, the violence and chaos that ensues in Bolivia could spill into Brazilian territory, and it may scare away investors who contemplate engaging in Brazil. Brazil is strong and getting stronger—but its neighbors are weak and some appear to be getting weaker. It is within this context that Brazil faces its biggest security challenges.[64]

While Brazil usually acts swiftly in the face of political instability, it is far more reluctant to intervene in places where democracy suffers from procedural problems—such as in Venezuela, where President Chávez used the state apparatus to promote his campaign, leading to an uneven playing field between him and his opponent, Henrique Capriles. One way to explain Brazil's reluctance to intervene in such cases is that they do not affect Brazil's economic interests in the region. Democracy promotion can thus be seen not necessarily as an end in itself, but rather an important element of Brazil's strategy to strengthen its growing economic presence in the region. Similar to the United States, democracy promotion thus largely aligns with Brazil's national interests as an emerging power.

The case of India

Considering the immense domestic challenges it faces, India is a great democratic success story.[65] Yet India, democratic since independence in 1947, has been traditionally reluctant to promote democracy actively abroad, and it continues to value the preservation of sovereignty over democracy promotion.[66] Similar to Brazil, Indian foreign policy thinking features a realist strand and an idealist one, which stand in continuous tension. During the Cold War, India's non-alignment and relative proximity to the Soviet Union made democracy promotion impossible, particularly because the idea was strongly associated with the Western struggle against communism at the time.[67] In addition, democracy promotion carried a connotation of intervention, anathema to India's foreign policy perspective.[68] Particularly the US intervention in Chile in 1973 had a profound impact on India's foreign policy thinking.[69]

Finally, relations between India and the world's leading promoter of democracy, the United States, were difficult and marked by misunderstandings for most of the second half of the twentieth century. In 1971, India intervened in East Pakistan to end genocide there committed by the Pakistani army, playing midwife to the creation of a democratic nation—a strategy for which India was, at the time, severely criticized by both the United States and the United Nations.[70] This move was motivated by India's desire to weaken Pakistan rather than by spreading democratic rule, yet the episode is continuously mentioned by Indian analysts in the context of democracy promotion. Siddharth Mallavaparu, for example, calls India's intervention a "success notwithstanding trials and tribulations of politics in the new state of Bangladesh since then."[71] Pratap Mehta writes that "India in effect applied what we would now call the 'responsibility to protect' (R2P) principle, and applied it well."[72]

In the 1980s, India intervened in Sri Lanka to protect the Tamil minority there, yet this occurred largely due to political pressure in Tamil Nadu, so it hardly counts as a case of democracy promotion. In 1988, in what can be regarded as the country's first pro-democracy intervention, India's Prime Minister Rajiv Gandhi sent Indian troops to the Maldives to avoid a *coup d'état*, helping the country's democratically elected president reassert power.[73] This move was both a genuine attempt to defend democracy as well as a way to reaffirm India's strategic presence in the Indian Ocean. More recently, India has turned into a significant provider of aid in Afghanistan, where it paid for most of the construction of the parliament in Kabul.[74] It has also carefully engaged Bangladesh, Nepal and Sri Lanka, providing economic aid that is likely to contribute to a strengthening of democratic institutions there.[75]

In most instances, India has been reluctant to promote democracy. India has for over a decade followed a so-called "constructive engagement" policy with Myanmar's (Burma) military junta in which it has not criticized the regime's human rights abuses even as it hosts large numbers of Burmese refugees and political exiles on its soil. Nor did New Delhi take much of a position one way or the other on the political turmoil in Myanmar in 2007, disappointing pro-democracy activists.[76] Raja Mohan argues that "democracy as a political priority has been largely absent from India's foreign policy,"[77] which may be partly explained by the fact that India is surrounded by unstable and often autocratic regimes. Delhi has no choice but to engage with its autocratic neighbors and it is skeptical that outside factors can democratize its largest neighbor, China. The growing Chinese presence was also one of the main reasons why New Delhi was unwilling openly to condemn the military regime in Rangoon for the suppression of the Saffron Revolution in 2007.

Yet Indian policy makers frequently express their commitment to democracy promotion, particularly in multilateral forums. In 2005, India's Prime Minister Manmohan Singh argued that "liberal democracy is the natural order of political organization in today's world," saying that "all alternative systems … are an aberration."[78] He also stated that "[a]s the world's largest democracy, it is natural that India should have been among the first to welcome and support the concept of a UN Democracy Fund."[79] Dan Twining points out "Indian officials recognize that the widespread appeal of their country's democratic values is a strategic asset for Indian diplomacy."[80] This notion also extended into the Indian public debate. Raja Mohan argued that democracy was as much an Indian value as a Western one, and that this convergence of values could be the key foundation of a strong bilateral partnership. India participated in the first ministerial conference of the Community of Democracies organized in Warsaw in June 2000, yet observers pointed out that rather than genuinely promoting democracy, India saw the initiative as a means to strengthen US-Indian ties.

Indian policy analysts see India's regional geopolitical context as one of the principal reasons why India does not promote democracy—providing a stark contrast to Brazil, which faces far fewer regional constraints. For example, Pratap Mehta argues that:

> … sheer economic necessity requires that India be circumspect in its policies regarding the Middle East. Countries in this region not only supply a large share of India's vast and growing energy needs, but also host millions of Indian workers. Thus whatever India's level of commitment to Middle Eastern democracy as a value, that commitment must be tempered by a weighing of concrete risks.[81]

In sum, we can argue that contrary to Brazil, where defending democracy is aligned with Brazil's project or regional hegemony by benefiting its strategic and economic interests, such logic does not apply to India in South Asia. Despite its dominant size and its theoretical capacity to exert influence over its neighbors' regime type, promoting democracy could potentially destabilize India's still largely non-democratic region. In South America, on the other hand, democracy has largely taken hold, and Brazil's task of merely keeping its neighbors from sliding back is far easier and safer than India's challenge to help its neighbors democratize.

The case of South Africa

As with other regional powers with global aspirations, South Africa sees itself as an important actor in the region's stability and development. Promotion of democracy in Africa has been one of the pillars of South African foreign policy since the country's democratization. Already in the mid-1990s, as leader of the ANC, Nelson Mandela set out his priorities for South African foreign policy: human rights, democracy promotion and international law. According to him, "human rights are the cornerstone of our government policy and shall not hesitate to carry the message to the far corners of the world."[82] He promised that human rights would be "the light that guides our foreign affairs," and Western observers at the time hoped South Africa would play a leading role in promoting democracy abroad.[83] Indeed, Mandela's release from prison in 1990 transformed South Africa and contributed to a wave of democratic revolutions across the continent. More than 30 African dictatorships organized multiparty elections in the decade that followed.[84] The narrative of South Africa's journey from apartheid to democratic rainbow nation provided inspiration at a time when the African continent was otherwise wracked by conflict and economic decline.[85] However, despite of Pretoria's rhetoric, South Africa's democracy promotion efforts have encountered many contradictions and dilemmas that have forced the government to adapt its approach.

The first test came in 1995, when Nelson Mandela failed to condemn General Sani Abacha for executing nine human rights activists, among them the internationally recognized Ken Saro-Wiwa. Human rights activists around the world were dismayed when Mandela refused to take a stand against the Nigerian generals, some of whom had supported the ANC during apartheid. The same dilemma explains Mandela's unwillingness to criticize Muhammar Gaddafi.[86] As Mandela himself once reminded an American audience, "One of the mistakes the western world makes is to think that their enemies should be our enemies."[87] Mandela also maintained close ties to Cuban dictator Fidel Castro, who sent arms to the ANC during the 1960s when it was an illegal political party.

Yet, it must be taken into account that promoting or defending democracy in Africa has been, over the past decades, a far harder task than in other regions such as Latin America. South Africa's democratization policy to influence other African states was a key aspect of the country's foreign policy. Since the end of apartheid, South African leaders have actively sought continental leadership and emphasized their commitment to African solidarity. Change in South Africa opened the way for the renegotiation of it relations with the rest of the subcontinent, presenting an opportunity for South Africa to go on a democratization offensive.[88] South African leaders have attempted to make peace by promoting democracy in countries such as Angola, Lesotho, Swaziland, Nigeria, Sudan, the Comoros and the Democratic Republic of the Congo (DRC).[89]

South African leaders—Mandela, Mbeki and Zuma—have been more favorably disposed toward preventive diplomacy than toward peace enforcement and peacekeeping, displaying a much keener interest in brokering peace deals and mediating between two or more antagonistic factions. The post-apartheid government first employed its preventive diplomacy strategy in response to a 1994 political crisis in Lesotho.[90] The strategy achieved a reasonably good effect in Swaziland in 1996, when President Mandela tried to explore ways of resolving tensions that had arisen in that country over the role of the monarchy. Both Mandela and his successor, Thabo Mbeki, have espoused an "inclusive" settlement of the more than two decades-old civil war in Angola.

As Landsberg points out, later, Pretoria faced a more delicate and tricky challenge during its diplomatic intervention in a rebellion against the DRC's self-declared new President Laurent Kabila. South Africa's presumed neutrality was questioned because of its policy of selling arms to Kabila's rivals, Uganda and Rwanda.[91] A subsequent South Africa-led intervention in Lesotho in 1998, ostensibly to protect a democratically elected government, also spurred accusations that South Africa was trying to act like a regional hegemon. Many states that had been on the receiving end of Pretoria's foreign democratic engagement questioned South Africa's alleged neutrality in conflict situations.

In 2003, South Africa's President Thabo Mbeki helped arrange the exit of Charles Taylor, a dictator, from Liberia. He also assisted in reversing a *coup d'état* in São Tomé and Príncipe. A year later, he helped avoid a coup in Equatorial Guinea. In 2005 alone, he traveled to Kenya, Sudan, Congo, Gabon and Côte d'Ivoire for peace negotiations.[92] He has also hosted negotiations between warring parties in Burundi and Côte d'Ivoire.[93]

Box 6.1 South Africa and the Mugabe regime

Zimbabwe's political and economic decline and political crisis since 2000 has been one of the major challenges for South African policy makers, testing Pretoria's ability to align contradictory narratives in its foreign policy discourse: on the one hand, a commitment to democracy and human rights, and on the other, liberation solidarity, the promotion of an African consensus and a residual anti-Western sentiment in the ruling ANC.[1] Given the historic ties between authoritarian President Robert Mugabe and the ANC, South Africa has been rather reluctant actively to promote democracy in Zimbabwe. Critics frequently point to the inability of South Africa's "quiet diplomacy" to have any discernible effect on the conduct of a despotic Mugabe in neighboring Zimbabwe.

The crisis in Zimbabwe has directly affected South Africa. The country bore the brunt of the hundreds of thousands of Zimbabwean refugees who fled across the border from the 2008 violence after the elections. Many stayed and their presence frequently leads to tensions in South African society. Yet, Mbeki not only failed to criticize, but actively supported Mugabe despite escalating human rights violations, which today is seen as decisive in helping the Zimbabwean president stay in power.[2]

In 2011, the South African government seemed to change its strategy under the newly elected President Zuma. Jacob Zuma said at a meeting of regional leaders that violence, intimidation and politically inspired arrests must stop and conditions for free elections in Zimbabwe be met.[3] Advisors to Zuma focused on the issue, bluntly declaring that it was time democracy came to Zimbabwe.[4] At the time, observers around the world wondered whether the ANC would finally leave its historical ties with Mugabe's ZANU-PF behind and help redemocratize Zimbabwe. In the apparent end of appeasement, South Africa then joined Zambia and Mozambique in adopting a strong statement in March 2011 condemning intimidation and violence in Zimbabwe and setting out a road map for free and fair elections that should involve regional facilitators more directly. This communiqué was adopted by the full Southern African Development Community (SADC) in June.[5]

Yet by 2013, it seemed that South Africa had again lost the interest it once had in free and fair elections in Zimbabwe. A "credible" poll (i.e. one not riddled with violence) was enough to satisfy Zuma.[6] In September 2013, the SADC observer mission head, Tanzanian Foreign Minister Bernard Member, announced the elections were "free, peaceful and generally credible," while Africa Union mission head and former Nigerian President Olusegun Obasanjo had already said the polls were "free, honest and credible"—a notion most other independent observers contested.[7]

If democracy returned to Zimbabwe, many would return to the country, and the foreign investment that would also return to Zimbabwe would help South Africa, which has been losing investor confidence. By contrast, renewed turmoil would bring a fresh wave of refugees to South Africa.[8]

Notes

1. James Hammill, "Democracy or Solidarity: South Africa's Zimbabwe Dilemma," *World Politics Review*, 15 April 2013, www.worldpoliticsreview.com/articles/12869/democracy-or-solidarity-south-africa-s-zimbabwe-dilemma.
2. Thomas Carothers and Richard Youngs, "Looking for Help: Will Rising Democracies Become International Democracy Supporters?" *Democracy and Rule of Law* (2011): 11.
3. Celia W. Dugger, "Zimbabwe's Mugabe Faces Pro-Democracy Push From Powerful Neighbor, South Africa," *The New York Times*, 10 June 2011, www.nytimes.com/2011/06/11/world/africa/11zimbabwe.html?_r=0.
4. Mmanaled Mataboge, "Rift Between Zanu-PF and SA Deepens," *Mail & Guardian*, 13 July 2013, mg.co.za/article/2013-07-12-rift-between-zanu-pf-and-sa-deepens/.
5. Carothers and Youngs, "Looking for Help."
6. "Zimbabwe's Election: Not So Fast," *The Economist*, 5 June 2013, www.economist.com/blogs/baobab/2013/06/zimbabwe-s-election.
7. "Sadc Ignores Own Guidelines on Zimbabwe," *Zimbabwe Independent*, 6 September 2013, www.theindependent.co.zw/2013/09/06/sadc-ignores-own-guidelines-on-zimbabwe/.
8. "Zimbabwe's Election: Not so Fast."

Given these experiences and the crisis of confidence and credibility afflicting its democratization policy, South Africa's recent advocacy for human rights and democracy has been more cautious. In order not to aggravate tension in the region still further, it has emphasized voluntary and multilateral mechanisms rather than bilateral confrontation.[94] South Africa has also contributed to multiple peacekeeping missions in Africa, and its presidents have taken active roles, with varying degrees of success, in mediating conflicts across the continent. Yet while sensitive to the need to reassure South Africa's neighbors, South African leaders insisted that the country would not be deterred from promoting democracy in Africa. Severe problems with South Africa's own democracy, however, have often limited its capacity. According to some analysts, freedom of the press is under threat. After winning power in 1994, the ANC enshrined freedom of expression as well as "the right to access any information held by the state" in the country's 1996 Constitution. Yet since the ruling ANC has come under strong criticism, several policy makers have attempted to curb South Africa's media. As a consequence, Freedom House rated South Africa as "partly free" for the first time in the 2010 analysis of press freedom.[95] In 2005, *The Economist*, while acknowledging Mbeki's achievements abroad, argued that "the face the president shows within South Africa is decidedly less benign. Domestic critics feel that he is becoming so over-mighty, and so intolerant of criticism, that he may undermine the vibrant democracy that the ANC helped create."[96]

Like other emerging powers, despite its determination to promote Africa's renewal through democratization, South Africa is eager to preserve its growing trade relationships with undemocratic countries.[97] Given its important economic ties with China, South Africa has been careful not to displease the regime in Beijing. That became clear in 2009, when the Dalai Lama, who wanted to attend a peace conference in South Africa, was denied an entry visa.[98]

As a consequence, South African foreign policy has often disappointed democracy and human rights advocates. Furthermore, South Africa has not consistently supported human rights in international forums. In its first Security Council term, South Africa voted against condemning Zimbabwe and Myanmar for human rights abuses and opposed the International Criminal Court's prosecution of Sudan's Omar al-Bashir.[99] However, South African foreign policy remains in a process of definition, and it is highly uncertain how far future leaders in South Africa may be open to a more assertive role on democracy and human rights.

There is great expectation among policy makers in Europe and North America that the IBSA countries will become active democracy promoters. This assumption to a large part explains why Brazil's, India's and South Africa's economic success is, contrary to China, rarely seen as a threat in the West. In fact, as stated above, Brazil has turned into a quite reliable defender of democracy in the region. India, for its part, was far more cautious, but acted in some rare instances, such as when a *coup d'état* occurred in the Maldives. In a similar vein, South Africa has often been reluctant to promote democracy openly. Thus, rather than a clash between countries that support democracy promotion and those that outright reject it, a more nuanced and complex debate is emerging about when and how democracy promotion is legitimate, and how it should take place. Not the concept as such, but its interpretation and application, will increasingly be open to contestation and competition between established and emerging democracies—as seen in Venezuela in 2002 or Honduras in 2009.

It is likely that in the context of the redistribution of global power, it will be increasingly difficult for US and European actors—both state and non-state—to control the international debate about democracy promotion.[100] While democracy as an international norm remains strong[101]—the call for democracy being one of the important issues during the recent revolutions in the Arab world—Europe's and the United States' relative declines may soon cause them to promote democracy less openly, or only in specific circumstances. This stands in stark contrast to the early years after the Cold War, when analysts marveled at an "unprecedented movement towards democracy."[102] Even in 2000 Cox, Ikenberry and Inoguchi confidently asserted that democracy was "increasingly the only legitimate means by which we can manage our political affairs effectively."[103]

One of the most striking differences between US or European democracy promotion on the one hand, and Brazilian, South African and Indian democracy promotion on the other is that the latter's civil societies are far less involved in the process. No civil society or government in the global South has developed the capacity to allocate thousands of democracy aid workers around the world, as is the case with European and US NGOs. As so-called "emerging donors," Brazil, South Africa and India do not use democracy-related conditionalities in their aid programs,[104] while the United States and Europe have in several instances integrated democracy promotion efforts into their development aid schemes. Democracy promotion neither seems to be part of a greater Brazilian, South African or Indian "liberal narrative," nor an important element of Brazil's or India's "mission." Rather, emerging powers are, by nature, suspicious of any pursuit of ideological convergence among states. None has developed any kind of *mission civilizatrice* or interest in expanding its particular ideological narrative across the world;[105] they are unlikely to elevate their own success into an ideological basis for their foreign policy.

One could assume that "new" democracies are not yet convinced enough of the strength of their own democratic system to promote democracy themselves. According to this logic, only "consolidated democracies" are interested in promoting democracy themselves, and emerging powers will slowly in turn adopt Western-style democracy promotion as their political system matures. Yet India has long been a consolidated democracy and its national identity is very much shaped by Enlightenment values.[106] The same can be said of Brazil and South Africa, whose cultures are based on the respect for human rights, democracy, constitutional government, and government by public reason. Fundamental differences are therefore likely to remain.

The normative approach used to explain Western democracy promotion, which points out that one of the main drivers is the urge to project one's democratic identity and recreate the world in one's own image,[107] thus does not apply to emerging democracies like India, Brazil and South Africa. This may suggest that in an increasingly multipolar world order, Western-style grassroots democracy promotion, partially driven by non-state actors, is thus bound to play a much less significant role. It also indicates that room for cooperation on a non-state level is limited. Brazil prefers to take preventive action on a political level—for example, through treaty clauses that punish countries which do not uphold democratic standards (Brazil in South America), or on the multilateral level. Not only is this high-level "political approach" of defending democracy less invasive, but it is also much cheaper and involves lower risk than having thousands of development workers—employed either by state or non-state actors—working in other countries.

Conclusion

As the analysis makes clear, IBSA members promote democracy as long as doing so is aligned with their overall strategic and economic interests, and if they are willing to adopt democracy promotion as a means to legitimize their growing influence—in this respect, their approach is similar to the Western practice. While promoting democracy may endanger India's foreign policy goal of maintaining regional stability, it is increasingly aligned with Brazil's national interests as a regional hegemon. Given that autocratic leaders are more likely to endanger Brazilian investments in the region—for example, by expropriating Brazilian investments—democracy promotion has become a key tool to contain threats against the legitimacy of the established order and to defend its growing economic presence in South America.

Yet the IBSA members fundamentally differ from established actors in that they rarely justify their democracy-related activities in the context of a larger liberal narrative often used by European and US policy makers. Brazil, India and South Africa remain suspicious of the at times sweeping Wilsonian liberal rhetoric and concepts used by European or US democracy promoters, which policy makers in the global South consider both ineffective and smacking of cultural imperialism. It is worth noting that despite their democracy-related activities, no Brazilian, Indian or South African policy maker or civil society representative describes them as "democracy promotion"—very much contrary to Europe and the United States, where the term is common. Therefore, it is no surprise that none of the emerging powers have embraced US ideas such as the "League of Democracies." As a consequence, observers in Europe and the United States have generally seen the scope for cooperation with rising democracies on democracy-related activities as limited.

Emerging powers' position matters greatly because they are located in regions of the world where democracy's footing is not yet firm. In addition, there are indications that emerging democratic powers' credibility among poor countries may exceed that of the rich world—perhaps precisely because they are rarely perceived as overly paternalistic or arrogant. What is perhaps most important, emerging powers' societal structures—high inequality, a high degree of illiteracy (in India's case) and pockets of poverty—are similar to many countries that struggle to establish democracy. Seen from that perspective, policy makers in the global South have much more experience in making democracy work in adverse environments. In Brazil's case, an additional asset is very recent experience of a successful transition to democracy. Emerging powers such as Brazil, India and South Africa would therefore be in a much better position to share experience about democracy than Europe or the United States, whose democratization lies in the distant past, and whose societies look very different from the rest of the world. Finally, in a world where an increasing number of national leaders look to China as an economic and political model to copy, India, South Africa and Brazil provide powerful counter-examples that political freedom is no obstacle to economic growth.[108] In this sense, as Pratap Mehta points out, their own success may do far more for democracy promotion than any overtly ideological push in that direction could ever hope to accomplish.[109]

Notes

1 Daniel Flemes, "Emerging Middle Powers' Soft Balancing Strategy: State and Perspectives of the IBSA Dialogue Forum," *GIGA Working Papers* 57 (2007), 25.

2 Rajiv Bhatia, "IBSA: Talking Shop or Powerhouse?" *The Hindu*, 12 October 2010, www.thehindu.com/opinion/lead/article825414.ece.

3 Sarah al-Doyaili, Andreas Freytag and Peter Draper, "IBSA: Fading out or Forging a Common Vision?" *South African Journal of International Affairs* 20, no. 2 (2013): 297–310, 298.

4 See, for example: Flemes, "Emerging Middle Powers' Soft Balancing Strategy," 25; Manish Chand, "IBSA: Ambitious Exercise in Transformational

Diplomacy," *Indo-Asian News Service*, 15 October 2008, www.ipc-undp. org/ipc/doc/ibsa/papers/ibsa4.pdf.

5 India-Brazil-South Africa Dialogue Forum (IBSA), "IBSA Ministerial Meeting at General Debate of UNGA 65," 25 September 2010, www.itam araty.gov.br/sala-de-imprensa/notas-a-imprensa/reuniao-ministerial-do-ibas -a-margem-do-debate-geral-da-65a-assembleia-geral-das-nacoes-unidas-2 013-nova-york-25-de-setembro-de-2010.

6 Ramesh Thakur, "World Holds Vested Interest in a Successful South Africa," *UNU Update*, October 2003, archive.unu.edu/update/archive/ issue28_11.htm.

7 Oliver Stuenkel, "Why Brazil Matters," *The Times of India*, 1 September 2010, articles.timesofindia.indiatimes.com/2010-09-01/edit-page/28229782_1_pres ident-luiz-inacio-lula-first-brazilian-president-brazilian-politics.

8 Quoted in Priya Chacko, "IBSA in the Foreign Policy of a Rising India," in *Contemporary India and South Africa: Legacies, Identities, Dilemmas*, ed. Sujata Patel and Tina Uys (New Delhi, India: Routledge, 2012), 285.

9 Thomas Carothers and Richard Youngs, "Looking for Help: Will Rising Democracies Become International Democracy Supporters?" *Carnegie Endowment for International Peace*, The Carnegie Papers, Democracy and the Rule of Law, July 2011, Introduction.

10 See, for example: Amichai Magen, Thomas Risse and Michael McFaul, ed., *Promoting Democracy and the Rule of Law: American and European Strategies* (Basingstoke: Palgrave Macmillan, 2009).

11 The term "rising democracies" refers to emerging powers under demo-cratic rule. The term is used by, among others: Ted Piccone, "Do New Democracies Support Democracy?" *Journal of Democracy* 22, no. 4 (2011): 139.

12 Simon Serfaty, "Moving into a Post-Western World," *The Washington Quarterly* 34, no. 2 (2011): 7–23.

13 Carothers and Youngs, "Looking for Help," Summary.

14 Democracy promotion can take many different forms, ranging from the enactment of pro-democracy clauses in regional bodies, political party development, electoral monitoring, supporting independent media and journalists, capacity building for state institutions, training for judges, civic group leaders and legislators, and offering development aid if the recipient takes steps towards democratization, to, in rarer cases, imposing sanctions on non-democratic regimes. Rather than merely by governments, democ-racy promotion began to be undertaken by specialized government agen-cies (such as USAID) or nongovernmental organizations such as Freedom House, the National Endowment for Democracy (NED) or the German Stiftungen.

15 Michael Doyle, "Peace, Liberty and Democracy: Realists and Liberals Contest a Legacy," in *American Democracy Promotion: Impulses, Strategies, and Impacts*, ed. Michael Cox, G. John Ikenberry and Takashi Inoguchi (Oxford: Oxford University Press, 2000).

16 See, for example: Jonas Wolff, "Theorie des Demokratischen Friedens— Politik der internationalen Demokratieförderung," in *Frieden durch Demokratie? Genese, Wirkung und Kritik eines Deutungsmusters*, ed. Jost Dülffer and Gottfried Niedhart (Essen: Klartext, 2007), 227–42.

17 Peter J. Schraeder, "The State of the Art in International Democracy Promotion: Results of a Joint European-North American Research Network," *Democratization* 20, no. 2 (2003): 21–44. See also G. John Ikenberry, "Why Export Democracy? The 'Hidden Grand Strategy' of American Foreign Policy," *The Wilson Quarterly* 23, no. 2 (1999): 56–65. Democracy's impact on poverty reduction is less clear. Ashutosh Varshney, for example, states: "Democracies … have prevented the worst-case scenarios from happening, including prevention of famines, but they have not achieved the best results; and the performance of dictatorships, in comparison, covers the whole range of outcomes: the best, the worst, and the moderate." In "Democracy and Poverty," Paper for the Conference on World Development Report, *UK Department for International Development, and the Institute of Development Studies*, 2000.

18 Michael W. Doyle, "Kant, Liberal Legacies, and Foreign Affairs," *Philosophy and Public Affairs* 12, no. 3 (1983): 205–35.

19 Georg Sørensen, "Liberalism of Restraint and Liberalism of Imposition: Liberal Values and World Order in the New Millennium," *International Relations* 20, no. 3 (2006): 251–72. See also: Hans-Joachim Spanger and Jonas Wolff, "Universales Ziel—partikulare Wege? Externe Demokratieförderung zwischen einheitlicher Rhetorik und vielfältiger Praxis," in *Schattenseiten des Demokratischen Friedens. Zur Kritik einer Theorie liberaler Außen-und Sicherheitspolitik*, ed. Anna Geis, Harald Müller and Wolfgang Wagner (Frankfurt and New York: Campus, 2007), 261–84.

20 Ibid., 261.

21 Pratap Bhanu Mehta, "Do New Democracies Support Democracy? Reluctant India," *Journal of Democracy* 22, no. 4 (2011): 102.

22 Michael W. Doyle, "A Few Words on Mill, Walzer, and Nonintervention," *Ethics & International Affairs* 23, no. 4 (2009): 349–69.

23 Samuel P. Huntington, *Political Order in Changing Societies* (New Haven, Conn. and London: Yale University Press, 1968).

24 Colin H. Kahl, "Constructing a Separate Peace: Constructivism, Collective Liberal Identity, and Democratic Peace," *Security Studies* 8, no. 2–3 (1998): 94–144.

25 Henry A. Kissinger, *A World Restored: Europe After Napoleon* (New York: Grosset & Dunlap, 1964).

26 Michael Cox, G. John Ikenberry and Takashi Inoguchi, ed., *American Democracy Promotion: Impulses, Strategies, and Impacts* (Oxford: Oxford University Press, 2000), 5.

27 William I. Robinson, "Globalization, the World System, and 'Democracy Promotion' in US," *Foreign Policy/Theory and Society* 25, no. 5 (1996): 615–65.

28 Ibid.

29 N. Scott Cole, "Hugo Chavez and President Bush's Credibility Gap: The Struggle against US Democracy Promotion," *International Political Science Review/Revue internationale de science politique* 28, no. 4 (2007): 493–507.

30 Robinson, "Globalization, the World System, and 'Democracy Promotion' in US."

31 Thomas Carothers, *Critical Mission: Essays on Democracy Promotion* (Washington, DC: Carnegie Endowment for International Peace, 2004), 11.

32 Randall Schweller, "Emerging Powers in an Age of Disorder," *Global Governance* 17, no. 3 (2011): 285–97, 293.

33 Carlos Santiso, "Promoção e Proteção da Democracia na Política Externa Brasileira," *Contexto int.* 24, no. 2 (2002): 397.

34 Brazilian Constitution, 5 October 1988, Title 1, Article 4, number 2, www.planalto.gov.br/ccivil_03/constituicao/constituicao.htm.

35 Santiso, "Promoção e Proteção da Democracia na Política Externa Brasileira," 397.

36 Ibid., 404.

37 Matias Spektor, "Intervenções no Brasil," *Folha de S. Paulo*, 19 March 2012, www1.folha.uol.com.br/colunas/matiasspektor/1063756-intervencoes-do-br asil.shtml.

38 Sean Burges and Jean Daudelin, "Brazil: How Realists Defend Democracy," *Promoting Democracy in the Americas*, ed. Thomas Legler, Sharon F. Lean, Dexter S. Boniface (Baltimore, Md.: Johns Hopkins University Press, 2007), 3.

39 Thomas Carothers, "Think Again: Democracy," *Foreign Policy* 107 (1997): 11–18. See also: Jonatas Luis Pabis, "O compromisso Brasileiro com a Promoção da Democracia," *RI*, September 2012; Arturo Valenzuela, "Paraguay: The Coup that Didn't Happen," *Journal of Democracy* 8, no. 1 (1997): 43–55.

40 Santiso, "Promoção e Proteção da Democracia na Política Externa Brasileira," 408.

41 Ibid., 413.

42 The norm of democratic solidarity postulates that the peoples of the Americas have a right to democracy and their governments have an obligation to promote and defend it. See Organization of American States, "Representative Democracy," Resolution adopted at the fifth plenary session, AG/RES. 1080 (XXI-O/91), 5 June 1991.

43 Burges and Daudelin, "Brazil: How Realists Defend Democracy," 1.

44 Santiso, "Promoção e Proteção da Democracia na Política Externa Brasileira," 415.

45 Fernando Henrique Cardoso, *A Arte da Política—A história que Vivi* (São Paulo, Brazil: Editora Civilização Brasileira, 2006), 636.

46 Burges and Daudelin, "Brazil: How Realists Defend Democracy," 8.

47 Santiso, "Promoção e Proteção da Democracia na Política Externa Brasileira," 422.

48 Burges and Daudelin, "Brazil: How Realists Defend Democracy." See also Santiso, "Promoção e Proteção da Democracia na Política Externa Brasileira," 422.

49 Amanda Sanches Daltro de Carvalho and Renata de Melo Rosa, "O Brasil e a Não-indiferença à Crise Haitiana: Solidariedade ou Retórica do Discurso?" *Universitas: Relações Internacionais* 9, no. 1 (2011): 487–509.

50 "OAS Members Balk at U.S. Intervention Plan," *CNN International*, 7 June 2005, edition.cnn.com//2005/WORLD/americas/06/06/oas/index.html?section=cnn_world.

51 Carothers, *Critical Mission*, 15. Others have argued quite the opposite, charging that Brazil did in fact help legitimize the ouster of a democratically elected government, yet most admit that the case falls into a grey area. See, for example: Burges and Daudelin, "Brazil: How Realists

Defend Democracy"; Santiso, "Promoção e Proteção da Democracia na Política Externa Brasileira," 8.

52 Carothers and Youngs, "Looking for Help," 6.

53 *Support by the United Nations System of the Efforts of Governments to Promote and Consolidate New or Restored Democracies, Report of the Secretary-General* (General Assembly document A/RES/61/226), 14 March 2007.

54 "UNDP Guinea-Bissau and Brazil's Electoral Supreme Court Signed Electoral Memorandum," *United Nations Integrated Peace-Building Office in Guinea-Bissau*, 11 July 2011, www.uniogbis.unmissions.org/Default.aspx? tabid=9919&ctl=Details&mid=12838&ItemID=11650&language=en-US.

55 *Report of the Secretary-General on Developments in Guinea-Bissau and on the Activities of the United Nations Integrated Peacebuilding Office in that Country, Report of the Secretary-General* (Security Council document S/2012/554), 17 July 2012.

56 Eleonora de Lucena, "Foi Golpe o que Aconteceu em Paraguai, Diz Alto Representante do Mercosul," *Folha de São Paulo*, 29 June 2012, www1. folha.uol.com.br/mundo/1112252-foi-golpe-o-que-ocorreu-no-paraguai-diz-alto-representante-do-mercosul.shtml.

57 Burges and Daudelin, "Brazil: How Realists Defend Democracy."

58 Sean Burges, "Consensual Hegemony: Theorizing Brazilian Foreign Policy After the Cold War," *International Relations* 22, no. 1 (2008): 65–84, 65.

59 Piccone, "Do New Democracies Support Democracy?" 140.

60 See, for example, Matias Spektor, "Silêncios," *Folha de S. Paulo*, 3 October 2012, www1.folha.uol.com.br/colunas/matiasspektor/1162958-silencios.shtml.

61 Matias Spektor, "O Regionalismo do Brasil," in *Brasil e América do Sul: Olhares cruzados*, ed. Bernardo Sorj and Sergio Fausto (São Paulo, Brazil: iFHC, Centro Edelweiss, Fundação Konrad Adenauer, 2011), 141–72, 144.

62 Ibid., 145.

63 Simon Romero, "Brazil's Long Shadow Vexes Some Neighbors," *The New York Times*, 4 November 2011, www.nytimes.com/2011/11/05/world/americ as/brazils-rapidly-expanding-influence-worries-neighbors.html.

64 Oliver Stuenkel, "Strategic Threats Surrounding Brazil," *International Reports Konrad-Adenauer-Stiftung*, 30 September 2010.

65 Mehta, "Do New Democracies Support Democracy?"

66 Siddharth Mallavaparu, "Democracy Promotion circa 2010: An Indian Perspective," *Contemporary Politics* 16, no. 1 (2010): 49–61, 49.

67 This sentiment is not only limited to India. See, for example: Carothers and Youngs, "Looking for Help," Summary.

68 Mallavaparu, "Democracy Promotion circa 2010," 53.

69 Mehta, "Do New Democracies Support Democracy?" 100.

70 Ramachandra Guha, *India After Gandhi: The History of the World's Largest Democracy* (New Delhi, India: Palgrave Macmillan, 2007).

71 Mallavaparu, "Democracy Promotion circa 2010," 49.

72 Mehta, "Do new Democracies Support Democracy?" 100.

73 Jorg Faust and Christian Wagner, "India: A New Partner in Democracy Promotion?" Briefing Paper 3-2010, German Development Institute, 3.

74 Carothers and Youngs, "Looking for Help," 8.

75 Carothers and Youngs, "Looking for Help," Introduction.

76 Raja C. Mohan, "India's Outdated Myanmar Policy: Time for a Change," *RSIS Commentaries* 103/07 (2007): 1.

77 Raja C. Mohan, "Balancing Interests and Values: India's Struggle with Democracy Promotion," *The Washington Quarterly* 30, no. 3 (2007): 99–115.

78 Ibid.

79 Mallavaparu, "Democracy Promotion circa 2010," 53. Indeed, India is the second largest contributor to the Fund. See Carothers and Youngs, "Looking for Help," 8.

80 Daniel Twining, "India's Relations with Iran and Myanmar: 'Rogue State' or Responsible Stakeholder?" *India Review* 7, no. 1 (2008): 1–37, 31.

81 Mehta, "Do New Democracies Support Democracy?" 98.

82 Chris Landsberg, "Promoting Democracy: The Mandela-Mbeki Doctrine," *Journal of Democracy* 11, no. 3 (2000): 107–21.

83 Carothers and Youngs, "Looking for Help."

84 Heidi Vogt, "Mandela Leaves Divided Legacy in Africa," *The Wall Street Journal*, 6 December 2013, online.wsj.com/news/articles/SB1000142405 2702303497804579241800418069602.

85 William Wallis, "Mandela Magic has its Limits in Africa," *Financial Times*, 10 December 2013, www.ft.com/intl/cms/s/0/3e910340-618d-11e3-b7f1-00144feabdc0.html.

86 Vogt, "Mandela Leaves Divided Legacy in Africa."

87 Ken Wiwa, "We Nigerians are Celebrating Mandela as the Kind of Hero we've Never Had," *The Guardian*, 8 December 2013, www.theguardian.com/commentisfree/2013/dec/08/ken-wiwa-on-nigeria-response-to-mandela.

88 Landsberg, "Promoting Democracy," 109.

89 Ibid., 109.

90 Ibid., 110.

91 Ibid., 111.

92 "Thabo Mbeki: A Man of Two Faces," *The Economist*, 20 January 2005, www.economist.com/node/3576543.

93 Ibid.

94 Landsberg, "Promoting Democracy," 116.

95 "The Media in Southern Africa: U-turn on the Long Walk to Freedom," *The Economist*, 16 December 2010, www.economist.com/node/17733679.

96 "Thabo Mbeki: A Man of Two Faces."

97 Carothers and Youngs, "Looking for Help," 11.

98 "Dalai Lama Denied Visa for South Africa Peace Conference," *CNN International*, 23 March 2009, edition.cnn.com/2009/WORLD/africa/03/23/south.africa.dalai.lama.visa/.

99 Carothers and Youngs, "Looking for Help," 11.

100 For an interesting case study of US democracy promotion in Venezuela, see: N. Scott Cole, "Hugo Chavez and President Bush's Credibility Gap: The Struggle Against US Democracy Promotion," *International Political Science Review/Revue internationale de science politique* 28, no. 4 (2007): 493–507.

101 Michael McFaul, "Democracy Promotion as a World Value," *The Washington Quarterly* 28, no. 1 (2004/2005): 147–63.

102 Larry Diamond, "Promoting Democracy," *Foreign Policy* 87 (1992): 25–46.

103 Cox *et al.*, ed., *American Democracy Promotion*.

104 Carothers and Youngs, "Looking for Help," 6.

105 Mehta, "Do New Democracies Support Democracy?" 101.

106 Ibid., 97.

107 Thomas Carothers, "Critical Mission: Essays on Democracy Promotion," *Carnegie Endowment for International Peace*, 2004, 17.
108 Oliver Stuenkel, "Why Brazil Matters," *Times of India*, 1 September 2010, articles.timesofindia.indiatimes.com/2010-09-01/edit-page/28229782_1_president-luiz-inacio-lula-first-brazilian-president-brazilian-politics#ixzz1145GSdPo.
109 Mehta, "Do New Democracies Support Democracy?" 101.

Conclusion

> IBSA is much more than just a diplomatic edifice. It is a natural expression of particular views on great international issues. It is also a concrete expression of the objectives shared by Brazil, India and South Africa. We are fully consolidated democracies that give an example of how the various ethnic groups and cultures that form our societies can co-exist in harmony. We are emerging economies, destined to have an ever more relevant international presence.
>
> (President Lula da Silva[1])

More than a decade after its launch, one can no longer claim that IBSA is still in its infancy. What has it achieved? Does the grouping have policy substance or does it amount to little more than a catchy acronym in the debate about global governance?

Irrespective of its policy relevance, the creation of the IBSA Forum symbolizes an important element in the debate about global affairs during the first decade of the twenty-first century. The IBSA initiative by three emerging democracies located in the global South must be understood in the context of a tradition of developing country clubs, but also in the context of a decade that was marked by an unprecedented process of multipolarization. Contrary to previous outfits such as the G77 or the NAM, IBSA's rhetoric was based on confidence in its members' newfound power and capacity to increasingly make rather than take international rules and norms. Interestingly enough, as this book has shown, IBSA's demands are also far less revolutionary and more status quo oriented than those of previous developing country alliances, which sought fundamentally to challenge the existing economic order.

The decision to create the IBSA grouping aimed at reducing rising powers' economic dependence on the industrialized world, promote political and economic South-South ties, and sought to increase member countries' leverage in international forums. The past 10 years have seen important advances for developing countries (such as historic IMF quota reforms), but also many disappointments (for example, no UNSC reform and continuing Western control over the process of selecting the World Bank and IMF leadership).

Still, the preceding chapters make clear that while most analysts are skeptical of the grouping, it would be wrong to describe IBSA as ineffective altogether. Rather, it significantly contributed to reorienting each country's foreign policy perspective and strengthened the significance of South-South cooperation. At the same time, a detailed analysis of intra-IBSA activities shows that many of them have only a very limited impact. Despite countless attempts to facilitate trade, barriers remain formidable, and there are few signs that this will change anytime soon. Intra-IBSA trade thus remains negligible, more than a decade after the creation of the grouping. Working groups are often ineffective, and they would almost certainly benefit from focusing on a smaller number of issue areas and from obtaining stronger political support at the highest level.

While Manmohan Singh was not prime minister during the IBSA Forum's inception in 2003, he can still, along with Thabo Mbeki and Lula da Silva, be considered a "founding member" of the grouping. With his recent departure, it remains to be seen how supportive the new generation of leaders is towards the IBSA concept. With both Brazil's Dilma Rousseff and South Africa's Jacob Zuma more concerned about domestic challenges, much depends on India's next prime minister.

In 2011, Flemes argued that "the IBSA Forum has impacted the global order in recent years as a powerful driver for change. India, Brazil and South Africa have contributed to an incremental global power shift in their favor. The southern coalition also induced a change in the character of multilateralism and, in particular, its procedural values."[2] While that may have been a convincing narrative for some, the three IBSA countries have yet to show how exactly they have been able to bring about a fundamental change in the character of multilateralism. Now that growth rates among IBSA countries are barely higher than those in the United States, it remains to be seen how far India, Brazil and South Africa can sustain their proactive South-South cooperation.

IBSA's slow progress on strengthening ties also shows that South-South cooperation, even that between ideologically similar actors, is no simple undertaking, and no panacea to the many challenges developing nations face as they seek to increase their benefit from an ever more integrated global economy. Internal protectionist forces make reducing trade barriers towards the South as difficult as opening up towards the North. This also shows that while the entire concept of South-South cooperation may find support among a group of high-level bureaucrats in India, Brazil and South Africa, the three countries' societies are far less likely to consider South-South cooperation as something different from trade relations with industrialized countries. That does not mean that they do not consider trade within the global South as important, but governments have clearly not yet been able to generate in their societies the excitement about the topic that often seemed to be present in their official declarations. The IBSA grouping remains a fringe topic even in India's, Brazil's and South Africa's foreign policy communities.

As IBSA countries seek to play a greater global role, their contested regional leadership claims hamper their capacity and legitimacy to speak in the name of the global South. As Vieira and Alden rightly note:

> This regional gap impacts significantly on the legitimacy of the IBSA trio in that their key claim to leadership is founded only on a shared platform of mutual recognition clothed loosely in the rhetoric of Global South solidarity. Lacking an equivalent endorsement of their leadership role from their region, the IBSA countries are nonetheless called on by established powers to play a seminal part in representing the region's economic interests and even managing emerging security challenges. These factors introduce important constraints on IBSA and its prospects to act as an effective diplomatic partnership aimed at influencing international processes.[3]

The analysis has also shown that while India, Brazil and South Africa seek to reform global order, they have no intention of undermining or seriously destabilizing it. While IBSA countries are at times called revisionist, leading policy makers in Brasília, Pretoria and New Delhi do not see themselves as challengers of the global order, even if in their minds it is often unjust and hegemonic. The solution, according to IBSA, lies in step-by-step reforms. No IBSA country wants to rock the boat—just to make it bigger and more balanced.[4] This has a number of reasons. First of all, the benefits the current system provides for emerging powers remain plentiful, and given the hegemon's dominance, hard balancing remains self-defeating. Second, emerging powers still lack the ideas to develop alternative paradigms that could rival those that undergird today's order. Still, there is a firm belief that working together in some areas could strengthen the IBSA countries' bargaining power in their quest to reform the global order.

Notes

1 *Speech by President Luiz Inácio Lula da Silva at the Opening Session of the First IBSA Summit*, Brasília, 13 September 2006.
2 Daniel Flemes, "India-Brazil-South Africa (IBSA) in the New Global Order: Interests, Strategies and Values of the Emerging Coalition," *International Studies* 46, no. 4 (2009): 401–21, 401.
3 Marco Antonio Vieira and Chris Alden, "India, Brazil, and South Africa (IBSA): South-South Cooperation and the Paradox of Regional Leadership," *Global Governance* 17, no. 4 (2011): 507–28, 508.
4 See, for example Matias Spektor, "A Place at the Top of the Tree," *Financial Times*, 22 February 2013, www.ft.com/intl/cms/s/2/9c7b7a22-27bb9-11e2-95b9-00144feabdc0.html.

Appendix

Timeline of events

Table A.1 IBSA timeline

Date	Location	Event
2003		
06/02/2003	Evian, France	Informal trilateral meeting at the G8 Summit
06/06/2003	Brasília, Brazil	First meeting of foreign ministers—the creation of IBSA
24/09/2003	New York, United States	Foreign Ministers Meeting at 58th UN General Assembly
2004		
02/12/2004	New Delhi, India	I IBSA Focal Points meeting
03/04/2004– 03/05/2004	New Delhi, India	I Foreign Ministers Trilateral Commission meeting (Comista)
29/11/2004– 30/11/2004	New Delhi, India	II IBSA Focal Points meeting
03/2004		Creation of the IBSA Fund
2005		
10/03/2005– 11/03/2005	Cape Town, South Africa	II Foreign Ministers Trilateral Commission meeting
10/03/2005– 11/03/2005	Cape Town, South Africa	IBSA Business Forum launched
10/03/2005– 11/03/2005	Cape Town, South Africa	III IBSA Focal Points meeting
10/03/2005– 11/03/2005	Cape Town, South Africa	II Foreign Ministers Trilateral Commission meeting (Comista)
08/03/2005– 09/03/2005	Rio de Janeiro, Brazil	IV Focal Points meeting
03/08/2005– 04/08/2005	Rio de Janeiro, Brazil	IBSA seminar on Economic Development and Social Equity
24/11/2005– 25/11/2005	Vereeniging, South Africa	V Focal Points meeting
2006		
28/03/2006– 30/03/2006	Rio de Janeiro, Brazil	Technical Regulations and Conformity Assessment

Table A.1 (continued)

Date	Location	Event
29/03/2006	Rio de Janeiro, Brazil	IBSA Trade and Investment Forum
30/03/2006	Rio de Janeiro, Brazil	III Foreign Ministers Trilateral Commission meeting (Comista)
21/06/2006– 22/06/2006	Brasília, Brazil	VI Focal Points meeting
17/08/2006– 18/08/2006	Brasília, Brazil	VII Focal Points meeting
13/09/2006	Brasília, Brazil	**First IBSA Summit**
13/09/2006	Brasília, Brazil	Academic Seminar
2007		
16/07/2007	New Delhi, India	IV Foreign Ministers Trilateral Commission meeting (Comista): IX Focal Points meeting
03/09/2007– 05/09/2007	Brasília, Brazil	Working Group on Public Administration meeting
16/09/2007– 18/09/2007	Sun City, South Africa	X Focal Points meeting
16/10/2007	Johanesbourg, South Africa	IBSA Business Council meeting
16/10/2007	Johannesburg, South Africa	XI Focal Points meeting
17/10/2007	Tshwane, South Africa	**Second IBSA Summit**
24/10/2007– 27/10/2007	Salvador, Brazil	First IBSA Music and Dance Festival
2008		
17/01/2008– 19/01/2008	New Delhi, India	Local Governance Forum
21/04/2008– 25/04/2008	Pretoria, South Africa	Working Group on Agriculture meeting
08/05/2008– 11/05/2008	Somerset West, South Africa	XII Focal Points meeting
11/05/2008	Somerset West, South Africa	V Foreign Ministers Trilateral Commission meeting (Comista)
07/07/2008– 08/07/2008	New York, United States	National Coordination meeting about the IBSA Fund
29/07/2008	New Delhi, India	Health Ministers Trilateral meeting
05/08/2008	Brasília, Brazil	Brazilian Coordination meeting about Naval Transport
06/08/2008– 07/08/2008	Pretoria, South Africa	Aeronautics Authorities meeting
13/08/2008	Brasília, Brazil	Brazilian Coordination meeting for the Science and Technology and Information Society Working Group

Table A.1 (continued)

Date	Location	Event
13/08/2008– 15/08/2008	Florianopolis, Brazil	IBSA Academic Seminar about Genetic Engineering, organized by the Working Group on Agriculture
13/08/2008– 16/08/2008	Florianopolis, Brazil	IBSA Academic Seminar, organized by the Working Group on Education
29/08/2008	Rio de Janeiro Brazil	IBSA Academic Seminar on the IBSA Forum, organized by the the Alexandre de Gusmão Foundation.
08/09/2008– 09/09/2008	New Delhi, India	Working Group on Human Settlements meeting
09/09/2008– 10/09/2008	New Delhi, India	Working Group on Transport meeting
10/09/2008	New Delhi, India	Working Group on Information Society meeting
10/09/2008– 11/09/2008	New Delhi, India	Working Group on Public Administration meeting
12/09/2008	New Delhi, India	Working Group on Environment and Climate Change meeting
13/09/2008– 14/09/2008	New Delhi, India	IBSA Academic Forum
13/09/2008– 14/09/2008	New Delhi, India	Parliamentary Forum
13/09/2008– 14/09/2008	New Delhi, India	IBSA Businessmen Forum
13/09/2008– 14/09/2008	New Delhi, India	IBSA Editors Forum
14/09/2008	New Delhi, India	IBSA Foreign Ministers meeting
15/09/2008– 16/09/2008	New Delhi, India	Working Group on Trade and Investment meeting
15/09/2008– 16/09/2008	New Delhi, India	Working Group on Tax and Customs Administration meeting
15/09/2008– 16/09/2008	New Delhi, India	II Diplomatic Academies Directors meeting
16/09/2008	New York, United States	IBSA Fund Board of Directors meeting
17/09/2008– 18/09/2008	New Delhi, India	Chiefs of Tax and Customs Administration meeting
18/09/2008– 19/09/2008	New Delhi, India	Working Group on Energy meeting
21/09/2008	Kochi, India	Working Group on Tourism meeting
29/09/2008	New York, United States	IBSA Foreign Ministers meeting
30/09/2008	New Delhi, India	Working Group on Health meeting
03/10/2008– 04/10/2008	New Delhi, India	IBSA Seminar on Social Development Strategy
07/10/2008	New Delhi, India	Working Group on Education meeting

Table A.1 (continued)

Date	Location	Event
08/10/2008	New Delhi, India	Working Group on Social Development meeting
10/10/2008	New Delhi, India	XIII Focal Points meeting
10/10/2008	New Delhi, India	Science and Technology Working Group Seminar on anti-HIV/AIDS Vaccines
10/10/2008–14/10/2008	New Delhi, India	IBSA Film Festival
10/10/2008–15/10/2008	New Delhi, India	IBSA Gastronomic Festival
13/10/2008	New Delhi, India	Working Group on Defense meeting
13/10/2008	New Delhi, India	Working Group on Science and Technology meeting
13/10/2008	New Delhi, India	Information Society Working Group Seminar on Eletronic Governance
13/10/2008–14/10/2008	New Delhi, India	IBSA Dance and Music Concerts
14/10/2008	New Delhi, India	IV IBSA Science and Technology Ministers meeting
15/10/2008	New Delhi, India	**Third IBSA Summit**
24/11/2008–28/11/2008	Mumbai, India	Working Group on Administration Technical meeting about Customs Valuation and Risk Management
24/11/2008–28/11/2008	New Delhi, India	Working Group on Administration Technical meeting about Transfer Prices
18/11/2008–22/11/2008	New Delhi, India	Tri-Nations Summit for Small Business Development
28/11/2008	Johannesburg, South Africa	IBSA Digital Inclusion Award given by IBM South Africa
2009		
22/01/2009	New York, United States	IBSA Fund Board of Directors meeting
24/01/2009	Cape Town, South Africa	Signature of the Joint Declaration that creates the IBSA Conference of Supreme Courts
05/02/2009–09/02/2009	New York, United States	IBSA Fund Board of Directors meeting
24/03/2009	Brasília, Brazil	National Entities involved in the work of the IBSA Coordination meeting, with the presence of the General Secretary of External Relations
08/04/2009	Baltimore, United States	IBSA country delegations meeting at the XXXII ATCM
04/05/2009–05/05/2009	New Delhi, India	Working Group on Public Administration meeting

Table A.1 (continued)

Date	Location	Event
07/09/2009	Ramallah, Palestine	Ceremony marking the beginning of the Sports Complex built with funds from the IBSA Fund
27/05/2009	New York, United States	IBSA Fund Board of Directors meeting
02/06/2009	Brasília, Brazil	National Coordination in preparation to the IBSA VI Joint Commission
14/07/2009–15/07/2009	Rio de Janeiro, Brazil	Working Group on Agriculture meeting
14/07/2009–15/07/2009	Rio de Janeiro, Brazil	Working Group on Transport meeting (Sea Segment) followed by technical visit
14/07/2009–15/07/2009	Rio de Janeiro, Brazil	Working Group on Information Society meeting
14/07/2009–15/07/2009	Rio de Janeiro Brazil	Working Group on Environment meeting
14/07/2009–15/07/2009	Rio de Janeiro, Brazil	Working Group on Education meeting followed by technical visit
14/07/2009–15/07/2009	Rio de Janeiro, Brazil	Working Group on Social Development meeting
14/07/2009–15/07/2009	Rio de Janeiro, Brazil	Working Group on Defense meeting
14/07/2009–15/07/2009	Rio de Janeiro, Brazil	Working Group on Culture meeting
14/07/2009–15/07/2009	Rio de Janeiro, Brazil	Working Group on Trade and Investment meeting followed by technical visit
14/07/2009–15/07/2009	Rio de Janeiro, Brazil	Working Group on Human Settlements meeting followed by technical visit
15/07/2009–16/07/2009	Rio de Janeiro, Brazil	XIV Focal Points meeting
10/08/2009–11/08/2009	São José dos Campos, Brazil	1st Antarctic IBSA Seminary, organized at INPE
24/08/2009–28/08/2009	Hyderabad and Thiruvananthapuram	2nd Seminar of IBSA Government Schools
31/08/2009–01/09/2009	Brasília, Brazil	Foreign Ministers meeting and closure of the VI Trilateral Commission (Comista)
10/09/2009–11/09/2009	São José dos Campos, Brazil	IBSA Seminar on Antartica
14/09/2009–15/09/2009	Pretoria, South Africa	Working Group on Revenue Administration meeting
16/09/2009–17/09/2009	Pretoria, South Africa	4th Meeting of IBSA Heads of Revenue Administration
21/09/2009	New York, United States	Foreign Ministers meeting at the 64th UN General Assembly
23/09/2009	New York, United States	IBSA Informal meeting on climate change

Table A.1 (continued)

Date	Location	Event
24/09/2009	São Paulo, Brazil	Working Group on Energy meeting
31/09/2009	Brasília, Brazil	Foreign Ministers meeting
06/10/2009	Astana, Kazakhstan	Working Group on Tourism meeting at the 18th Session of World Tourism Organization
20/10/2009	New York, United States	IBSA Fund Board of Directors meeting
21/10/2009	Durban, South Africa	IBSA Science an Technology Ministerial Meeting at the XI TWAS General Conference (The Academy of Sciences for the Developing World)
01/12/2009– 03/12/2009	Nairobi, Kenya	Exposition "IBSA initiatives of Cooperation" at UN Headquarters
01/12/2009– 03/12/2009	Nairobi, Kenya	Exposition "IBSA initiatives of Cooperation" at UN High Level Conference about South-South Cooperation
03/12/2009	Nairobi, Kenya	Presentation about the IBSA Fund during the official panel of the UN High Level Conference about South-South Cooperation
08/12/2009	New York, United States	Debate about the IBSA Fund project on Haiti
17/12/2009	New York, United States	IBSA Fund Board of Directors meeting
2010		
23/02/2010	Johanesbourg, South Africa	Working Group on Tourism meeting, at the T-20 Meeting
09/04/2010	Brasília, Brazil	Working Group on Science and Technology meeting
12/04/2010	Brasília, Brazil	Coordination meeting with UNDP about the IBSA Fund
12/04/2010	Brasília, Brazil	XV Focal Points meeting
12/04/2010– 13/04/2010	Brasília, Brazil	IBSA Academic Forum
13/04/2010	Brasília, Brazil	Working Group on Energy meeting
13/04/2010– 14/04/2010	Brasília, Brazil	IBSA Parliamentary Forum
13/04/2010– 14/04/2010	Brasília, Brazil	Debate on IBSA Intergovernmental Relations
14/04/2010	Rio de Janeiro, Brazil	IBSA and BRIC Business Forum
14/04/2010– 15/04/2010	Brasília, Brazil	IBSA Women's Forum
14/04/2010	Brasília, Brazil	IBSA Editors Forum

Table A.1 (continued)

Date	Location	Event
14/04/2010	Brasília, Brazil	Meeting of CEOs of organizations to promote IBSA small and medium enterprises
14/04/2010	Brasília, Brazil	Presentation Ceremony of the panels: "IBSA South-South Cooperation Initiatives"—Exposition about the IBSA Fund
15/04/2010	Brasília, Brazil	**Fourth IBSA Summit**
15/04/2010	Brasília, Brazil	Release of the IBSA Bibliographic Catalogue
16/07/2010	New York, United States	IBSA Fund Experts Meeting
17/08/2010– 18/08/2010	São José dos Campos, Brazil	IBSA seminars on: 1 IBSA Satellite; 2 Micro-satellites; and 3 Earth Observation
09/09/2010– 26/09/2010	South African Coast	II IBSAMAR
17/09/2010	New York, United States	IBSA Fund received the 2010 MDGs Award for South-South Cooperation
25/09/2010	New York, United States	Foreign Ministers meeting at the 65th UN General Assembly
04/10/2010– 05/10/2010	Salvador, Brazil	7th & 8th Revenue Administration Steering Group (RASG) meeting
06/10/2010– 07/10/2010	Salvador, Brazil	5th Heads of Revenue Administration Working Group (HRAWG) meeting
2011		
11/02/2011	New Delhi, India	VII Foreign Ministers Trilateral Commission meeting (Comista)
04/03/2011	New Delhi, India	IBSA Working Group on Culture meeting
04/03/2011– 07/03/2011	New Delhi, India	IBSA Working Group on Public Administration meeting
07/03/2011	New Delhi, India	IBSA Working Group on Trade and Investment meeting
10/08/2011	Damascus, Syria	IBSA mission to Syria
01/09/2011– 02/09/2011	Rio de Janeiro, Brazil	IBSA Seminar on Global Internet Governance
23/09/2011	New York, United States	Foreign Ministers meeting at the 66th UN General Assembly
11/10/2011– 12/10/2011	Pretoria, South Africa	IBSA Working Group on Defense meeting
11/10/2011– 13/10/2011	Pretoria, South Africa	IBSA Working Group on Human Settlements meeting
12/10/2011	Pretoria, South Africa	IBSA Working Group on Energy meeting
12/10/2011– 13/10/2011	Pretoria, South Africa	IBSA Working Group on Agriculture meeting

Table A.1 (continued)

Date	Location	Event
13/10/2011	Pretoria, South Africa	IBSA Working Group on Public Administration meeting
13/10/2011	Pretoria, South Africa	IBSA Working Group on Transport and Infrastructure meeting
13/10/2011– 14/10/2011	Pretoria, South Africa	IBSA Women's Forum
14/10/2011	New Delhi, India	IBSA Working Group on Revenues Administration meeting
14/10/2011– 15/10/2011	Pretoria, South Africa	IBSA Working Group on Information Society meeting
14/10/2011– 15/10/2011	Durban, South Africa	IBSA Academic Forum
15/10/2011	Pretoria, South Africa	IBSA Working Group on Science and Technology meeting
15/10/2011	Pretoria, South Africa	IBSA Working Group on Trade and Investment meeting
16/10/2011	Pretoria, South Africa	IBSA Intergovernmental Relations and Local Governments Forum
16/10/2011	Pretoria, South Africa	IBSA Editors Forum
16/10/2011– 17/10/2011	Pretoria, South Africa	IBSA Small and Medium Business Forum
17/10/2011	Pretoria, South Africa	IBSA Business Forum
18/10/2011	Pretoria, South Africa	**Fifth IBSA Summit**
2012		
01/02/2012	Video Conference	IBSA Working Group on Human Settlements meeting
01/03/2012– 03/03/2012	New Delhi, India	International Workshop on South-South Cooperation on "Innovations in Public Employment Programmes and Sustainable Inclusive Growth"
12/03/2012	New York, United States	IBSA Fund Board of Directors meeting
15/03/2012	New York, United States	IBSA Fund Board of Directors meeting
16/04/2012– 17/04/2012	Pretoria, South Africa	IBSA Conference on Culture and Development
18/04/2012	Pretoria, South Africa	IBSA Working Group on Culture meeting
31/07/2012	South Africa	IBSAMAR—III Final Planning Conference
09/2012	New York, United States	20th IBSA Focal Point Meeting on the margins of UN General Assembly

Table A.1 (continued)

Date	Location	Event
06/09/2012–11/09/2012	São José dos Campos, Brazil	IBSA Seminar on Defense Industry
06/09/2012–11/09/2012	Bangalore, India	Technical meeting on the IBSA satellite
11/09/2012		IBSA Working Group on Trade and Investment meeting
03/10/2012–05/10/2012	Cape Town, South Afria	Workshop on Viticulture, organized by the Working Group on Agriculture
10/10/2012–14/10/2012		IBSA Working Group on Revenue Administrations meeting
09/10/2012–26/10/2012	South African Coast	III IBSAMAR
23/10/2012–26/10/2012	Bangalore, India	Technical meeting on the IBSA satellite
2013		
11/01/2013		IBSA Working Group on Health meeting
18/03/2013–19/03/2013	Brasília, Brazil	IBSA Working Group on Environment meeting
08/04/2013–09/04/2013	New Delhi, India	IBSA Local Governance Forum
11/04/2013–11/04/2013	Rio de Janeiro, Brazil	IBSA meeting on Tax and Customs
29/04/2013–30/04/2013	New Delhi, India	IBSA Working Group on Culture meeting
29/04/2013–30/04/2013	New Delhi, India	IBSA Working Group on Education
10/05/2013	New Delhi, India	IBSA Working Group on Agriculture meeting
17/05/2013–18/05/2013		IBSA Working Group on Human Settlements meeting
23/05/2013		IBSA Working Group on Trade and Investment meeting
23/05/2013–24/05/2013		IBSA Working Group on Defense meeting
29/05/2013	New Delhi, India	IBSA Working Group on Energy meeting
29/05/2013–30/05/2013		IBSA Working Group on Transport and Infrastructure meeting
30/05/2013–31/05/2013	New Delhi, India	IBSA Working Group on Science and Technology meeting
10/06/2013	Video Conference	IBSA Working Group on Public Administration
30/07/2013–31/07/2013	New Delhi, India	IBSA Working Group on Education
25/09/2013	New York, United States	Foreign Ministers meeting at 68th UN General Assembly

Table A.1 (continued)

Date	Location	Event
04/11/2013–08/11/2013	Rio de Janeiro, Brazil	IBSA Working Group on Revenue Administrations meeting

Select bibliography

Chris Alden and Marco Antonio Vieira, "The New Diplomacy of the South: South Africa, Brazil, India and Trilateralism," *Third World Quarterly* 26, no. 7 (2005): 1077–95. The first academic article about the IBSA Forum.

Thomas Carothers and Richard Youngs, "Looking for Help: Will Rising Democracies Become International Democracy Supporters?" *Carnegie Endowment for International Peace*, The Carnegie Papers, Democracy and the Rule of Law, July 2011. Analysis of the role of emerging democratic regimes for the future of democracy in the world.

Daniel Flemes, "India-Brazil-South Africa (IBSA) in the New Global Order: Interests, Strategies and Values of the Emerging Coalition," *International Studies* 46, no. 4 (2009): 401–21. Interesting theoretical analysis of the implications of the IBSA grouping for the future of global order.

Kevin Gray and Craig N. Murphy, "Introduction: Rising Powers and the Future of Global Governance," *Third World Quarterly* 34, no. 2 (2013): 183–93. Interesting theoretical considerations about the impact of emerging powers on international institutions.

Daniel Kurtz-Phelan, "What is IBSA Anyway?" *Americas Quarterly*, Spring 2013, www.americasquarterly.org/content/what-ibsa-anyway. One of the few recent analyses of IBSA's relevance in the mainstream foreign policy debate.

Philip Nel and Ian Taylor, "Bugger thy Neighbour? IBSA and South-South Solidarity," *Third World Quarterly* 34, no. 6 (2013): 1091–110. Important analysis of trade between developing countries.

Carlos Aurélio Pimenta de Faria, Joana Laura Marinho Nogueira and Dawisson Belém Lopes, "Coordenação Intragovernamental para a Implementação da Política Externa Brasileira: O Caso do Fórum IBAS," *DADOS—Revista de Ciências Sociais, Rio de Janeiro* 55, no. 1 (2012): 173–220. Excellent summary of IBSA's institutional structure which includes details about the IBSA working groups (in Portuguese).

Folashadé Soule-Kohndou, "The India-Brazil-South Africa Forum a Decade On: Mismatched Partners or the Rise of the South?" *Global Economic Governance Programme Working Paper* 2013/88, University of Oxford, November 2013. One of the most detailed working papers of the IBSA grouping's importance, then years after its creation.

Marco Antonio Vieira and Chris Alden, "India, Brazil, and South Africa (IBSA): South-South Cooperation and the Paradox of Regional Leadership," *Global Governance* 17, no. 4 (2011): 507–28. This paper analyzes the regional leadership challenges each IBSA country faces, which is one of the key limitations to the grouping's claim to represent the developing world.

Sean Woolfrey, "The IBSA Dialogue Forum Ten Years On: Examining IBSA Cooperation on Trade," *Tralac Trade Brief* No. S13TB05/2013, August 2013. One of the key articles that analyzes intra-IBSA trade relations between 2003 and 2013.

Index

Afghanistan 106, 138
agriculture 2, 7, 26, 29, 30–31, 36,
    40, 44, 53–54, 67–72, 80, 86,
    102–4, 107, 111, 113, 159, 160,
    162, 165–66
Ahmadinejad, Mahmoud 50
AIDS 29, 74, 86, 161
Al-Assad, Bashar 7
Alden, Chris 19, 30, 156, 157
Algeria 35
Amorim, Celso 1, 6, 25, 27, 37,
    40–42, 45–46, 48, 50, 52, 63, 72,
    120, 129, 135
Angola 141
Antarctica 67, 77, 162
ANVISA 74
apartheid 12–14, 140–41
Argentina 18, 33, 45, 104, 136
arms 40, 72, 140, 141
arms industry 40, 72
Asia 20–21, 38, 42, 86, 105, 122, 139
Australia 103

Bandung conference 18, 118
Bangladesh 138
Beijing 144
Berlin 121
Bhatia, Rajiv 71, 86, 93, 105
biofuels 73
biosecurity 77
biotechnology 72, 77, 82
Bolivia 78, 134, 137
Bolsa Família 78, 85
Brasília 1–2, 6, 25–26, 42–44, 47, 50,
    52–53, 67, 81, 84, 88, 105, 121,
    135, 156, 158–59, 161–66

Brasília Declaration 1, 16, 60, 88
Braveboy-Wagner, Jacqueline Anne 18
Brazilian Ministry of Foreign Affairs
    17, 20, 38–39, 59, 71, 80, 133–37
BRIC 48–52, 105–7
BRICS 5–6, 47–48, 58–59, 99, 103,
    105–12, 118–19, 121
BRICS Development Bank 111, 121
budget 72, 80, 108, 133
Burges, Sean 134–35
Bush, George W. 132
business 18, 51, 58, 61, 63–64, 78,
    91–94, 109–12, 137
Business Forum 41, 43, 67, 81, 82,
    94, 158, 163, 165

Cambodia 86
Cardoso, Fernando Henrique 14–16,
    133–34, 136
Chávez, Hugo 134, 137
China 2–3, 5–6, 26, 42, 47, 53–54,
    71, 95, 105–12, 118–19, 130
civil society 4, 49, 51, 60, 64, 75,
    87–88, 93, 99, 108, 145, 146
civil war 141
climate change 2, 25, 73, 106, 160, 163
Cold War 11–12, 16–20, 59, 117,
    122, 132, 137, 145
Collor de Mello, Fernando 133
communism 137
Conectas 87
Congo 141
Constitution 133–34, 144
coup d'etat 134–35, 138, 141, 144
culture 26, 46, 49, 67–71, 80, 115,
    162–66

Daudelin, Jean 134–35
declarations 7, 19, 49, 101, 118, 129, 134, 156
defense 2, 20, 26, 44, 67–72, 80, 89, 130–31, 161–62, 164, 166
democracy 56–57, 111, 129–47
development 17–21, 25–26, 39–40, 46–49, 51, 54–57, 66–69, 72–87, 100–101, 111, 118–21, 126, 136, 140–42, 145–46, 158, 160–62, 165
dictatorship 15, 132, 140, 149
diplomacy 20, 26, 47, 58, 71, 99, 139–42
diversification 94, 98–99, 117
Dlamini-Zuma, Nkosazana 1, 25, 27, 40, 42, 45–48
Doha Round 29, 36, 102
Durban 71, 75, 121, 163, 165

earthquake 51
economy 3, 12, 17, 23, 28, 47, 51, 56, 69, 118, 120, 122, 155
education 7, 19, 26, 27, 40, 41, 44, 67, 68, 72, 78, 80, 82, 97, 107, 160, 162, 166
Egypt 24, 58
election 50, 109, 129, 134–36, 140, 142
elite 2, 81, 132
Embraer 3
emerging markets, 2–3, 12–16, 50, 102, 105–6, 122–25
emerging powers, 1–6, 19–20, 23, 31, 103, 106, 117–18, 145, 147, 156
energy 2, 26, 53, 67, 68, 69, 71, 73, 77, 80, 86, 105, 139, 160, 163–64, 166
environment 2, 4, 20, 68–69, 73, 77, 79–80, 107, 160, 162, 166
equity 18, 43, 51, 85, 117, 125, 158
Europe 2, 16, 20, 29–31, 57, 79, 104, 106, 130, 136, 144–47
European Union 31, 93, 95, 103, 122
Evian 1, 24, 158

failed states 2, 106
Fernandes, Ottoni 83
Figueiredo, Luiz Alberto 60
Financial crisis 28, 49–50
Fiocruz 74
Florianópolis 160

Focal Points 28, 38–42, 66, 85, 158–65
Fome Zero 78
food security 73–74, 78
Fujimori, Alberto 134
Fundação Alexandre de Gusmão (FUNAG) 44

G20, 3, 29–31, 106–8
Gabrielli, José Sérgio 45
Gaddafi, Muhammar 140
Gandhi, Rajiv 138
Geisel, Ernesto 13
geopolitical 47, 83, 131, 139
Germany 34–36, 42, 103–4, 133, 148, 151
Global governance 4–5, 20, 23, 30, 66, 72, 82, 118, 154
globalization 20, 26, 39, 51, 106, 118
Graham, Suzanne 11
Guimarães, Samuel Pinheiro 22

Haiti 86, 133, 135, 163
Havana 44
health 7, 26–27, 29, 44, 46, 59, 67, 68, 69, 74, 77, 80, 86, 100, 107, 111, 159–60, 166
Hirst, Mônica 20
Honduras 134, 145
human rights 6, 26, 56–57, 87, 108, 121, 129, 133, 138, 140–45
human settlements 68, 75, 80, 160, 162
hunger 27, 78, 85, 110

IBSA Fund 25, 27–28, 40, 43, 46, 52, 58–60, 66, 77, 85–88, 111, 158–65
Ikenberry, G. John 4, 109, 145
illiteracy 147
IMF 22, 60, 126, 155
impeachment 135
imperialism 5, 105, 146
Indonesia 7, 53
inequality 6, 18, 19, 66, 78, 82, 97, 147
information society 68, 75, 80, 160, 161–62
infrastructure 13, 68, 121, 124, 165–66
international
forums 2, 59, 78, 102–3, 129, 154

institutions 3, 4, 18, 20, 24, 31, 34, 57
law 26, 140
media 27, 52, 58, 66
International Monetary Fund 22,
    35, 57, 60, 126, 154–55
internet 76, 164
intervention 4, 131–38, 141, 150
Israel 52, 58
Itamaraty *see* Brazilian Ministry of
    Foreign Affairs

Jaguaribe, Hélio 18
Jaguaribe, Roberto 38, 110
Japan 35, 42, 95, 104
Johannesburg 159, 161, 163

Kabila 141
Kant, Immanuel 109, 115, 130
Katju, Vivek 38
Kazakhstan 163
Kenya 141, 163
Khullar, Shri Dinkar 38
Khurshid, Salman 60
King, Stephen 117
Kornegay, Francis 20, 85
Krasner, Stephen 4
Krishna, S. M. 50–55, 85
Kumar, Nagesh 101

Lagarde, Christine 57
Landsberg, Chris 24, 101, 141
Laos 86
Latin America 13, 30, 42, 52, 118,
    122, 140
League of Arab States 58
League of Democracies 132, 147
legitimacy 2, 21, 106, 146, 156
Lesotho 141
liberalism 4–5, 109–10, 130–31
Liberia 141
Lima, José Graça 38
livestock 40
Lula da Silva, Luiz Inácio, 1, 17,
    22–24, 37–60, 69, 82, 110, 134–36,
    154–56
Lyal, White 87, 101

Mahmoud, Ahmadinejad 50
Maldives 138, 144
Mallavaparu, Siddharth 138

Mandela, Nelson 59, 140–41
Mbeki, Thabo 1, 23–24, 41, 43, 46,
    141–44, 155
media 27, 38, 44, 51–52, 58–59, 66,
    70, 83–84, 99, 103, 129, 136, 144,
    148, 152
Medvedev, Dmitry 50, 63
Mehta, Pratap 131, 138–39, 147
Mercosur 38, 45, 46, 51, 79, 123–24,
    133–35
Mexico 7, 24, 30, 103–4
Middle East 20, 38, 56, 139
middle powers 3, 20, 21, 33–36,
    113–14, 124, 128, 147
military 3, 15, 40, 71–72, 104, 106,
    110–11, 133, 138
Millennium Development Goals 86,
    120
MINUSTAH 135
Mohan, Raja 20, 127, 138–39
Motlanthe, Kgalema 48
Mozambique 142
Mugabe, Robert 141–43
Mukherjee, Pranab 25, 27, 40, 45–48
multilateralism 18, 27, 30, 143
multipolar 3, 7, 20, 106, 129, 146
multipolarity 48
Mumbai 71, 161
Myanmar 138, 144

Nairobi 119, 163
nanotechnology 77
Narayanan, Kocheril Raman 17
naval 48, 71–72, 89, 159
neocolonialism 23
New Delhi 2, 6, 12, 37–42, 45,
    48–49, 55, 59, 72, 77, 80–81, 84,
    105–8, 123, 138, 156–61, 164–66
New York 27, 40, 46, 50, 52, 54–55,
    60, 83, 88, 103, 158–67
Nicaragua 134
Nigeria 24, 104–5, 141
North America 16, 144
north-south trade 9, 117–18, 120,
    122, 125

O'Neill, Jim 105
OAS 133–35
Obama, Barack 130
Oceania 38

OECD 76, 126
oil 45, 95, 121
Oviedo, Lino 134

Pakistan 104, 137–38
Palestine 52–53, 58, 86
Paraguay 38, 133–36
Partido dos Trabalhadores (PT) 84
patriarchal 85
Patriota, Antônio de Aguiar 55
peacekeeping 40, 72, 135, 141, 143
Peru 134
Petrobras 3, 45
Pimentel, José Vicente 83
port-au-prince 86
portuguese language countries 135
poverty 2, 26–27, 44, 66, 78, 85, 88,
    106, 110, 127–28, 130, 147, 149
Prebisch, Raul 18
Pretoria 2, 39, 42, 46–47, 56, 75, 77,
    104–5, 141, 156, 159, 162, 164–65
protests 59, 121
Pu, Xiayou 106
public administration 46, 68, 76, 80,
    90, 159–61
Puig, Juan Carlos 18

Qobo, Mzukisi 20, 33
Quito 134

Ramallah 52, 86, 162
realism 4, 131, 137
Responsibility to Protect 138
rising powers *see* emerging powers
Russia 5–6, 42, 50–52, 106–8, 111
Rwanda 141

Salvador 70, 159, 164
Santiso, Carlos 134
Sanya 105
São Tomé e Príncipe 141
Sarney, José 133
Saudi Arabia 24, 25, 132
Schweller, Randall 106
science and technology 26, 53,
    67–69, 74, 77, 80, 108, 159, 161,
    163
SEBRAE 79
settlements 52, 68, 75, 80, 160, 162,
    164–66

shanghai cooperation organization 50
singapore issues 29
Singh, Manmohan 11, 26, 39–53, 56,
    81, 102, 105, 109, 130, 138, 155
social development 26, 39, 68–69,
    75, 78, 80, 160–62
socialism 131
solidarity 11, 21, 23, 30, 34, 117,
    119–20, 122, 125–26, 134, 140–41,
    150, 156
Somerset West 2, 48–49, 159
Sotero, Paulo 101–2
Soule-Kohndou, Folashadé 68, 94
South America 28, 105, 133–36,
    146
South-South trade 3, 37, 94–99,
    117–26; *see also* emerging
    markets
sovereignty 119–20, 132–34, 137
soybean 69
Spektor, Matias 20
sports 52, 67, 86, 162
Sri Lanka 138
subgroup 67, 73, 76, 79
subgroups 67, 77
Sudan 141, 144
summit 1, 7, 24, 27, 38, 41, 43–44,
    46–60, 66, 70, 81–84, 88, 103,
    105–8, 121, 123, 158–59, 161,
    164–65
Surie, Nalin 38
Swaziland 141
Syria 7, 56, 57, 164

tax and revenue administration 68,
    76, 107
Taylor, Charles 107, 141
terrorism 5, 25, 39, 114
Thailand 35
tourism 26, 67, 68, 69, 70, 78–80,
    100–101, 160, 163
transport 13, 26, 53, 68, 78–80, 124,
    159, 160, 162, 165–66
trilateral commission 39–42, 45, 48,
    50–51, 55, 80, 158–59, 162
TRIPS Agreement 28–29
Tshwane 2, 46, 54, 57, 81, 100, 159
Tshwane declaration 46, 54, 57, 81,
    100
Turkey 7

Uganda 141
United Kingdom 9, 73, 118
United Nations
General Assembly 22, 27, 38, 40, 42,
   44, 46, 50–53, 55, 58, 60, 108, 130,
   134
Security Council 3, 20, 22, 25–26,
   39–44, 53–55, 74–75, 104, 108,
   133, 144
United States 2, 15, 18, 27, 29, 31,
   40, 42, 46, 50, 52, 54–55, 60, 73,
   79, 93, 103–6, 111, 122, 130–32,
   134, 136–38, 145, 147, 155
urbanization 19, 75, 97

Vajpayee, Atal Bihari, 1, 37–38
Vale 3
venezuela 104, 132, 134–37, 145
Vietnam 86
violence 56–57, 58, 84, 85, 137, 142
visa 125, 144

Waisbich, Laura 87
Warsaw 139

Washington, DC 107
Wasmosy, Juan Carlos 134
well-being 40, 120
Western world 2, 5, 38, 44, 50, 56,
   106, 121, 126, 129–32, 137, 139,
   140, 144–46, 155
wilsonian 146
women 81, 84–85, 90
Woolfrey, Sean 47, 95–96, 102–3,
   124
working group 2, 19, 25, 28, 39,
   42–44, 46, 49, 58, 66–88, 97–100,
   107–8, 159–67
World Bank 22, 57, 75, 83,
   155
World Trade Organization 23, 25,
   28–31, 102–3, 120, 125

Yekaterinburg 48, 50, 105

Zambia 142
Zimbabwe 104, 142–44
Zuma, Jacob 25, 27, 40–41, 48,
   52–53, 56, 59, 141–42, 155

Routledge Global Institutions Series

89 India-Brazil-South Africa Dialogue Forum (IBSA) (2014)
The rise of the global South?
Oliver Stuenkel (Getulio Vargas Foundation)

88 Making Global Institutions Work (2014)
Power, accountability, and change
Edited by Kate Brennan

87 Post-2015 UN Development (2014)
Making change happen
*Edited by Stephen Browne (FUNDS Project) and Thomas G. Weiss
(CUNY Graduate Center)*

86 Who Participates in Global Governance? (2014)
States, bureaucracies, and NGOs in the United Nations
Molly A. Ruhlman (Towson University)

85 The Security Council as Global Legislator (2014)
*Edited by Vesselin Popovski (United Nations University) and Trudy Fraser
(United Nations University)*

84 UNICEF (2014)
Global governance that works
Richard Jolly (University of Sussex)

**83 The Society for Worldwide Interbank Financial Telecommunication
(SWIFT) (2014)**
Cooperative governance for network innovation, standards, and
community
*Susan V. Scott (London School of Economics and Political Science) and
Markos Zachariadis (University of Cambridge)*

82 The International Politics of Human Rights (2014)
Rallying to the R2P cause?
*Edited by Monica Serrano (Colegio de Mexico) and
Thomas G. Weiss (The CUNY Graduate Center)*

81 Private Foundations and Development Partnerships (2014)
American philanthropy and global development agendas
Michael Moran (Swinburne University of Technology)

**80 Nongovernmental Development Organizations and the Poverty
Reduction Agenda (2014)**
The moral crusaders
*Jonathan J. Makuwira (Royal Melbourne Institute of Technology
University)*

79 Corporate Social Responsibility (2014)
The role of business in sustainable development
Oliver F. Williams (University of Notre Dame)

78 Reducing Armed Violence with NGO Governance (2014)
Edited by Rodney Bruce Hall (University of Oxford)

77 Transformations in Trade Politics (2014)
Participatory trade politics in West Africa
Silke Trommer (Murdoch University)

76 Committing to the Court (2013)
Rules, politics, and the International Criminal Court
Yvonne M. Dutton (Indiana University)

75 Global Institutions of Religion (2013)
Ancient movers, modern shakers
Katherine Marshall (Georgetown University)

74 Crisis of Global Sustainability (2013)
Tapio Kanninen

73 The Group of Twenty (G20) (2013)
*Andrew F. Cooper (University of Waterloo) and
Ramesh Thakur (Australian National University)*

72 Peacebuilding (2013)
From concept to commission
Rob Jenkins (Hunter College, CUNY)

71 Human Rights and Humanitarian Norms, Strategic Framing, and Intervention (2013)
Lessons for the Responsibility to Protect
Melissa Labonte (Fordham University)

70 Feminist Strategies in International Governance (2013)
Edited by Gülay Caglar (Humboldt University, Berlin), Elisabeth Prügl (the Graduate Institute of International and Development Studies, Geneva), and Susanne Zwingel (the State University of New York, Potsdam)

69 The Migration Industry and the Commercialization of International Migration (2013)
Edited by Thomas Gammeltoft-Hansen (Danish Institute for International Studies) and Ninna Nyberg Sørensen (Danish Institute for International Studies)

68 Integrating Africa (2013)
Decolonization's legacies, sovereignty, and the African Union
Martin Welz (University of Konstanz)

67 Trade, Poverty, Development (2013)
Getting beyond the WTO's Doha deadlock
Edited by Rorden Wilkinson (University of Manchester) and James Scott (University of Manchester)

66 The United Nations Industrial Development Organization (UNIDO) (2012)
Industrial solutions for a sustainable future
Stephen Browne (FUNDS Project)

65 The Millennium Development Goals and Beyond (2012)
Global development after 2015
Edited by Rorden Wilkinson (University of Manchester) and David Hulme (University of Manchester)

64 International Organizations as Self-Directed Actors (2012)
A framework for analysis
Edited by Joel E. Oestreich (Drexel University)

63 Maritime Piracy (2012)
Robert Haywood (One Earth Future Foundation) and Roberta Spivak (One Earth Future Foundation)

62 United Nations High Commissioner for Refugees (UNHCR) (2nd edition, 2012)
Gil Loescher (University of Oxford), Alexander Betts (University of Oxford), and James Milner (University of Toronto)

61 International Law, International Relations, and Global Governance (2012)
Charlotte Ku (University of Illinois)

60 Global Health Governance (2012)
Sophie Harman (City University, London)

59 The Council of Europe (2012)
Martyn Bond (University of London)

58 The Security Governance of Regional Organizations (2011)
Edited by Emil J. Kirchner (University of Essex) and Roberto Dominguez (Suffolk University)

57 The United Nations Development Programme and System (2011)
Stephen Browne (FUNDS Project)

56 The South Asian Association for Regional Cooperation (2011)
An emerging collaboration architecture
Lawrence Sáez (University of London)

55 The UN Human Rights Council (2011)
Bertrand G. Ramcharan (Geneva Graduate Institute of International and Development Studies)

54 Responsibility to Protect (2011)
Cultural perspectives in the global South
Edited by Rama Mani (University of Oxford) and Thomas G. Weiss (The CUNY Graduate Center)

53 The International Trade Centre (2011)
Promoting exports for development
Stephen Browne (FUNDS Project) and Sam Laird (University of Nottingham)

52 The Idea of World Government (2011)
From ancient times to the twenty-first century
James A. Yunker (Western Illinois University)

51 Humanitarianism Contested (2011)
Where angels fear to tread
Michael Barnett (George Washington University) and
Thomas G. Weiss (The CUNY Graduate Center)

50 The Organization of American States (2011)
Global governance away from the media
Monica Herz (Catholic University, Rio de Janeiro)

49 Non-Governmental Organizations in World Politics (2011)
The construction of global governance
Peter Willetts (City University, London)

48 The Forum on China-Africa Cooperation (FOCAC) (2011)
Ian Taylor (University of St Andrews)

47 Global Think Tanks (2011)
Policy networks and governance
James G. McGann (University of Pennsylvania), with Richard Sabatini

46 United Nations Educational, Scientific and Cultural Organization (UNESCO) (2011)
Creating norms for a complex world
J.P. Singh (Georgetown University)

45 The International Labour Organization (2011)
Coming in from the cold
Steve Hughes (Newcastle University) and
Nigel Haworth (University of Auckland)

44 Global Poverty (2010)
How global governance is failing the poor
David Hulme (University of Manchester)

43 Global Governance, Poverty, and Inequality (2010)
Edited by Jennifer Clapp (University of Waterloo) and
Rorden Wilkinson (University of Manchester)

42 Multilateral Counter-Terrorism (2010)
The global politics of cooperation and contestation
Peter Romaniuk (John Jay College of Criminal Justice, CUNY)

41 Governing Climate Change (2010)
Peter Newell (University of East Anglia) and
Harriet A. Bulkeley (Durham University)

40 The UN Secretary-General and Secretariat (2nd edition, 2010)
Leon Gordenker (Princeton University)

39 Preventive Human Rights Strategies (2010)
Bertrand G. Ramcharan (Geneva Graduate Institute of International and Development Studies)

38 African Economic Institutions (2010)
Kwame Akonor (Seton Hall University)

37 Global Institutions and the HIV/AIDS Epidemic (2010)
Responding to an international crisis
Franklyn Lisk (University of Warwick)

36 Regional Security (2010)
The capacity of international organizations
Rodrigo Tavares (United Nations University)

35 The Organisation for Economic Co-operation and Development (2009)
Richard Woodward (University of Hull)

34 Transnational Organized Crime (2009)
Frank Madsen (University of Cambridge)

33 The United Nations and Human Rights (2nd edition, 2009)
A guide for a new era
Julie A. Mertus (American University)

32 The International Organization for Standardization (2009)
Global governance through voluntary consensus
*Craig N. Murphy (Wellesley College) and
JoAnne Yates (Massachusetts Institute of Technology)*

31 Shaping the Humanitarian World (2009)
*Peter Walker (Tufts University) and
Daniel G. Maxwell (Tufts University)*

30 Global Food and Agricultural Institutions (2009)
John Shaw

29 Institutions of the Global South (2009)
Jacqueline Anne Braveboy-Wagner (City College of New York, CUNY)

28 International Judicial Institutions (2009)
The architecture of international justice at home and abroad
Richard J. Goldstone (Retired Justice of the Constitutional Court of South Africa) and Adam M. Smith (Harvard University)

27 The International Olympic Committee (2009)
The governance of the Olympic system
Jean-Loup Chappelet (IDHEAP Swiss Graduate School of Public Administration) and Brenda Kübler-Mabbott

26 The World Health Organization (2009)
Kelley Lee (London School of Hygiene and Tropical Medicine)

25 Internet Governance (2009)
The new frontier of global institutions
John Mathiason (Syracuse University)

24 Institutions of the Asia-Pacific (2009)
ASEAN, APEC, and beyond
Mark Beeson (University of Birmingham)

23 United Nations High Commissioner for Refugees (UNHCR) (2008)
The politics and practice of refugee protection into
the twenty-first century
Gil Loescher (University of Oxford), Alexander Betts (University of Oxford), and James Milner (University of Toronto)

22 Contemporary Human Rights Ideas (2008)
Bertrand G. Ramcharan (Geneva Graduate Institute of International and Development Studies)

21 The World Bank (2008)
From reconstruction to development to equity
Katherine Marshall (Georgetown University)

20 The European Union (2008)
Clive Archer (Manchester Metropolitan University)

19 The African Union (2008)
Challenges of globalization, security, and governance
*Samuel M. Makinda (Murdoch University) and
F. Wafula Okumu (McMaster University)*

18 Commonwealth (2008)
Inter- and non-state contributions to global governance
Timothy M. Shaw (Royal Roads University)

17 The World Trade Organization (2007)
Law, economics, and politics
Bernard M. Hoekman (World Bank) and
Petros C. Mavroidis (Columbia University)

16 A Crisis of Global Institutions? (2007)
Multilateralism and international security
Edward Newman (University of Birmingham)

15 UN Conference on Trade and Development (2007)
Ian Taylor (University of St Andrews) and
Karen Smith (University of Stellenbosch)

14 The Organization for Security and Co-operation in Europe (2007)
David J. Galbreath (University of Aberdeen)

13 The International Committee of the Red Cross (2007)
A neutral humanitarian actor
David P. Forsythe (University of Nebraska) and
Barbara Ann Rieffer-Flanagan (Central Washington University)

12 The World Economic Forum (2007)
A multi-stakeholder approach to global governance
Geoffrey Allen Pigman (Bennington College)

11 The Group of 7/8 (2007)
Hugo Dobson (University of Sheffield)

10 The International Monetary Fund (2007)
Politics of conditional lending
James Raymond Vreeland (Georgetown University)

9 The North Atlantic Treaty Organization (2007)
The enduring alliance
Julian Lindley-French (Center for Applied Policy, University of Munich)

8 The World Intellectual Property Organization (2006)
Resurgence and the development agenda
Chris May (University of the West of England)

7 The UN Security Council (2006)
Practice and promise
Edward C. Luck (Columbia University)

6 Global Environmental Institutions (2006)
Elizabeth R. DeSombre (Wellesley College)

5 Internal Displacement (2006)
Conceptualization and its consequences
Thomas G. Weiss (The CUNY Graduate Center) and David A. Korn

4 The UN General Assembly (2005)
M.J. Peterson (University of Massachusetts, Amherst)

3 United Nations Global Conferences (2005)
Michael G. Schechter (Michigan State University)

2 The UN Secretary-General and Secretariat (2005)
Leon Gordenker (Princeton University)

1 The United Nations and Human Rights (2005)
A guide for a new era
Julie A. Mertus (American University)

Books currently under contract include:

The Regional Development Banks
Lending with a regional flavor
Jonathan R. Strand (University of Nevada)

Millennium Development Goals (MDGs)
For a people-centered development agenda?
Sakiko Fukada-Parr (The New School)

The Bank for International Settlements
The politics of global financial supervision in the age of high finance
Kevin Ozgercin (SUNY College at Old Westbury)

International Migration
Khalid Koser (Geneva Centre for Security Policy)

Human Development
Richard Ponzio

The International Monetary Fund (2nd edition)
Politics of conditional lending
James Raymond Vreeland (Georgetown University)

The UN Global Compact
Catia Gregoratti (Lund University)

Institutions for Women's Rights
Charlotte Patton (York College, CUNY) and
Carolyn Stephenson (University of Hawaii)

International Aid
Paul Mosley (University of Sheffield)

Global Consumer Policy
Karsten Ronit (University of Copenhagen)

The Changing Political Map of Global Governance
Anthony Payne (University of Sheffield) and
Stephen Robert Buzdugan (Manchester Metropolitan University)

Coping with Nuclear Weapons
W. Pal Sidhu

Twenty-First-Century Democracy Promotion in the Americas
Jorge Heine (The Centre for International Governance Innovation) and
Brigitte Weiffen (University of Konstanz)

EU Environmental Policy and Climate Change
Henrik Selin (Boston University) and
Stacy VanDeveer (University of New Hampshire)

Global Governance and China
The dragon's learning curve
Edited by Scott Kennedy (Indiana University)

The Politics of Global Economic Surveillance
Martin S. Edwards (Seton Hall University)

Mercy and Mercenaries
Humanitarian agencies and private security companies
Peter Hoffman

Regional Organizations in the Middle East
James Worrall (University of Leeds)

Reforming the UN Development System
The politics of incrementalism
Silke Weinlich (Duisburg-Essen University)

The United Nations as a Knowledge Organization
Nanette Svenson (Tulane University)

United Nations Centre on Transnational Corporations (UNCTC)
Khalil Hamdani and Lorraine Ruffing

The International Criminal Court
The politics and practice of prosecuting atrocity crimes
Martin Mennecke (University of Copenhagen)

The Politics of International Organizations
Views from insiders
Edited Patrick Weller (Griffith University) and
Xu Yi-chong (Griffith University)

The African Union (2nd edition)
Challenges of globalization, security, and governance
Samuel M. Makinda (Murdoch University),
F. Wafula Okumu (African Union), and
David Mickler (University of Western Australia)

BRICS
João Pontes Nogueira (Catholic University, Rio de Janeiro) and
Monica Herz (Catholic University, Rio de Janeiro)

Expert Knowledge in Global Trade
Edited by Erin Hannah (University of Western Ontario),
James Scott (University of Manchester), and
Silke Trommer (Murdoch University)

Past as Prelude?
Wartime History and the Future United Nations
Edited by Dan Plesch (SOAS, University of London) and
Thomas G. Weiss (CUNY Graduate Center)

The European Union (2nd edition)
Clive Archer (Manchester Metropolitan University)

Governing Climate Change (2nd edition)
Peter Newell (University of East Anglia) and
Harriet A. Bulkeley (Durham University)

Contemporary Human Rights Ideas (2nd edition)
Betrand Ramcharan (Geneva Graduate Institute of International and
Development Studies)

Protecting the Internally Displaced
Rhetoric and reality
Phil Orchard (University of Queensland)

The Arctic Council
Within the far north
Douglas C. Nord (Umea University)

For further information regarding the series, please contact:
   Craig Fowlie, Publisher, Politics & International Studies
   Taylor & Francis
   2 Park Square, Milton Park, Abingdon
   Oxford OX14 4RN, UK
   +44 (0)207 842 2057 Tel
   +44 (0)207 842 2302 Fax
   Craig.Fowlie@tandf.co.uk
   www.routledge.com

For Product Safety Concerns and Information please contact our
EU representative GPSR@taylorandfrancis.com Taylor & Francis
Verlag GmbH, Kaufingerstraße 24, 80331 München, Germany